Creating the
Prairie Xeriscape

University Extension Press
University of Saskatchewan

Dean of the Extension Division: Gordon Thompson

Managing Editor of the Press: Bertram Wolfe

Associate Editor: Roberta Mitchell Coulter

Coordinator of Agricultural/Horticultural Publications:
  Bruce Hobin

Drawings (unless otherwise indicated): Jocelyn Young

Proofreader: Allison Muri

This book was made possible by a grant from the
Canada Saskatchewan Agriculture Green Plan Agreement.

Creating the Prairie Xeriscape

Low-maintenance, water-efficient gardening

Sara Williams

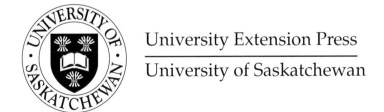

University Extension Press
University of Saskatchewan

To my son, David Saul Williams,

And to those who broke trail: George Bugnet,
Henry Marshall, Bert Porter, Isabella Preston,
Robert Simonet, Frank Skinner, and Percy Wright

Cover photograph by Sara Williams.

While every effort has been made to ensure that the information contained in this publication is correct, the author and
the publisher caution against the use of the information
contained in this publication in any particular application
and accept no responsibility or liability for errors, omissions,
or representations, expressed or implied, contained herein or
in any written or oral communication associated with this
publication. Errors brought to the attention of the publisher
will be corrected in periodic updates to this book.

Printed in Canada

06   05   04   03   02   01   00   99   98   97   5   4   3   2   1

Canadian Cataloguing in Publication Data

Williams, Sara, 1941–

   Creating the prairie xeriscape

   Includes bibliographical references and index.
   ISBN 0–88880–357–5

1. Xeriscaping – Prairie Provinces.   2. Drought-
tolerant plants – Prairie Provinces.   3. Prairie
gardening.   I. University of Saskatchewan.   Extension
Division.   II. Title.

SB439.8.W544 1997   635.9'52'5   C97–920049–0

Contents

Preface   vii

Chapter 1   Introduction   1

Part 1   Xeriscape Fundamentals   7

Chapter 2   Design   9

Chapter 3   Soil   30

Chapter 4   Irrigation   41

Chapter 5   Mulch   60

Chapter 6   Lawns   73

Part 2   Xeriscape Plants   91

Chapter 7   Ornamentals   93

    Trees & Shrubs   97

    Perennials   131

    Vines   160

    Bulbs   165

    Annuals   168

    Native Plants   190

Chapter 8   Native Plants in the Xeriscape   191

Chapter 9   The Edible Xeriscape   199

Part 3   Appendices   205

    Appendix 1   Implementing Change in
      Your Community   206

    Appendix 2   Ornamental Plant
      Charts   213

    Appendix 3   Glossary   239

Index   243

Preface

I began practicing these concepts—water and soil conservation, reduced pesticide use, recycling organic material into mulch or soil amendments—long before I heard the term xeriscape. To me, they seemed to encapsulate good garden practice—they simply made sense.

I live on five acres of sand with limited water. Weeding, cultivating, and watering are not high on my list of favorite activities. I'd rather spend my time in the garden creatively—planing, building, propagating, and designing.

Having practiced xeriscape, I began to share the concept with others, at first informally and then through workshops, and soon the idea for a book on xeriscape written specifically for the prairies—from the smallest of urban yards to the most expansive of farmyards, from public parks to parking lots—began to develop. With the generous assistance and patience of the Canada Saskatchewan Agriculture Green Plan, administered through the Prairie Farm Rehabilitation Administration, this has become a reality.

Our gardens are a small portion of this planet, but they are the only part over which we alone hold stewardship. I hope this book inspires you in the creation of your own prairie xeriscape.

My sincere thanks to the following individuals and institutions who have so unstintingly contributed photographs and slides, landscape designs, technical review, and written material for this book. It would not have been possible without them.

Photographs, slides, and line drawings: • Brian Baldwin, Department of Horticulture Science, University of Saskatchewan • Brendan Casement, Edmonton, Alberta • Allan Daku, Honeywood Lilies, Parkside, Saskatchewan • Buck Godwin, Olds, Alberta • John G. N. Davidson, Beaverlodge, Alberta • International flower Bulb Center • Hugh Knowles, Professor Emeritus, University of Alberta • Louis Lenz, Faculty of Agricultural and Food Sciences, University of Manitoba • M.P.M. Nair, Saskatoon, Saskatchewan • National Garden Bureau, Downers Grove, Illinois • Brian Porter, Saskatchewan Agriculture and Food, Regina, Saskatchewan • Chris Powter, Reclamation Research Technical

Advisory Committee, Alberta Land Conservation and Reclamation Council, Edmonton, Alberta • Gail Rankin, Edmonton, Alberta • Connie Reavie, Carrot River, Saskatchewan • Ed Reid, AQUALTA, Edmonton, Alberta • Bill Remphrey, Faculty of Agricultural and Food Sciences, University of Manitoba • Saskatchewan Waste Reduction Council • Hugh Skinner, Skinner's Nursery, Roblin, Manitoba • Steven Still, Professor of Landscape Horticulture, Ohio State University • Ed Toop, Professor Emeritus, University of Alberta.

Landscape designs: • Terry Klassen, KLA Group, Inc., Saskatoon, Saskatchewan • Eugene Lin, Country Gardens Landscape Ltd., Calgary, Alberta • Arnie Theissen, Crosby Hanna & Associates, Saskatoon, Saskatchewan • Charles Thomsen, Department of Landscape Architecture, University of Manitoba • Jocelyn Young, horticultural and design consultant, Saskatoon, Saskatchewan.

Technical review: • Marie Boehm, Department of Soil Science, University of Saskatchewan • Brian Baldwin, Department of Horticulture Science, University of Saskatchewan • Helen Buchanan, Battleford, Saskatchewan • David Calam, Municipal Engineering, City of Regina, Regina, Saskatchewan • Randi Derdall, Utilities Technician, City of Kamloops, Kamloops, British Columbia • Grace Berg, garden designer, Saskatoon, Saskatchewan • Phyllis Hanson, Wood Mountain, Saskatchewan • Dennis McKernon, Olds College, Olds, Alberta • Ed Reid, AQUALTA, Edmonton, Alberta • Rod Reid, Public Works, City of Saskatoon, Saskatoon, Saskatchewan • Bill Schroeder, PFRA Shelterbelt Centre, Indian Head, Saskatchewan • Doug Shearer, Crosby Hanna & Associates, Saskatoon, Saskatchewan • Hugh Skinner, Skinner's Nursery, Roblin, Manitoba • Erl Svendsen, Department of Horticulture Science, University of Saskatchewan • Arnie Theissen, Crosby Hanna & Associates, Saskatoon, Saskatchewan • Doug Waterer, Department of Horticulture Science, University of Saskatchewan • Jeannette Wickstrand, Battleford, Saskatchewan • Brenda Winny, Sovereign, Saskatchewan.

Written material: • Brian Baldwin, Department of Horticulture Science, University of Saskatchewan • Eugene Lin, Country Gardens Landscape Ltd., Calgary, Alberta • Lee and Mack Miller, Millers Native Plants, Saskatoon, Saskatchewan • Native Plant Society of Saskatchewan • Robin Smith, Saskatoon, Saskatchewan • Arnie Theissen, Crosby Hanna & Associates, Saskatoon, Saskatchewan • Charles Thomsen, Department of Landscape Architecture, University of Manitoba • Tom Ward, Department of Horticulture Science, University of Saskatchewan.

Special thanks for efforts beyond the call of duty and friendship to Brian Baldwin, Roberta Coulter, Arnie Theissen, and Jocelyn Young.

eople are delighted
with a landscape
that is pleasing to
the eye, kind to the
environment and undemanding
in time, chemicals, and water."
David Calam

Chapter 1

Introduction

Xeriscaping is an environmentally friendly approach to
your yard and garden which leaves your portion of
the world in as good or better shape than when you
assumed stewardship. As well, a xeriscape yard frees you
from much of the repetitive maintenance we have come to
accept as normal in conventional landscaping. Instead of
weeding, watering, and mowing, you'll be able to spend
quality time in your garden, doing whatever gives you
pleasure: designing, planting, or just enjoying your garden.

Creating the Prairie Xeriscape

What Is Xeriscape?

The word *xeriscape* was coined from the Greek *xeros*, meaning
dry, and *scape*, from the Anglo-Saxon word *schap*, meaning
view. The word is misleading—it conjures up visions of a dry,
desert-like landscape, but in fact a xeriscape landscape can be
just as lush and green as a conventional landscape. It is not
rocks and plastic. It is high-quality, attractive landscaping.

Xeriscape is not a limited style of landscaping, but an

approach which can employ many and varied styles. The difference lies in that way water is used.

There are many approaches to xeriscaping: naturalization using native plant material; cottage gardening; layered mixed borders; or more conventional designs using plants both introduced and native. It can be applied to condominiums, urban yards, farms, acreages, and public spaces ranging from libraries and schools to parks and parking lots.

The Principles

Xeriscape is a concept that includes several principles. Many prairie gardeners have been using some of these practices for years. The principles and practices of xeriscape are what sound gardening is all about.

Design for water conservation

Xeriscape yards provide us with beauty, privacy, and protection from the elements, but they also conserve water. Plants with similar water needs are grouped together and watered appropriately. Grading directs water to planting beds or pond-like areas where it can be held until needed.

Improve soil

Improving the ability of your soil to hold water and nutrients before planting goes a long way to reducing maintenance and inputs later. Xeriscape provides practical solutions to soils that are too shallow, too heavy, too light, or lack organic matter.

Reduce lawn areas

Reducing the area of lawn, changing its shape to conform to irrigation patterns, using more drought-tolerant grasses, and changing the way you water, mow, and fertilize reduces your labor considerably and saves water.

Appropriate plant selection

We think of our water-intensive landscapes as normal, but the disparity between the water needs of our landscapes and natural precipitation is perhaps nowhere greater than on the prairies. In many areas of the prairies, average annual precipitation is less than 30 cm (12 in.), yet many of our landscape plants are more suited to the lush, green gardens of England.

There is an extensive selection of drought-tolerant trees, shrubs, vines, bulbs, annuals, and perennials that are hardy on the prairies. Some of these may already be a part of your landscape, but because they are located beside less drought-tolerant plants, they may be receiving a lot more water than they need.

Efficient irrigation

Much of the water now applied to our landscape is either not needed or is wasted. Understanding how and when plants need water, where most wastage occurs, and how irrigation systems work will not only save you time and money, it will conserve water and reduce maintenance.

Mulching

An organic mulch is placed on the soil surface to conserve water, reduce weeding, and improve the soil. There are many types of mulching material—from grass clippings to post peelings—and most of these are available free or at little cost.

Why Xeriscape?

Landscapes composed of plants with water needs proportional to that of natural precipitation are easier and cheaper to maintain and are much more likely to survive drought and water restrictions.

One of the greatest benefits of xeriscape is reduced maintenance. Liberated from much of the drudgery of weeding, mowing, and watering, we can spend our garden time in more creative pursuits. While there is no such thing as "no maintenance," xeriscaping does offer "low maintenance."

Less watering

Drought-tolerant plants are able to survive with less water. Once a mulch layer is in place and plants are grouped according to their water needs, less water and less frequent watering are needed. Soil amended with organic matter is able to hold a greater volume of water, again resulting in less frequent watering. Irrigation is more efficient, reducing water waste.

Less weeding

The mulch layer greatly reduces the time spent weeding. Weeding is also reduced because you are no longer watering and encouraging the growth of weeds in "non-target" areas. Denser plantings of ground covers leave less space for weeds. A higher mowing height in lawns results in deeper-rooted and more vigorous grass which is better able to compete with lawn weeds.

Less fertilizing

Drought-tolerant plants generally require fewer nutrients, reducing the need for fertilizer. As well, deeper watering encourages deeper rooting, allowing roots to obtain nutrients from a larger soil volume. Because the soil has been amended with organic matter, more nutrients are available within the soil. Mulching also reduces fertilizer inputs because as the mulch layer slowly decays over the years, still more nutrients are released into the soil. Leaving clippings on the lawn also reduces fertilizer needs.

Less pruning

Drought-tolerant plant material that is watered deeply but less frequently generally has less succulent growth and therefore requires less pruning. By leaving trees and shrubs in their natural form (rather than hedging), pruning and trimming are further reduced. Finally, knowing the mature height and width of a tree or shrub and planting it in an appropriate site reduces pruning substantially.

Less mowing

By reducing the area of grass to that which is *actually used* as lawn and replacing the remainder with drought-tolerant ground covers or hard surfaces you eliminate a great deal of mowing. The grass that remains is mowed less frequently because a xeriscape lawn is usually cut at 10 cm (4 in.) rather than at the conventional 7.5 cm (3 in.). Less-frequent mowing results in a deeper root system able to withdraw water from a greater volume of soil. As well, slightly taller grass will shade the soil surface, reducing evaporation.

Less pesticides

Succulent plant growth encourages disease because cells are thinner and more easily penetrated by disease organisms. Since drought-tolerant plants generally require less water and fertilizer, their growth is less succulent, making them less vulnerable to disease. As well, because the xeriscape landscape encourages biodiversity—the use of a wide range of plants—rather than a monoculture of just a few types of plants, it also encourages insect predators and a balance of insects. In addition, the use of drip irrigation leaves foliage dry, reducing fungal diseases. Finally, there are fewer weeds (which often act as alternate hosts for both diseases and insects), which in turn lowers the incidence of pest problems.

The Rewards

The rewards of xeriscape are many.

Lower maintenance means spending quality time in your landscape. Working creatively is so much more satisfying than the drudgery of spraying or pushing a lawn mower.

Xeriscape also means a lower water bill. Water savings vary between 20 and 80 percent of a pre-xeriscape landscape.

Along with conserving water, fewer pesticides and fertilizers are used.

And if drought should occur and water restrictions are imposed on the landscape, your landscape will survive.

How to Use This Book

The extent to which individuals follow xeriscape principles is one of choice based on philosophy, time, cost, and household use of the landscape. As individuals we can apply these principles to the degree that we feel comfortable. We can use any or all of them. They are adaptable and can be modified to fit the household use of our yards, our personal philosophy, our sense of what is beautiful, and the time and money we wish to commit.

The intention of this book is to guide homeowners, landscape professionals, developers, and municipal planners through the implementation of xeriscape principles. The book may be read in its entirety or used as a reference manual. It is designed to allow you to create a prairie xeriscape of your own.

Each of the five chapters in Part 1 is based on a xeriscape principle. Applicable maintenance is discussed within each chapter. Part 2 gives detailed descriptions of the hardy, drought-tolerant plants that form the prairie xeriscape. The sections on ornamentals includes trees and shrubs, vines, perennials, bulbs, and annuals. Sections on native plants and the edible xeriscape follow. Don't overlook the appendices, which include how to implement change in your community, plant reference charts, and a glossary.

Begin with the design chapter, but remember, there are landscape design plans for specific applications throughout the book. Line drawings and photographs provide a visual picture of xeriscape possibilities.

When you need information about a particular plant and when you're ready to get down to selecting specific plant material for your prairie xeriscape, turn to chapter 7 and the reference charts in appendix 2.

Chapter 7 includes detailed information and photographs of almost 200 annuals, perennials, bulbs, vines, shrubs, and trees that form part of the prairie xeriscape. All of these plants (except, of course, the annuals) are considered hardy at least to zone 2b unless stated otherwise. Those accompanied by the icon Ψ are extremely drought tolerant. Once "established" (i.e., by their second or third growing season), they will seldom if ever need supplemental water. Among this group are caragana, clary sage, *Anthemis tinctoria*, gaillardia, *Yucca glauca*, and lilac. The remainder of the plants listed are moderately drought tolerant. During dry, hot, windy periods, supplemental water will be needed. (A third category—not included in this book—are those plants that will always need supplemental water, such as tea roses, hostas, primroses, hydrangeas, birch, and lindens.)

Within each category, the plants are listed alphabetically

Further Reading
General

Xeriscape Programs for Water Utilities, by Ken Ball (American Water Works Association, Denver, Colorado, 1990).

Every Drop Counts, edited by Dan Shrubsole and Don Tate (Canadian Water Resources Association, Cambridge, Ontario, 1994).

"It's Your Yard: A practical guide to low-water, low-maintenance landscaping," video (Minds Eye Pictures, Regina, Saskatchewan, 1996).

Last Oasis: Facing Water Scarcity, by Sandra Postel (W. W. Norton & Company, New York, 1992).

Xeriscape Gardening, by Connie Ellefson, Tom Stephens, and Doug Welsh (Macmillan Publishing Company, New York, 1992).

by botanical name. (If you don't know the botanical name, all plants are listed by their common names in the index.) Each descriptive entry is accompanied by one or more color photographs.

Much of the information in the plant descriptions is also summarized in reference charts in appendix 2, which also includes propagation information. These charts are particularly useful if you are looking for a tree or shrub of a particular height, or a flower of a particular color.

Part 1

Xeriscape Fundamentals

onsider the extent to which you wish to carry out xeriscape principles. Do you want to make these changes immediately and to your entire yard, or slowly and to only portions of your yard?

Chapter 2

Design

Designing your xeriscape

This chapter explains the basics of landscape design, with emphasis on xeriscape principles which save water and result in a low-maintenance landscape.

It leads you through the process of design, step by step, from paper to reality. Using chapter 7 as a reference, you can then fill in the details of garden walls, floor, and ceiling.

The implementation of a xeriscape design demands a careful observation of the topography and microclimates of your landscape, and sometimes the modification of problem areas such as slopes to make the landscape a more hospitable place for both your plants and yourself. Some areas of your yard may require careful selection of plant material appropriate to the existing microclimate there.

Proper placement of plants is critical. Xeriscape design emphasizes beds and borders rather than individual or scattergun plantings. It uses mixed plantings of drought-tolerant annuals, perennials, bulbs, biennials, vines, trees, and shrubs within a single bed, thereby creating a "layered look." Plants with similar water needs are grouped together to conserve water.

A mixed layered border on a sloped corner lot replaces much of the lawn and lends more interest. Spruce provide the backbone, while Oriental poppies, daylilies, and snow-in-summer add color.

Also in this chapter are found different approaches to xeriscape, complete with landscape designs: mixed layered borders, winter color, and birds; large-scale landscaping using mass plantings in rural yards; and a new concept in shelterbelts.

Introduction to Landscape Design

Many decisions go into landscape planning. You may do the design and installation yourself or hire professionals, but it is *your yard*. Like any other endeavor, the more you know, the more comfortable you'll be in making these decisions.

Why Are You Doing This?

We want our landscapes—whether conventional or xeriscape—to be functional as well as provide us with beauty, privacy, protection from the elements, convenience, safety, and low maintenance. The difference in a xeriscape landscape is the emphasis on water conservation—lower maintenance is a bonus.

Beauty is, of course, in the eye of the beholder. What you like is very personal and probably different from your neighbor. And so it should be!

Our landscape gives us privacy. We plant trees and shrubs and build fences so that our neighbors aren't privy to the comings and goings of our daily lives. This is particularly true of our back yards, which we use as outdoor living space. Remember too that whatever you see outdoors from your house or yard is also part of your landscape, whether you happen to own it or not. It is your choice to include or exclude views through landscaping. If a neighbor has an exceptionally beautiful tree, emphasize it by "framing" it with other plant material. If there is an ugly shed or garage, hide it. In the words of architect Frank Lloyd Wright: "The physician can bury his mistakes, but the architect can only advise his client to plant vines"—or a tree, shrub, trellis, or fence.

Landscaping provides protection from the elements. We use plant material to modify our environment, creating microclimates that are warmer, calmer, more humid, and that conserve moisture. Trees with large canopies such as Manitoba maple and green ash provide shade. So can arbors or decks laced

Virginia creeper draws the house into the landscape. The front lawn has been partially replaced with yarrow, coral bells, and juniper.

Landscape design makes use of foliage as well as flowers. Purple-leafed cistena cherry, silver artemisia, and golden marguerite provide contrast and color while replacing a front lawn.

with vines. Dense shrubs and coniferous trees, placed to buffer prevailing winds, increase our comfort and decrease our heating bills. Shrub plantings reduce dust, traffic glare, pollutants, and, to a lesser extent, noise.

Be flexible when planning your landscape. Allow for a variety of activities to take place in a single area. Consider recreational and social use of space and allow for changing use of outdoor areas as the family grows and changes. What might begin as a sunken sandbox/play area could later be converted to a sunken patio or pond area.

Starting Points

The hardscape

Convenience and safety are important elements of landscaping. The placement of walkways and gateways should be determined by a logical "traffic" pattern through different areas of the yard. Both should be wide enough to accommodate the largest piece of machinery (e.g., rototiller, snow blower) that has to move over or through them. A minimum width of 1.25 m (4 ft) to accommodate two people walking side by side is recommended. Steps should have treads of 30 cm (12 in.) and risers of 15 cm (6 in.). Steps and walks should be safe and well lit.

Driveways should be wide enough to accommodate vehicles as well as people entering and leaving them. Plantings along driveways can be used to soften harsh concrete or asphalt, but should be low enough not to block the view of the driver. Nor should they trap snow, hinder snow removal, or be vulnerable to damage caused by snow dumping or salt used to melt ice. Hedging along driveways and sidewalks can make snow removal difficult if not impossible. To reduce areas of concrete or asphalt—and the amount of the time spent shovelling snow—place garages as close to the property line as possible.

Placement of plant materials: The layered look

Most of us have a lawn area which includes flower beds, trees, and shrubs. Placing trees and shrubs around the perimeter of our yards allows us to view them in their entirety from the lawn, patio or deck; provides maximum screening for enclosure and our sense of privacy, as well as reducing wind, noise, glare and dust; allows them to serve as a visual backdrop for flower beds; gives the illusion of more space; and leaves space for "people" activities. Trees are also positioned to provide shade for specific areas such as decks, patios, play areas, and dog runs.

The placement of plants affects maintenance. Trees and shrubs should be planted in beds or groupings rather than in a "scattergun" pattern. A yard in which trees and shrubs have

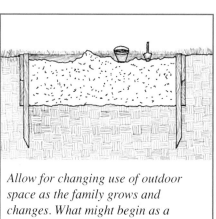
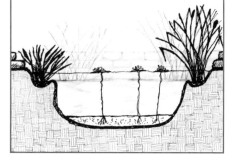

Allow for changing use of outdoor space as the family grows and changes. What might begin as a sunken sandbox/play area could later be converted to a sunken patio or pond area.

A mixed layered border may include trees, shrubs, perennials, bulbs, and annuals.

been planted singly here and there within the lawn can be an obstacle course in which to play or socialize and a near impossibility to mow.

For visual interest and variety, develop mixed borders with a layered look. A mixed border is composed of a mixture of plants: trees, shrubs, annuals, biennials, perennials, bulbs, and even vines. The border itself is generally (but not always) free-form and curved rather than formal with straight lines.

Curved beds are more informal, can be made to "fit" any space, and are more in keeping with today's lifestyles. When planning, use a garden hose to determine the curve. Ensure that your mower will fit the lawn side of curved beds.

Add various heights or layers to this concept and you have a mixed layered border. There are many advantages to a mixed layered border. Mowing around a single large bed is much easier than mowing around a multitude of smaller beds or scattergun-planted trees. The different layers provide year-round interest in terms of height, color, and texture. By grouping plants with the same water needs in the same bed, you conserve water.

The highest layer consists of a backbone of taller shade trees or conifers. Some of these may already exist in your yard and have merely to be incorporated.

Below these are taller shrubs, usually 1 to 2 m (4–6 ft) in height. For greater visual impact and ease of maintenance, these are planted in informal groupings. Each group consists of the same type of shrub, traditionally—but not necessarily—of an odd number such as three, five, or seven, depending on the overall size of the border. (According to ancient Oriental traditions, odd numbers are supposed to have more visual impact than even.) These are generally toward the back of the border in relation to where it is usually viewed.

Also below the canopy trees but toward the center and front of the border is a layer of lower shrubs or tall annuals or perennials, usually 0.5 to 1.25 m (2–4 ft) in height.

On the edge of the border and visually tying it together is a ground cover layer, generally less than 0.5 m (2 ft) in height. This layer can consist of annuals, perennials, and low shrubs. Shorter flowering plants are usually placed in pockets where they can be appreciated from the direction from which the border is most commonly viewed.

Flower borders can be incorporated toward the front of these beds facing a lawn, deck, or patio. In small urban yards the dominant feature of a mixed layered border may be a single crabapple or Russian olive. In larger rural landscapes, these borders may be

This front lawn has been entirely eliminated and replaced with drought-tolerant perennials, shrubs, and trees.

Sara Williams

several hundred meters and include many trees and shrubs.

Scale, focal points, and unifying elements

Scale refers to the relative size of plant material in relation to the size of the house and lot. Just as large, overstuffed furniture tends to make a small room appear even smaller, large trees will further reduce the apparent size of a small house. Conversely, using smaller trees will make a large house appear even larger. It is important that the size of plantings be in proportion to the size of buildings. Know the mature size (height and width) of plants, especially trees and shrubs. The smaller the area, the more satisfactory are trees, shrubs, flowers, and ground covers that are not only small to medium in overall size, but have small- to medium-sized leaves and flowers.

Each major area of a yard should contain a focal point or visual point of interest. This could be a particularly beautiful tree (such as a Swiss stone pine), a vine-draped trellis, a pond, bird bath, flower bed, formal herb garden, piece of sculpture, or sundial.

To unify the landscape as a whole, repeat plant species within an area and from one area of the yard to another. One might repeat a grouping of shrub roses in several places, a favorite vine such as 'Rosy O'Grady' clematis, daylilies, or an underplanting of junipers. This does not imply that one side of the lot should be a mirror image of the other. Rather, that several species form a theme of plant material around which the total design is based.

Some of us delight in the development of a "horticultural zoo," compulsively seeking out the new, the unusual, the just-possibly-hardy. For the less demented, 20 plant species may suffice in a smaller yard.

Nonplant material—the hardscape of walkways, fences, and walls—should also be repeated, thereby unifying house and yard. If your house is constructed of brick, why not use brick for walks, patios, and retaining walls? If you own a cedar house, use cedar for a garden bench, a lamp post, fencing, or a trellis. If your house is faced with stone, why

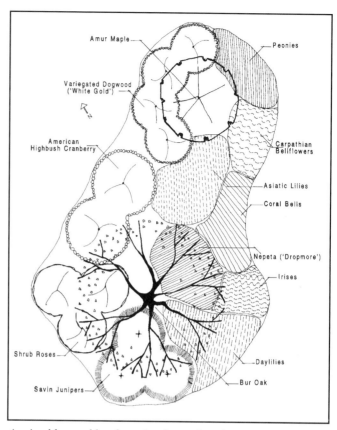

A mixed layered border using bur oak and Amur maple as the canopy. The middle layer has American highbush cranberry, dogwood, shrub roses, and savin junipers. Perennials, including daylilies, iris, Nepeta, *coral bells, lilies, Carpathian bellflowers, and peonies, are planted at the front of the bed.*

The birdbath in the curved tree-shrub border serves as a focal point and is part of an attractive habitat for birds.

A mixed layered border in a rural setting integrates native plants with introduced ones and acts as a transition zone between the more manicured yard and the bush beyond.

not use stone for your walks, patio flooring, or garden walls?

Bylaws

Prior to any landscape construction, major plantings, or building, find out about local bylaws. These may concern what may be planted or built on boulevards; lighting requirements; distance within property lines on which construction is permitted; required fencing around pools; management of drainage patterns; and even the overhang of trees onto neighboring property. A phone call to city hall or the rural municipality office before you begin can save a lot of grief.

Also ensure that your property lines are where you think they are. A survey is less costly and less emotionally exhausting than constructing a fence or planting a tree-shrub border only to find you've encroached on a city boulevard or a neighbor's lot. Check into any utility easement which may cross your property, and find out about bylaws that restrict the height of fences (especially on corner lots) or their placement toward the perimeter of your property.

Main Divisions of the Home Landscape

Yards have conventionally been divided into three main use areas: the public or entrance area, the service or utility area, and the private area. Although these have long been discussed as separate entities, in reality they are usually somewhat merged.

The Public Area

In North America, the front yard is usually considered a public or entrance area. Highly visible, it should be inviting, and remain attractive with minimal maintenance. Street numbers or name plates should be well lit, not obscured by plant material, and large enough to be visible from the street or road.

Walks and driveways

Centered front walks date from the era when garages were located at the back of the lot.

Drought-tolerant perennials soften a brick walkway and provide spring color.

Most garages are now attached to the house. Place the sidewalk parallel and next to the driveway and from the driveway to the front door, following the logical foot traffic pattern. This avoids cutting up and visually shrinking the front yard.

To soften a sidewalk, gently curve it and plant low evergreens, ground covers, or perennials adjacent to it to bring it "into the landscape." Choose plants that are drought tolerant, noninvasive, and will not interfere with snow removal.

The minimum grade across a driveway should be 2 cm per m (0.25 in./ft). This ensures adequate drainage and minimizes standing surface water which would otherwise be lost to evaporation. The grade should direct water from the driveway onto planting beds.

If the concrete is slightly textured, it is less slippery when wet and less reflective, thus creating a more hospitable environment for people as well as nearby plants.

Foundation plantings

Foundation plantings are those near the house which give the illusion that the house is a part of the natural landscape. They should achieve visual balance without formal symmetry or a mirror image. Plant shrubs and trees as groupings rather than narrow, monotonous lines of the same plant parallel to the house. Pay particular attention to the mature height and width of the plant material used. A 1-m (3 ft) spruce planted in front of your picture window will mature to 12 to 15 m (40–50 ft), fully blocking the view you once had.

Because your front yard is seen throughout the year by many people, think in terms of the winter landscape when selecting plants. Use evergreen and deciduous trees and shrubs with colorful bark or retained fruit which are attractive in themselves and will attract resident birds. (See p. 18)

Use larger, heavier shrubs at the corners of the house. Planting a small tree will extend the width of the house, soften corners and draw the house into its setting. Remember the idea of scale: a large, two-storey house will need larger trees and shrubs than a bungalow.

Trees and shrubs should be planted 1 to 2 m (4–6 ft) from foundations. Although this seems a wide expanse when the landscape is young, small plants do mature. This distance gives them room to grow and the homeowner space in which to paint siding, wash windows, and make repairs. At this spacing, roots are less likely to interfere with foundations, and the plants are less likely to "bump their heads" under the roof overhang and more likely to catch rain water. They will also

Often a container of annuals on the front landing or an attractive hanging basket is all that is needed to visually draw attention to the front entrance and announce a cheerful welcome.

Foundation plantings give the illusion that the house is a part of the natural landscape.

A front lawn replaced by drought-tolerant trees, shrubs, and perennials.

Drought-tolerant verbascum, lilies, and poppies dominate a cottage-type border and sharply contrast with the traditional front lawns on either side.

benefit from staying out of the hot, dry microclimate of reflected heat and light from white or reflective aluminum siding or stucco walls during their first few years when the root systems are relatively small and less able to absorb large quantities of water.

Flower beds

Flowers require higher maintenance than trees and shrubs. Depending on how and where you wish to spend your garden time, you may wish to limit the number of flower beds in the front yard. (Or you may decide to throw caution to the wind and replace the entire lawn with flowers.) Often a container of annuals on the front landing or an attractive hanging basket is all that is needed to visually draw attention to the front entrance and announce a cheerful welcome. If your house faces north, use begonias, impatience, coleus, and other plants that do well in the shade. If it faces south, use annuals tolerant of hot, dry conditions. Plants in containers will need more frequent watering than those in the ground. Increasing the organic matter in the soil mix or adding synthetic polymers will increase the water-holding capacity of container mixes.

Using xeriscape principles to their full extent in a front yard can be both challenging and creative, and will certainly grab the attention of your neighbors. Conventional lawn areas which are seldom if ever actually used as lawns can be entirely replaced with mixed beds of more drought-tolerant shrubs, perennials, and ground covers.

Service or Utility Area

This is the catchall term for everything from the clothesline to the dog run. The utility area may include the garage, garbage containers, storage sheds, greenhouse, cold frame, compost pile, vegetable garden, pad for a recreational vehicle, and the satellite dish.

These structures are sometimes located in a single area, separated and screened from the remainder of the lot; they may be in several different areas as convenient; or they may be part and parcel of the back yard and family living space. When planning service areas, consider accessibility to back lanes and the occasional delivery of bulk materials such as manure.

If the utility area is subjected to heavy wear, think about using a hard surface such as concrete, gravel, or brick. If the hard

Shrubs with green, gold, purple, and grey foliage replace a traditional front lawn.

surface covers a large area, grade it so that water is directed to plantings. If the area is not pleasing to look at, consider screening it with plants (vines, a hedge, or shrubs); a fence, wall, or lattice; or a combination of both. Install power, gas, and water to outbuildings such as garden sheds or greenhouses prior to landscaping.

The Private Area

The private area is almost always in the back yard. It is the outdoor living area for you, your household, and guests. It is usually fenced and screened for privacy.

Decks and patios

An area intended for more intensive use is usually located immediately next to the rear entrance of the house, close to both the living room and kitchen. Ideally, it's an extension of the indoor living area into the outdoors and at the same level as the indoor living area. It usually has a hard surface (wood, brick, stone, or concrete) and takes the form of a deck or patio.

A word about decks. They originated in areas where houses were often built on hillsides or foothills overlooking oceans, valleys, or large lakes. They were designed to have a view while maintaining privacy, to take advantage of the

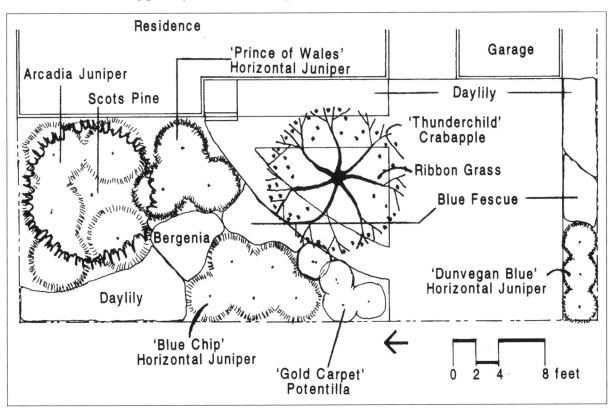

A sample design for a front yard in which the lawn has been entirely replaced with drought-tolerant trees, shrubs, perennials, and ornamental grasses.

Winter color, birds, and xeriscape design

Designing for the birds involves situating a border in a location where the housebound gardener will derive the most pleasure from the interaction of the birds with the color of the winter landscape, and where the birds will have food, shelter, and the safety in which to enjoy both. A well-located feeder is a bonus for both birds and gardener.

What we're after is a border that is easily viewed from the sidewalk or inside of the house, and that has a "layered look"—one or two canopy trees to provide shelter, a safe perch with a good view, and perhaps seed, fruit, or rough, furrowed, insect-containing bark for foraging; a middle layer of shrubs varying from 0.5 to 1.5 m (2–5 ft), selected for shelter, seeds, and berries; and a bottom layer consisting of ground cover, also selected for provision of food or shelter. The border as a whole is adjacent to a lawn or other open area that is easily viewed (this is a bird's eye view we're considering here) for cold-hardy cats and other predators.

Begin with what you have

If you have an established yard, you probably already know which trees and shrubs attract birds during the winter. Crabapple is obvious. Less obvious are pine, spruce, and Russian olive. If these plants are easily viewed from windows where you spend your wintertime, then begin with them. The average urban lot will need only one or two canopy trees for a winter bird border. A rural yard can be more expansive. Think of plants that retain their fruit through fall and all or part of winter. Color is an added bonus in a part of the world where the towing season exceeds the growing season.

Sara Williams

wolf willow, sea buckthorn, buffaloberry, honeysuckle, elder

Shorter shrubs
gooseberry, shrub roses, snowberry, juniper, golden/alpine currant

Annuals
corn, sunflower, wheat, barley, ornamental thistle

Ground covers
Manitoba grape, Virginia creeper, creeping juniper

Plants for the winter landscape
Canopy trees
Manitoba maple, green ash, Scots pine, Colorado spruce, crabapple, bur oak, Russian olive, hawthorn

Taller shrubs
lilac, saskatoon berry, pincherry, chokecherry,

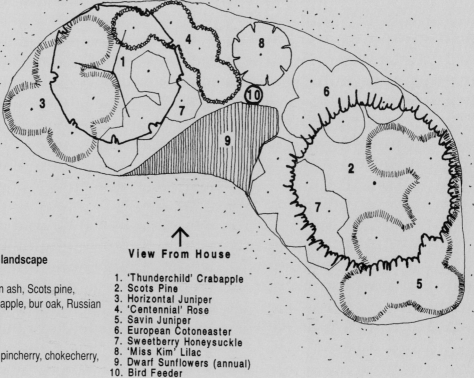

View From House

1. 'Thunderchild' Crabapple
2. Scots Pine
3. Horizontal Juniper
4. 'Centennial' Rose
5. Savin Juniper
6. European Cotoneaster
7. Sweetberry Honeysuckle
8. 'Miss Kim' Lilac
9. Dwarf Sunflowers (annual)
10. Bird Feeder

natural contours of the land, and were often built on a hillside so that what was the ground floor level on one side of the house was the second floor on the other.

Architectural styles do not always move gracefully from one geographic area to another. In a land noted for its prevailing winds, a raised deck is open to wind and wind-carried grit in early spring from surrounding agricultural land. In urban areas, the view from the deck is usually limited—at best, a neighbor's house, and at worst, a freeway. And it is usually anything but private—you're able to peer into your neighbors' yards, and your neighbors (from the sides and perhaps the back) can see everything on your deck. So, if it's not too late, consider alternatives—a patio, a sunken patio, or a deck of less than a meter (a few feet) in height—or at least effective screening against both wind and neighbors.

Whether you decide on a patio or a deck, think in terms of an area about 3.5 m by 4.5 m (12 ft x 15 ft). A deck should function as an outdoor room capable of seating six to eight adults and be roughly equivalent in shape to your living or dining room—more square than long and narrow. Humans tend to gather in groups that are oval or circular (around a dining room table or in a living room), and a deck that is the length of your house but only 1 to 1.5 m (4–5 ft) wide does not lend itself to socializing.

If the deck or patio is only slightly higher than the surrounding lawn and easily accessible with broad steps, it is easier for larger groups to spill over onto the adjoining lawn.

Flooring may be wood (if a deck) or patio squares, cement, stones, or bricks laid on sand and level with the lawn. As in the front yard, repeating the same construction materials in the patio or deck that are used in the house lends a sense of unity to the landscape.

Containers of plants can break up large expanses of hard surface while adding color. Vines help to visually lower a raised deck, pulling it into the landscape. They can also be used effectively as ceilings over decks and patios.

The back yard

A larger area, intended for less intensive use, is adjacent to the deck or patio and easily accessible from it. It is a place for the family or, on occasion, a large number of people to

This deck is covered with golden clematis, hanging baskets, and planters, providing shade, privacy, shelter, and beauty.

A brick patio is softened by drought-tolerant ground covers 'Dropmore' Nepeta (left) and 'Silver Brocade' Artemisia (right).

In a xeriscape design, raised beds should be only slightly higher than the surrounding soil, with soil amended downward to a depth of 45 cm (18 in.).

gather for a special occasion. It is usually level, grassed, and the scene of a variety of social and recreational activities.

As in the front yard, avoid a scattergun planting of trees and shrubs. It limits use of the lawn, makes the area appear visually smaller and more cut-up, hinders mowing, and increases maintenance. It is generally appropriate to use curves rather than straight lines to separate lawns from flower, tree, and shrub borders. A border that curves gently out of sight toward the edge of a property gives the illusion of greater distance and a larger yard than actually exists.

Flower beds may be separate from tree and shrub plantings or part of a mixed layered border that includes annuals, biennials, perennials, bulbs, vines, as well as trees and shrubs.

Raised beds are easy to work in, delineate and limit the space in which the soil is to be amended, are well drained, involve less bending and stooping on the part of the gardener, usually have fewer weed problems, and warm up quickly in the spring. Aesthetically, they are more visible than beds at ground level, especially for alpine plants which are of low stature. These beds add interest by varying height. If placed around a patio, they provide wind protection for the patio area, extra seating if their edges are wide enough, and if planted appropriately, a degree of privacy. If near a deck, they help to lower and tie the deck to its landscape.

From a xeriscape perspective, however, raised beds lose water much more quickly through surface and side evaporation than beds at ground level. They need a larger quantity of water applied more frequently. A compromise might be to include beds raised no more than 10 to 15 cm (4–6 in.) in your plan. Soil is then amended downward into the earth by about 45 cm (18 in.).

Designing Your Own Xeriscape: From Paper to Reality

Step 1: What Is

The first step in designing a landscape is to make an inventory of what you have. Sometimes referred to as "site analysis," it involves using graph paper and a soft pencil and making a plan: drawing to scale the existing features in your yard. One square may equal 1 m² (1 yd²). Ensure that your property lines are "real" and not assumed. These include boundaries between your lot and your neighbors', as well as municipal boulevards, back lanes, and public walkways. Use the list in the sidebar opposite to ensure you have included visible structures, traffic patterns, hidden structures, and plants to be retained. Make several photocopies of your base plan.

Once you have made a base plan of visible and hidden structures and plant material to be retained, using tracing paper, do an overlay which emphasizes topography and microclimate. You may wish to supplement the base plan with photographs of the yard as it is now.

Step 2: A Wish List

How you use your yard will depend largely on the needs and activities of your household. Make a wish list: what each member of your household wants from the available outdoor space. This might include a vegetable garden, barbecue area, play area, dog run, winter ice rink (situated on the vegetable garden or water catchment area—ice rinks are very detrimental to lawns and permanent plantings), swimming pool, a hidden corner retreat, pond, tennis court, bike rack, perennial border, herb garden, or whatever.

Your list should also include associated maintenance—a realistic assessment of the time each area or project will involve in the future.

Also consider the extent to which you wish to carry out xeriscape principles. Do you want to make these changes immediately and to your entire yard, or slowly and to only portions of your yard? Think about costs: those of professionals you may wish to hire, as well as the cost of materials and labor for grading, soil amendments, plants, irrigation, mulch, and hardscape such as decks, walks, or patios.

Consider which existing elements will aid you in developing your new landscape. Then prioritize the wish list based on time and budget considerations—and the degree to which your household operates democratically!

Step 3: Function and Use

Place tracing paper over the graph paper on which you have drawn the existing features of your yard and the overlay for topography and microclimate. Now is the time to place the ideas you came up with during the wish list phase. Think in terms of function and use, not specific plant material. The task is to make decisions about "screening the neighbor to the east," not "I want a lilac there." Think "play area" (can you utilize an existing Manitoba maple for a tree house with a slide descending into a sandbox?), "good place for moisture-loving plants," or "potential pond site." Use the Checklist for Change in the sidebar on page 22 as a guide.

Also consider features of your present landscape which will help you in developing your future landscape. Think of

---

Site analysis: What to include

Visible structures
- house (showing windows, doors, and downspouts)
- garage (showing windows, doors, and downspouts)
- driveway, sidewalks
- fence, gates
- utility poles (power and telephone), overhead wires
- satellite dish
- back lane
- garden shed, greenhouse, cold frame, compost pile
- pool
- dog run
- garbage stand
- patio, deck, barbecue
- outdoor lighting

Existing human and vehicle traffic patterns

Hidden structures
- cable TV lines, underground power lines, gas lines, sewer lines
- irrigation lines
- wells, septic tank
- any easements associated with above

Plant material to be retained
- trees (note height, spread, type of root system)
- shrubs
- flower beds
- lawns
- orchard
- vegetable garden
- shelterbelt
- native bush or prairie

Physical features
- north, south, east, west
- direction of prevailing winds
- slopes, ditches, areas of poor drainage/water catchment
- areas of permanent shade, hot, dry areas, areas where snow lingers
- frost pockets
- sheltered areas
- areas of root competition
- heat retentive surfaces, areas with reflective light
- soil type (texture, pH, salinity, organic matter)

your landscape through the different seasons of the year. What aspects of the winter landscape (when deciduous trees have dropped their leaves, the winds blow, and the snow drifts) do you want to modify? Think of sun/shade and microclimate at the time of day when you're most likely outside and enjoying your yard.

If you already have an underground irrigation system, determine what modifications, if any, it will require to accommodate your new landscape. Think about soils in your yard that have low water-holding capacity due to texture, lack of organic matter, or shallow depth. Amending these soils prior to planting will save a great deal on your water bill in future years. Alternatively, use drought-tolerant plants in areas with poor soil.

Think about your lawn area. How much of it is currently used as lawn? How much is there by default? What parts of it could be reduced and replaced with drought-tolerant shrubs, ground covers, or flower beds?

Determine traffic patterns. How is one area of your yard linked to another? Are these routes safe (well lit? slippery or icy? steep?) Are they convenient and direct? Are they wide enough?

Step 4: Filling In the Details

The final step in your plan, also on paper, involves filling in the details. To select plant material, you need to do your homework (see chapter 7), but it's also the most fun and probably the most satisfying part of landscape design. For example, you've already decided that you want a mixed border on the west side of your yard which will give you shade from the late afternoon sun and be visually pleasing. Now you decide exactly what that border will consist of.

Each area of your yard will need "walls," a "ceiling," and "flooring" in much the same way as the rooms of your house. These can be of plant or nonplant material or a combination of both.

Walls

The "walls" of your yard ensure privacy; increase your comfort by reducing dust, wind, noise, and glare; provide a pleasing backdrop for other plantings; and mark property boundaries. They enclose and define not only the yard as a whole, but the use areas within it. To do this, the material used should be fairly tall (1.5–2 m/5–6 ft), and, especially on smaller lots, take up as little width as possible. Walls are the vertical dimension of your yard and may be in the form of trees, shrubs, hedges, vines, fencing, trellises, or traditional walls of stone or brick.

Large-scale landscaping: Mass plantings in rural yards

Although the principles are the same, landscaping on a large scale is different because the space we must deal with is greater. Water conservation and reduced maintenance assume a larger role. Mixed layered borders and mass plantings of drought-tolerant perennials, ground covers, and ornamental grasses are two approaches to consider.

Mass plantings can be used to define and separate the intensively landscaped area of your farm or acreage from the nonirrigated rough grass or bush beyond. A single large bed can contain one or several different groupings. The beds themselves are usually curved and informal. They serve as a transition zone between the more manicured part of the yard and the less manicured portions. Plants used in these beds should not only be drought tolerant but have the ability to reseed or have an aggressive growth habit. Dead foliage can be left standing in the fall to act as its own windbreak and snow catchment area. Snow will pile up to insulate the plants over winter and provide added moisture in the spring. The bed can then be mowed in early spring.

Perennials useful for massed beds:

yarrow, *Artemisia* 'Silver King,' gaillardia, tansy, perennial cornflower, snow-in-summer, golden marguerite, Iceland poppies, tawny or lemon daylily, perennial blue flax, goutweed, comfrey, goldenrod

Ornamental grasses useful for massed beds:
blue fescue, ribbon grass, 'Skinner's Golden' bromegrass, blue lyme grass

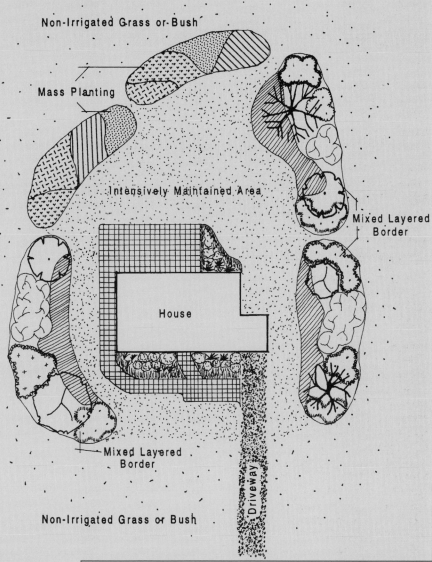

Non-Irrigated Grass or Bush

Mass Planting

Intensively Maintained Area

Mixed Layered Border

House

Mixed Layered Border

Driveway

Non-Irrigated Grass or Bush

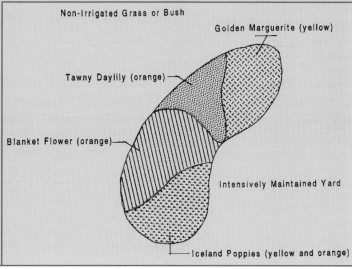

Non-Irrigated Grass or Bush

Golden Marguerite (yellow)

Tawny Daylily (orange)

Blanket Flower (orange)

Intensively Maintained Yard

Iceland Poppies (yellow and orange)

Hedges

Hedges are trees or shrubs, selected for their density, which are planted in straight lines, and usually require one or more annual shearings. Their initial cost is low, but it takes five or six years to form a good hedge. During this period they must be trained through shearing. A hedge takes up more space than a wall or fence—something to be considered on a smaller lot—and involves a very high degree of maintenance.

Shrubs

Shrubs may also form the walls of a yard. Left untrimmed in their natural shape, they should form informal shrub groupings rather than be planted in an evenly spaced straight line. Select several species for year-round interest, considering mature height and width, site requirements, disease and insect resistance, fruit, flowers, bark color and texture, leaf texture, and seasonal color changes. Shrubs need less maintenance than hedges but occupy more space; they are, however, far more interesting, much less labor intensive, and an invitation to birds to take up residence.

Trees

Know the mature height and spread of the trees you select. Choose species that are long lived and have year-round landscape value. Avoid planting trees with large, spreading, or shallow root systems (poplars, Manitoba maples, elms, and spruce) near gardens, swimming pools, walks, driveways, house foundations, septic systems, and sewer lines. Do not plant Siberian (or Manchurian) elms or large poplars on small urban lots. Although their fast growth is widely publicized, they are short lived and expensive to remove. Siberian elms self-seed generously, and poplars sucker readily. Both have weak limbs prone to wind and storm damage and are susceptible to insect infestation and disease. And both are very competitive for moisture with other plants within their root zones. Better trees are available.

Columnar trees such as upright juniper and Swedish columnar aspen are a good choice for screening, especially between properties on smaller urban lots.

Spruce and pine can be used to screen for privacy, provide a barrier, and act as a background planting through the entire year. They will deflect prevailing winds if placed on the north and west of the house and yard. They act as a snow fence, so plant them far enough from walks and buildings to prevent snow accumulation on driveways or walks.

Vines

Vines may be used to hide unsightly buildings or soften and break up an otherwise solid expanse of wall or fence. They can disguise guy wires and hide power and telephone poles. Most need some sort of support and are usually used in combination with a wall, fence, trellis, or arbor (or even allowed to drape over a dead tree). When selecting vines, consider the type of support they will need—do they have tendrils which will need something to wind around, or do they have holdfasts which will cling to brick but may damage painted surfaces?

Fencing

The advantage of fencing is its narrow spatial requirement—a few centimeters (an inch) compared to a meter (a few feet) for hedges, or a few meters (yards) for shrubs and trees. Other advantages include the "instant" quality of its installation and its relative permanency. From a xeriscape point of view, a fence may need repainting, but never watering. Its disadvantages are its initial expense and periodic maintenance.

Masonry walls

Walls are traditionally constructed of brick or stone. Choose a material that has already been used on your house or in your land-scape for walkways or patio flooring. Walls require skill to build but are relatively perma-nent. Aesthetically, they lend an Old World charm to your landscape, giving privacy and wind protection.

Garden ceilings

Garden ceilings provide shade, shelter, and the beauty of color and texture. Trees, vines, roof overhangs, awnings, pergolas, and trellises may all be used to advantage.

Trees

When deciding on the placement of shade trees, think of where you want shade and the direction of the sun at the time of day you'll most likely be using that area. Use deciduous trees to provide shade for patios, decks, or the south- and west-facing walls of a house. There, they provide shade and cooler tem-peratures during the heat of summer, but allow the warmth of the sun to penetrate during winter and early spring when their boughs are bare.

A deck or patio may be constructed to include an existing tree, or a space may be left so that a young one may be planted. Your design should allow for the expanding trunk diameter of the tree as well as its water requirements. Interlocking bricks are easily removed as the growth of the trunk requires.

Avoid selecting "messy" shade trees or nuisance trees near

Sara Williams

Slopes and banks are ideal locations for rock gardens, giving the plants the perfect drainage they require, lifting them visually, and preventing runoff and soil erosion.

A deck built around an existing tree.

patios or decks. Among these are Manitoba maples (honey-dew from aphids, twig and seed drop), elms (aphids, canker-worms, self-seeding), willows (self-prune during strong winds), poplars and cottonwoods (seed, sucker, drop twigs and some "fluff"), and large-fruited crabapples that drop their fruit in fall rather than retaining it through the winter.

Trellises, arbors, pergolas, and roof overhangs
These types of garden ceilings are usually draped with vines. They provide summer shade yet do not interfere with air circulation beneath. Manitoba grape, Virginia creeper, clematis, and honeysuckle allow the spring and early summer sun to warm a deck or patio while still providing shade and cooler temperatures during the heat of summer.

Flooring for outdoors
Like walls and ceiling, flooring used in the landscape can be of plant and nonplant materials. While grass is the most common flooring in conventional landscapes, in a xeriscape design lawn is replaced with drought-tolerant ground covers and, in intensively used areas, with nonplant material. There is extensive use of decks and patios, which may require some upkeep on your part, but never water!

Hard surfaces
Nonplant materials commonly used as flooring in the landscape include wood (decks), crushed stone or gravel (informal paths), and natural stone, brick, concrete block, poured concrete, and interlocking concrete or clay brick (patios, walkways, and driveways). Select materials which reflect the materials used in your house and which reflect the formality or informality of your landscape. Avoid hard surfaces which reflect light or absorb an undue amount of heat.

Lawns
Lawns are pleasant to look at, resilient, comfortable to sit and walk on, and safe for children. But they require more water than any other part of the landscape and are often planted much more extensively than their use dictates. In xeriscape designs, lawns are reduced to that area which is actually used as a lawn (rather than an expanse of green turf that is only looked at), shaped to conform to the delivery pattern of the sprinkler used to irrigate them, and cared for just a bit differently than conventional lawns—all in an effort to conserve water. (See chapter 6.)

Ground covers
Ground covers may consist of low evergreen or deciduous shrubs, ornamental grasses, vines,

Sara Williams

Ribbon grass replaces lawn where it can be contained by a walkway and large rocks.

or perennials. They are useful where lawns are not practical, where a different color, texture, or height is desired, or where a lower type of continuous plant material is needed to unify several trees and shrubs within a planting. In a xeriscape design, ground covers are chosen for their drought tolerance.

Low junipers and sedums are useful on terraces or steep slopes where lawns would be difficult to establish and maintain and would be wasteful of water. More aggressive plants such as goutweed, ribbon grass, or bigfoot geranium excel in this situation.

Although we think of vines as vertical, Virginia creeper and Manitoba grape are also useful horizontally, and make excellent ground covers, especially on slopes or banks.

Bergenia, creeping juniper, and sedums can unify tree-shrub borders while simultaneously preventing weed establishment and controlling erosion. When planted around a specimen tree or group of trees (such as daylilies at the base of a bur oak, or bergenias under a flowering crabapple tree), ground covers tend to emphasize that tree or grouping as a focal point.

Thyme, dwarf veronica, smaller sedums, and other flowering alpine or rockery plants may be planted on the edge of and among paving stones, interlocking bricks, patio blocks, or conventional bricks to soften and add color to an otherwise large expanse of hard surface forming a patio, walk, driveway, or garden stairway. These should not be planted in the direct line of traffic, as they will not tolerate being trampled.

Bigfoot geranium is an excellent perennial ground cover in sun or shade.

Mulches

Organic mulches used to cover the soil surface in planting beds (see chapter 5) also constitute flooring material, and in many instances serve a design function. They provide color and texture, unify a large planting bed, especially when the plant material is still young and small, and in a subtle way announce that this area has indeed been landscaped and would be better walked around than across! In beds with smaller plants or plants of low stature, use finer mulches or top-dress coarse mulching materials with coarse peat moss. Where plants are larger, coarser mulches may be applied. Mulches such as wood chips and post peelings can be used for informal paths and walkways.

Wood chips or post peelings can be used to mulch an informal walk made of disks of trees. The disks should be a minimum of 20 cm (8 in.) thick to prevent splitting. The mulch controls weeds and protects the soil.

Too aggressive for an irrigated border, goutweed is more constrained when used as a ground cover under established trees where little else will grow.

Sara Williams

Grouping by water needs

Using your site analysis, divide your yard into separate areas for plants with low, moderate, and high water needs.

Use the most drought-tolerant plants (indicated by the icon Ψ in chapter 7) in the following areas:

- areas with higher elevation
- southern or western exposures
- areas with the least water-retentive soil (soil that is sandy or lacks organic matter)
- areas with reflected light (from white or aluminum siding, stucco, or a white fence), especially from south- or west-facing structures
- near heat-retentive surfaces (asphalt or concrete)
- on slopes
- in the path of prevailing winds
- on the perimeter of rural properties
- near mature trees with competitive roots
- in full sun.

Drought-tolerant plants in these areas will need irrigation during establishment, but will later require little if any supplemental water.

At the opposite extreme are plants with high water needs, including willows, birch, primroses, tea roses, and strawberries. Group these in the following areas:

- areas with moisture-retentive soils (clay, loam, or those containing generous quantities of organic matter)
- areas of lower elevation
- purposely contoured water catchment areas
- northern or eastern exposures
- areas that are shaded or partially shaded and sheltered from prevailing winds
- areas with no root competition from established trees
- areas where snow accumulates in winter and melts slowly in spring, or where water lingers after a heavy rain or irrigation.

This grouping of plants with higher water needs is relatively small and is situated as close to the house as possible to make watering easier and more convenient.

Use plants that have moderate water requirements between these two extremes. Moderately drought-tolerant plants (also listed in chapter 7) will need supplemental water during extended hot, dry periods. Direct water from catchment areas toward beds containing these plants.

Further Reading

Design

Landscaping for Water Conservation: Xeriscape!, edited by Kimberly Knox (City of Aurora, Colorado, 1989).

Landscaping for Wildlife, by Carrol L. Henderson (Minnesota Department of Natural Resources, 1987).

Wildlife Gardening in Saskatchewan: Building Backyard Biodiversity, by Karen Scalise (Wildlife Branch, Saskatchewan Environment and Resource Management, 1996).

Throwing a curve at shelterbelts

More than a century ago, surveyors laid out the Prairies in a grid, and we still think in terms of sections and half-sections. Living on the Prairies gives us a geometrical mind-set. Everything, including shelterbelts, is done on the square.

Shelterbelts are planted for utilitarian reasons: to provide wind protection, conserve moisture, protect buildings and farm yards, conserve heat, and prevent topsoil from blowing away. It is hard to imagine what our landscape would be like without them.

Shelterbelts are almost invariably laid out in rigidly straight lines with one tree or shrub species per line and no consideration for aesthetics, yet there is no reason why they cannot be beautiful as well as functional.

In the last decade, thoughts on shelterbelts have begun to change. Wildlife and "agro-forestry" plantings have become accepted. It's time we threw a curve at the prairie grid and added beauty.

Use those trees and shrubs listed in chapter 7 designated as very drought tolerant (Ψ) or those available from PFRA. Maintain the within-the-row and between-the-row spacings recommended by your supplier. Design the inner two or three rows as "groupings" of one species rather than using one plant species per row. (Note: poplar are removed once green ash have become established.) Then curve the entire shelterbelt to fit your farm or acreage yard.

The initial planning and planting will take a little more time and effort, but contrary to popular opinion, cultivators can make curves. The payoff? It's the view from your deck, patio, driveway, or kitchen window. All of the functions a shelterbelt was designed for are retained, but the groupings will present a visual image of changing flowers, fruit, and foliage through the seasons. You'll have gained the dimensions of color, scent, songbirds, and fruit.

An informal tree-shrub border in a rural setting provides bright fall color and low maintenance. The brilliant orange-red of the untrimmed cotoneaster contrasts with the silver of Russian olive.

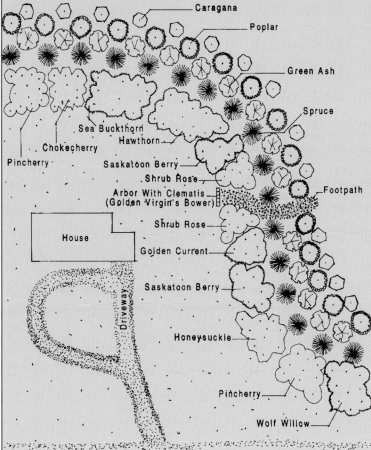

irt is what's tracked onto your kitchen floor. Soil is what plants grow in.

Chapter 3

Soil

——

From the Ground Up

Soil is basic to the concept of xeriscape. Soil that has been amended so that it readily absorbs and holds water makes a big difference to the health of your plants, the frequency with which you must irrigate, and the efficient use of water.

We tend to take soil for granted, but more plant problems are related to soil than any other factor. All too often, we would rather look for a quick fix, like an insecticide or synthetic fertilizer, than deal with problems related to soil. It's more effective, however, to start from the ground up and ensure that the soil you work with has the capacity to supply plants with the needed oxygen, water, and nutrients.

Soil *is* important. It provides mechanical or physical support for plants—quite simply, a medium in which they can grow. Soil water is required for the hundreds of biochemical reactions which take place within a plant. It prevents plants from wilting, and provides nutrients and a cooling system.

What Is Soil?

Soil forms a relatively shallow layer on the earth's surface. It is dynamic. It has changed over the millennia since its formation, and to a lesser degree over the past few days. These changes may involve moisture, temperature, organic matter content, microorganisms, or nutrient levels. These often have an effect on how well plants grow.

Rock, Organic Matter, Water, and Air

Contrary to its appearance, only 50 percent of soil is solid. Most of this is formed from rock which has been worn down, broken up, and eroded to form smaller and smaller particles of mineral matter of various sizes. A smaller percentage of the solid portion of the soil, usually up to 5 percent by volume, is made up of organic matter, which is or was alive. It is mostly composed of decayed vegetation contributed by the roots of native grasses, aided by earthworms, ants, and pocket gophers. Microorganisms play a key role in the decay process. This process recycles nutrients, making them continually available to plants.

Along with the clay content of the soil, organic matter gives soil its ability to absorb and hold water and the nutrients that are dissolved in the soil water. It improves the tilth (workability) of the soil and provides a slow release of nutrients. It also helps to maintain the pore structure of the soil—the spaces in between the solid soil particles. This affects the soil's porosity—its ability to allow water to infiltrate through the pores—and its aeration and water-storing capacity. The higher the organic matter content, the greater the soil's ability to hold and store water and nutrients.

Of the remaining 50 percent of the soil's volume, ideally 25 percent is water and 25 percent air. The soil atmosphere, located in the pore spaces among the solid particles, is variable but generally consists of 20 percent oxygen, 79 percent nitrogen, and 1 percent carbon dioxide. All plant cells, including those of the roots, need oxygen. When soils are waterlogged and water fills the pore space, oxygen is unavailable and plants suffer.

The relationship of air, water, soil, and plants is discussed in chapter 4.

Origins

Most of our soils were deposited by the Wisconsin Glacier over 10,000 years ago. In the northern shield it stripped existing soil, leaving only bedrock. Since its retreat, little new soil has formed. On the prairies, the ice sheet melted and deposited a thick layer of glacial till: the combination of soil, stones, and bedrock brought from the north. Only the higher elevations of the Cypress Hills of Alberta and Saskatchewan were missed.

Climate and vegetation have also influenced our soils. Due

to greater precipitation, forests developed in the north. Because of their longevity (usually over 100 years), the root systems of forest trees contributed relatively little to the organic matter of northern soils, but the leaves and needles they shed fell on the soil surface and formed a thin layer of organic material called leaf litter.

In the south, where moisture was limited, perennial grasses predominated. Each year a proportion of the extensive root system of these grasses died and decayed, contributing to the organic matter of the soil. These root systems often exceeded 3 m (9 ft) in depth. The organic matter found in southern soils is much greater and deeper than the thin leaf-litter layer of the north.

Soil Texture: Sand, Silt, and Clay

Soil texture refers to the relative proportion of sand, silt, and clay in a given soil. The rock or mineral portion of soil is classified and described in terms of the size of these individual particles. Loam has almost equal proportions of sand, silt, and clay. It is the preferred soil texture for horticulture because of its ease of workability.

Sand has the largest particles (0.05–2.0 mm in diameter). They are visible to the naked eye, irregular in shape and size, and gritty to the touch when wetted. A sandy soil drains easily and quickly after rain or irrigation, is easily worked, and warms up quickly in the spring. But it has a very low moisture-holding capacity and must be watered frequently. It also has a low nutrient-holding capacity and must be fertilized more often than a clay soil. When vegetative cover or mulch is lacking, it is subject to wind and water erosion.

Silt particles are intermediate in size (0.002 to 0.05 mm in diameter). They are irregular in shape and visible only with the aid of a microscope. Silt particles feel smooth and slippery to the touch when wetted.

Clay particles are smallest of all (less than 0.002 mm in diameter) and only visible with the aid of an electron microscope. Clay particles consist of plate-like layers, giving them a relatively large external surface, at least 1,000 times that of sand. They attract positively charged water ions as well as nutrients such as calcium, magnesium, and potassium. When wet, clay is sticky to the touch.

Clay soils hold large amounts of water and nutrients, but are often poorly drained. They warm up more slowly in the spring, which means a delay of a week or two in planting, shortening an already limited growing season. Because of their large water-holding capacity, they are subject to expansion and contraction with alternate freezing and thawing in spring and fall, causing root damage and heaving of plants out of the soil. Crusting and cracking are also common

Soil Particles

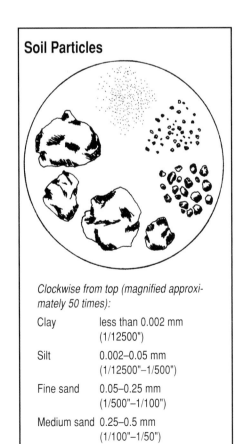

Clockwise from top (magnified approximately 50 times):

Clay	less than 0.002 mm (1/12500")
Silt	0.002–0.05 mm (1/12500"–1/500")
Fine sand	0.05–0.25 mm (1/500"–1/100")
Medium sand	0.25–0.5 mm (1/100"–1/50")

problems in clay soils. Crusting impedes water percolation and seedling emergence and encourages runoff. Cracking damages and dries out roots. Clay soils are often difficult to work if their moisture content is not optimal. If too wet, they are gummy and impossible. If too dry, they can be similar to concrete.

Problems with Soil

Besides being too sandy or too clay-like, soils may have poor structure, or problems associated with pH or salt. Plants grow poorly on soils that lack aeration or drainage. They also do poorly on soils that are unable to hold water or nutrients, are unduly acidic or alkaline, or are saline.

As gardeners, we have a choice. We can limit the plants we grow to those to which our soil is suited, or change the soil and grow the plants we want to grow. Incorporating soil amendments alleviates many problems, enormously increasing the workability and productivity of these soils.

Hardpans

Hardpans are compacted layers usually less than a meter (a few inches or feet) below the soil surface. They impede root penetration and water percolation and usually contribute to poor drainage and aeration. If the hardpan is immediately below the soil surface, the effective soil depth is limited, resulting in poor plant growth.

Compaction problems are often the result of repeated use of heavy machinery on wet soils. Compaction destroys the aggregation, or structure, of soil particles, thus reducing the pore space capable of holding air and water.

Improving these soils requires digging below the hardpan, breaking it up and thoroughly incorporating generous amounts of organic matter. Alternatively, raised beds containing amended soil may be constructed above the hardpans. This is often an easy and effective alternative, but it is not conserving of water. The higher a bed is raised, the greater the amount of water lost to evaporation.

pH

pH is a measure of the acidity or alkalinity of a soil, measured on a scale of 0 to 14, with 0 being the acidic end of the scale, 7 neutral, and 14 the alkaline end. The pH scale is logarithmic rather than geometric: A pH of 6 is 10 times more acidic than a pH of 7. A pH of 5 is 100 times more acidic than a pH of 7.

The pH of a soil is largely determined by the rock from which it originated, not the forest trees which grow there.

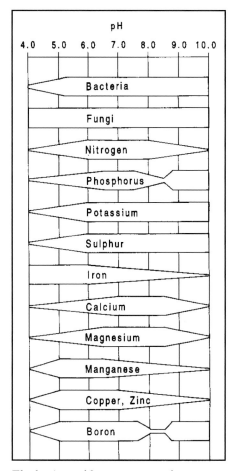

The horizontal bars represent the availability of nutrients and the level of activity of microorganisms at various pH levels. Fungi are active at all pH levels. The availability of iron decreases dramatically at a pH of over 7.0. (See "Iron Chlorosis" on the following page.)

pH is important because it indicates availability of nutrients. At a neutral pH (7), most nutrients in the soil water are in a soluble form and can be absorbed and used by plants. Soil bacteria and fungi are also active in this range. A pH of 6 to 7.5 is considered ideal for horticulture. As the pH moves further away from this range, some nutrients become less soluble in the soil water and thus less available for plant use. Bacterial activity, important to the availability of nitrogen and other nutrients, is also reduced.

Most prairie soils are basic, or alkaline (with a pH greater than 7). This means that iron, an essential trace element, although present in the soil, is often tied up in an insoluble form and unavailable for plant use. At a pH much above 8, phosphorus, manganese, zinc, copper, cobalt, and boron may also be unavailable.

Northern forest soils tend to be acidic. Although most plants grow well at a neutral pH, blueberries and azaleas will only grow in more acidic soils. Even if soil is generously amended with peat moss, eventually the pH rises due to the alkalinity of rain and the surrounding soil.

It is difficult to permanently raise or lower the pH of soils. Lime is used to raise the pH of acidic soils; elemental sulfur, ammonium sulfate, peat moss, and organic matter are used to lower the pH of alkaline soils. Apply these in accordance with recommendations from a soil-testing laboratory based on the results of a soil test.

Salinity

Salinity is the measure of salts within a soil. It often occurs where the water table is relatively close to the soil surface. Salts are wicked to the surface through evaporation and capillary action during the summer, when the evaporation rate is often greater than the precipitation rate. Over time, these salts accumulate and plant growth is adversely affected.

Saline soils are not conducive to plant growth because instead of water moving from the soil into the plant, water is pulled from the relatively pure solution within the plant into the more concentrated solution of the saline soil water. Bathing in the Dead Sea or a mineral spa would do the same thing to our skin—dry it out! As water is pulled out of the plant, a water deficiency is created and the plant wilts and dies.

Saline soils can be improved by providing better drainage, deep watering, and incorporating generous quantities of well-rotted organic material. Adding fresh manures with ammonia salts will make them worse. A soil test will indicate the presence of salinity.

Making Better: Soil Amendments

Soil amendments are organic or inorganic materials added to the soil to improve its productivity. They do this by improving aeration (ability to permit air flow through soil), drainage, nutrient- and water-holding capacity, and generally tilth (workability or friability). They may be added to large planting beds or individual planting holes, depending on their cost, availability, the plant material, and the existing soil.

Always thoroughly incorporate amendments into the existing soil. Never leave them as a surface layer. When soils of different textures are layered, capillary movement of water from one layer to the next is impeded. This leads to saturation of the upper layer and lateral rather than downward movement of the water before the second layer is wetted. Root penetration is often impeded, leading to shallow root development, leaving plants more vulnerable to cold, heat, and drought. Thorough incorporation of soil amendments—so that a gradation exists from the amended topsoil to the subsoil—encourages water percolation and root development into the lower soil depths.

If large quantities of amendment are to be added to a planting bed or vegetable garden, it may be beneficial to spread a 5 to 7.5 cm (2–3 in.) layer, thoroughly incorporate it by tilling, then add another layer, and perhaps even a third, rather than adding all of the amendment at once.

Organic Amendments

All organic soil amendments will eventually break down through microbial action. When conditions are consistently warm and moist this happens more quickly. Under dry prairie conditions and our limited growing season, this process is relatively slow. Organic matter breaks down sooner if the soil is frequently tilled.

As organic matter breaks down, it releases nutrients. It also improves the physical structure of the soil, its aeration, and water- and nutrient-holding abilities.

It is relatively easy to document nutrients released by organic matter. It is more difficult to place an economic value on improved soil structure, so as significant as this may be in the life of a gardener, its value is often ignored.

Bacteria and fungi play a critical role in decomposition. The more diverse the microbial population, the less likely is the uncontrolled spread of a single harmful microbe. Some beneficial microbes are able to "fix" atmospheric nitrogen in a form usable by plants. Others, within plant root zones, stimulate plant growth by secreting hormones. Organic

Amending planting holes

It is often more economical of time and money to amend only the planting holes of trees and shrubs rather than an entire planting bed. Some studies in the United States, however, have shown that it may be detrimental to add organic matter to planting holes. Plants on heavy clay soils have fared poorly because too much water is held by the amendment and the roots lack oxygen. Once the amendments dry out, they are difficult to rewet. Roots do not move out into the poorer surrounding soil, thus reducing the soil volume from which they can absorb water and nutrients.

If amendments in a planting hole are thoroughly incorporated with the existing soil, both in depth and laterally, these problems will be decreased.

Sandy soils will usually benefit from the addition of organic matter to planting holes and clay soils from a mixture of organic matter and *very coarse* sand. Alternatively, entire beds may be amended.

Aggregation and organic matter

An aggregate is made up of many individual soil particles. It is the crumb-like structure seen with our naked eye. Aggregation of soil particles improves and increases the pore structure of the soil, facilitating water infiltration and drainage. The addition of organic matter increases the aggregation of soil: microbes themselves produce a gelatinous substance that holds soil particles together; fungal hyphae wrap around soil particles; and humic acids form complexes with clay particles.

Synthetic fertilizers

A fertilizer supplies elements (such as nitrogen, phosphorus, and potassium) essential for plant growth. Synthetic fertilizers are usually less expensive per unit weight of nutrient than organic fertilizers. They are usually water soluble, have a predictable rate of release, and are consistent in the percentage of nutrients they contain.

Synthetic fertilizers add nutrients to the soil but do not improve its texture or structure. Their solubility can lead to inefficient use, leaching below the root zones of plants, and contamination of groundwater. Slow-release fertilizers are available but more expensive.

matter supplies both habitat and nutrients for microorganisms, thereby increasing the level of microbial or biological activity.

As organic matter decomposes, it forms humus, a form of humic acid, which holds potassium, calcium, magnesium, and hydrogen in the soil solution in a form that is readily available to plants but is not easily leached. The addition of organic matter to sandy soils can dramatically improve nutrient availability and reduce nutrient leaching. Because humus attracts water molecules, a soil's water-holding capacity is also increased by the addition of organic matter. Organic matter can hold almost twice as much water as clay.

Compost

Compost is living material on its way to becoming humus—the dark, crumbly, sweet-smelling stuff that is the result of decomposition. Composting recycles organic materials from your landscape by speeding up normal biological processes. It does this by providing optimum conditions of oxygen and moisture for the raw materials. The end product is an excellent soil conditioner and slow-release fertilizer which would otherwise be lost forever to garbage dumps and landfills.

The soil microorganisms that do the work require oxygen, water, and a balance of nitrogen ("green stuff," such as grass clippings, fresh kitchen waste, and garden refuse) and carbon ("yellow stuff," such as dry grass and leaves and straw). Soil and the materials that go into the compost pile usually contain enough microorganisms. Commercial inoculants are available but a shovelful of soil will usually suffice.

There are various methods of composting. Sheet composting involves spreading out the raw materials on the soil surface and incorporating them with a spade or a tiller. This is best done in the fall on a garden area. In trench composting, a trench 45 cm (18 in.) in depth and the same width is dug in a garden area and filled with kitchen scraps or grass clippings as they become available, and then covered. The location of the trench itself is rotated from season to season.

Compost piles are a more concentrated method of composting. The finished product can be used anywhere in the landscape. Urban residents are more likely to use bins because of concerns about aesthetics and space. Many building plans are available as well as ready-made commercial composters. Compost may simply be put in a pile. The minimum effective size is 1 m³ (1 yd³). Smaller piles are prone to moisture and heat loss.

Traditionally, the contents of a pile or bin are layered, 10 to 20 cm (4–8 in.) deep, alternating high-carbon materials and high-nitrogen materials with a few centimeters (approximately an inch) of soil in between. Enough water is added to keep the pile moist but not waterlogged. The pile should be

---

Troubleshooting the compost pile

Problem	Solution
Foul-smelling	Not enough oxygen. Turn the pile. Cover with soil for immediate relief.
Ammonia vapors	Nitrogen is escaping. Probably too many high-nitrogen raw materials. Turn the pile and add some "yellow stuff."
Not working	Pile lacks moisture or nitrogen-rich raw materials. Add water and grass clippings. Turn the pile.

What can be composted?

• kitchen scraps such as fruit, vegetables, tea bags, coffee grounds, egg shells
• leaves
• grass clippings
• garden refuse without seed heads
• livestock manures

What not to compost

• meat and bones
• weeds that have gone to seed
• cat, dog, pig, and human feces
• diseased garden refuse

---

turned so that oxygen is present. If organic materials decay without oxygen (anaerobic decomposition), they will smell much like silage.

To be effective, piles should heat to 70°C (160°F), hot enough to kill most weed seeds and decompose raw materials. On the prairies, it generally takes a full growing season to yield usable compost, but this depends on the materials used, their size (smaller particles decompose more quickly), the moisture and oxygen content of the pile, and ambient temperature.

Manures and other animal by-products

Organic fertilizers—for the most part farm animal manures—hold nutrients in a less leachable form and release them slowly.

Manures may not be readily available in urban areas and are labor-intensive to spread. Their nitrogen content decreases with age, exposure to wind and rain, and the degree of microbial activity to which they have been subjected. Much is lost by leaching and volatilization (evaporation). Bedding and litter mixed with manures lower the percent of nitrogen by dilution but increase the amount of organic matter. If immediately incorporated into a vegetable garden or planting bed in the fall, nitrogen loss is reduced.

Fresh manure is high in ammonia and salts and will "burn," or desiccate, plants. It should be aged or composted for at least a year. Composting allows the ammonia to volatilize into the air, salts to be leached out by rain, and weed seeds to heat to the point where they are no longer viable.

Manures are variable in their nutrient content depending on the type of animal, the feed of the animal, and the age and storage conditions of the manure. Commercially dried manures are more costly than bulk manures.

Blood meal, bone meal, and hoof and horn meal are all by-products of the slaughterhouse. They contain a higher concentration of nutrients (including trace elements) but less organic matter than many other amendments mentioned. Blood meal and hoof and horn meal contain quick-release forms of nitrogen; bone meal has a slowly released form of phosphorous. These products are relatively expensive and not always available, as many have been diverted into animal feeds.

Peat moss

Peat moss improves soil aeration, increases its ability to hold nutrients and water, and adds organic matter to the soil. It decomposes at a moderate rate, but the coarser the material, the slower the decomposition. Peat moss is very low in nutrient value, containing up to 3 percent nitrogen but few other nutrients. Its pH is between 3.0 and 4.5, making it useful for acid-loving plants and for lowering the pH of alkaline soils. It is a consistent and lightweight product, but

Average percentage of available nitrogen, phosphorous, and potassium in animal manures and by-products

Product	N	P	K
fresh cow manure			
with bedding	0.5	0.3	0.5
dried poultry manure	4.0	3.0	3.0
dried rabbit manure	2.4	0.6	0.05
fresh sheep manure	1.0	0.4	0.2
fresh horse manure	0.4	0.2	0.4
blood meal	10–15	1.3	0.7
bone meal	2–4	22–24	0.2
hoof & horn meal	10–14	1–2	0

Myth and reality: Nitrogen depletion, toxicity, and acidity

Wood products suffer from bad publicity regarding their effects on nitrogen, their toxicity to other plants, and their "acid" nature.

Wood shavings decompose slowly due to their high carbon and lignin content and generally do not tie up nitrogen. Sawdust decomposes more rapidly and may temporarily tie up soil nitrogen. Sawdust of deciduous trees decomposes more quickly and is more likely to be a problem than that of coniferous trees. Extra nitrogen may be added to the soil at the rate of 1 kg (2 lb) per 45 kg (100 lb) of wood amendment. Or, sawdust, shavings, and bark may be composted before being added to the soil.

Monitor plants for signs of nitrogen deficiency when using wood amendments. Look for overall pale green or yellow foliage, especially on older growth. If these symptoms appear, treat the nearby soil with a water-soluble form of nitrogen.

Except for a few species, none of which are grown on the prairies, toxicity is not considered a problem. Trees with phytotoxic properties include: western red cedar, white pine (bark), black walnut, hemlock (bark), and redwood. Bark or sawdust from green, newly milled trees will be more toxic. Allowing these products to leach for six weeks reduces their toxicity. Toxic substances are usually destroyed by soil bacteria and fungi within a few weeks after the addition of sawdust or shavings to soil.

Although most sawdust is slightly acid, it has no harmful effect on soils. Organic acids formed during decomposition break down quickly and the final effect on soil pH is negligible.

large quantities can be expensive. Peat moss should be moistened prior to use.

Leaf mold

Leaf mold is a valuable soil amendment consisting mainly of decayed leaves, which all too often we bag and send to the dump. Leaves may be mowed with a lawn mower in the fall and immediately spread and incorporated into a vegetable garden or annual flower bed, piled separately for later use, or added to a compost pile.

Mushroom compost

This is the material that remains after mushrooms have been harvested. It generally begins as a mixture of animal manures and straw and has usually been heated enough to kill any soil organisms that would compete with the mushroom themselves. It has a low level of nutrients but is an excellent soil conditioner. It may contain salts.

Wood products: sawdust, chips, and ash

Per tonne (ton), sawdust contains about 1.8 kg (4 lb) of nitrogen, 0.9 kg (2 lb) of phosphorus, 1.8 kg (4 lb) of potassium, 2.7 kg (6 lb) of calcium and 0.2 kg (0.5 lb) of magnesium. Sawdust and bark chips may be added to clay soils to improve aeration and to sandy soils to increase their water- and nutrient-holding abilities.

Wood ash is 25 percent calcium, 5 to 10 percent potassium, and 1 to 2 percent phosphorus by weight, plus trace elements. If used in large quantities (over 10 kg per 100 m^2/20 lb per 1,000 ft^2), it may raise the pH of the soil to which it is applied. Do not apply it near acid-loving plants such as azaleas or blue berries. Avoid direct contact with young plants and germinating seeds.

Green manures

Green manures, sometimes called cover crops, are seeded in summer and turned under once mature (but prior to seed formation) in late fall or spring of the following year. If left over winter, they protect the soil and trap snow. When incorporated, they add nutrients and organic matter to soil. They are usually grown a full year prior to the area being planted. They are inexpensive (the only cost is seed), but take time and labor. Fall rye, alfalfa, sweet clover, oats, peas, lentils, millet, and buckwheat have been used for this purpose.

Topsoil

If topsoil is thin, it is often beneficial to add more. Topsoil is extremely variable from source to source. If you're investing in a large quantity, obtain a sample and have it tested to determine its texture, the amount of organic material present, and its salt content. If it's an agricultural soil, you can often detect the presence of herbicides by a germination test using fresh pea or bean seeds. If seeds fail to germinate, it may indicate herbicide contamination.

Further Reading

Soil

The Nature and Properties of Soils, by Nyle C. Brady (Macmillan Publishing Co., Inc., New York, 1974).

Inorganic Amendments

Inorganic soil amendments are added to improve soil texture, aiding aeration and drainage. They must be purchased and hauled, are variable in their durability, and usually provide little or no nutrient value.

Sand

Sand is sometimes used in combination with an equal volume of organic material to lighten heavy clay soils. The sand used should be coarse-textured (with a particle diameter greater than 0.5 mm) and of irregular shape—not small, rounded particles. If small, rounded particles of sand are added directly to clay, the resultant soil is similar to concrete. Washed, coarse silica sand (also called builders' sand) is recommended. Sand improves drainage by creating larger pores. Very large quantities of coarse sand and organic matter are required to make a significant change. Experiment with a small area to determine the optimum amount to be incorporated.

Perlite

Perlite is manufactured from a granite-like, volcanic rock which is first crushed and then heated to 980°C (1800°F), causing its granules to expand and fill with air. It is white, inert, lightweight, has a neutral pH, and holds few nutrients. Its surface is covered with tiny pores that trap moisture. It is used almost exclusively in greenhouses and indoors in soilless media. In the short term, it increases soil aeration and drainage. It is usually too expensive for landscape use and is not long-lasting. Lacking mechanical strength, it soon becomes crushed in outdoor soils and then impedes rather than enhances drainage. It is dusty, and a mask should be used when mixing it or working with it.

Vermiculite

Vermiculite is an inert, lightweight, and consistent product. It is manufactured by heating particles of raw mica to 870°C (1600°F), expanding them up to 12 times their normal volume. It can bind and release nutrients, has some potassium and magnesium, and a pH of 6.0 to 6.5. It is used extensively indoors in soilless media. It increases the soil's ability to absorb water, but is expensive and not economical to use in the landscape. Nor is it long-lasting. Like perlite, it lacks

Hydrogels and soils: The jury is still out

Hydrogels are sometimes used in sandy soils, incorporated to a depth of 15 cm (6 in.). The expansion and contraction of the gels is also thought to provide aeration and improved drainage to clay soils. Along with water, they are able to store dissolved nutrients, reducing leaching losses. They are said to last about 10 years within the soil.

But problems have been observed when hydrogels absorb iron, magnesium, or calcium. These minerals, present in most prairie soils, cause hydrogels to break down, destroying their structure. In soil, this breakdown results in decreased pore space and insufficient oxygen availability to plant roots. The end result has been described as a slimy mass that fills the pore spaces and results in conditions far worse than if hydrogels had not been incorporated. Caution is advised when incorporating hydrogels into outdoor soils.

mechanical strength, and in outdoor soils it soon collapses, impeding rather than enhancing drainage.

Hydrogels

Also called water-absorbing polymers or cross-linked polyacrylamides, these are inert polymer crystals that swell with water that is then released slowly to plants as needed, preventing or delaying drought stress. They are presumed capable of soaking up and storing a hundred times their own weight in water. Full expansion of the polymers may take up to six hours. *Plants will still need the same amount of water.* The use of hydrogels reduces the frequency of irrigation. They are best used in containers such as hanging baskets.

In xeriscape design, plants are separated into zones according to their water needs.

Chapter 4

Irrigation

Every Drop Counts

Irrigation water supplements natural precipitation when landscape plants need more water than nature can provide. Until the last decade, both homeowners and the irrigation industry focused on the delivery of water rather than water conservation. As water for landscape use becomes more scarce and restrictions are placed upon its use, we are becoming more conscious of the need to design irrigation systems that conserve water.

While your choice of plants influences how much extra water will be needed, in a geographic area like the prairies with an average annual precipitation of 30 to 50 cm (12–20 in.), most conventional lawns and many other plants will require some degree of irrigation.

The philosophy of xeriscape irrigation is to satisfy the needs of plants without wasting water. This can be accomplished with a hose or by installing a fully automated underground irrigation system, or any combination of the two. Appropriate irrigation can reduce water use by a *minimum* of 20 percent. In order to do this one should design the landscape, consider irrigation options, and then coordinate and fine tune both so that little water is wasted.

Knowing the relationship between soil and water and understanding why plants need water and how they absorb, store, and conserve water will help you irrigate in a manner which encourages optimum plant growth while minimizing water waste and reducing water costs.

The Science of Water and Soil

As explained in the chapter on soils, only about 50 percent of the volume of an average soil is composed of solid matter. Most of this is mineral material—broken down rocks varying in size from large particles of very coarse sand (0.5 to 2.0 mm in diameter) to microscopic particles of clay which are less than 0.002 mm in diameter.

The ideal soil volume is about 50 percent solid, 25 percent liquid, and 25 percent air. The liquid and air portion take up the pore space between the solid soil particles. The larger air spaces are called macropores, the smaller spaces micropores.

When You Water or When It Rains...

Water, whether from rainfall or irrigation, percolates into the soil from the surface, filling the pore spaces between the solid soil particles and forming a "wetting front." As water is applied, either through rainfall or irrigation, the soil moisture content increases, displacing the air within the pore spaces, until the soil has reached the "saturation point" and both the macropores and micropores are filled with water. The saturation point usually occurs for only short periods during and immediately after rain or irrigation. At saturation, air space is reduced and water moves readily downward under the force of gravity.

Typical Landscape Water Waste

Much of the water directed toward plants never reaches them. The majority is lost to evaporation and runoff. Some of it ends up on nontarget—unplanted—areas and some is leached below the root zones of plants and effectively lost to their use.

Evaporation losses are affected by temperature, relative humidity, wind, droplet size, and water pressure. While it's impossible to control temperature and relative humidity, wind can be decreased by shelterbelts, screening with trees and shrubs, and fencing. Evaporation losses can also be reduced by irrigating when it's calm and cool and the relative humidity is high, usually in the very early morning.

A spray directed at a higher angle covers a greater area, but considerably more water is lost to evaporation and wind drift because the water is in the air longer and wind becomes stronger with increased height. The lower the "angle of trajectory," the less wind drift and evaporation. In windy areas, an angle of no more than 25° above the horizon is recommended.

Higher pressure usually breaks up the stream of water into smaller droplets which are more easily lost to evaporation and wind drift.

Runoff is water that is not absorbed by the soil to which it is applied and flows from the target area. Runoff usually occurs when water is applied more quickly than it can be absorbed by the soil. Infiltration rates are determined by soil texture and slope. In any given soil texture, water infiltrates quite readily when the soil is dry. Once the larger pore spaces are filled with water, the absorption rate falls off rapidly.

Select a sprinkler with a delivery rate compatible to the soil's infiltration rate. If your existing irrigation system produces runoff, schedule "off" periods during the course of the irrigation to allow for infiltration. Slopes of more than 10 percent are particularly vulnerable to runoff and may require an alternate on/off irrigation schedule or terracing to reduce runoff.

Overspray is water that is delivered beyond the landscaped area, usually to adjacent driveways, walks, decks, patios, or nonplanted areas. Overspray can be reduced by lowering water pressure, changing the spray head location or type, the method of irrigation, or changing the shape of the planted area.

Leaching occurs during and after excessive rainfall or irrigation when water and mineral nutrients dissolved in the soil water are washed below the plant's root zone. This represents a loss of both water and nutrients to the plant and possible contamination of groundwater.

Once the pore spaces closest to the soil surface are filled, the water moves downward, filling up the next layer of pores. Water molecules are attracted to each other and to the solid surfaces of the soil particles. This makes capillary action—the movement of water within the larger pores both vertically (usually downward) and horizontally—possible. Gravity pulls the water downward, removing excess water from the larger pore spaces of the upper soil layers for up to 48 hours after a heavy rain or irrigation.

From Field Capacity to Permanent Wilting Point

Once the macropores have been drained of water, the soil is said to be at "field capacity." It is moist because there is water in the micropores, but excess water will no longer drain from it. Below the wetting front, the soil remains dry. Once the soil is wet to a particular depth, the water in the pore space is either used by plants or evaporates from the soil surface into the atmosphere.

Optimal plant growth occurs when soil water is kept near field capacity and the pore space is approximately 50 percent air and 50 percent water. Gravity has drained excess water from the macropores and its place has been taken by air. The remaining water is held in the micropores. Little water moves within the soil, and moisture is used by plants or evaporates from the soil surface.

Plants can remove moisture from the soil quite rapidly until the soil particles and tiny micropores hold the remaining water so tightly that it is no longer available for plant use and soil is said to be at the "permanent wilting point." If there is no rainfall or irrigation, plants usually die at this point.

Water that has moved below the rooting zone of plants is also unavailable to plants and is basically lost to their use.

Different Soils Absorb and Hold Water at Different Rates

The infiltration rate is the rate at which water is absorbed into the soil. If water is applied faster than it can be absorbed, runoff or ponding (puddling) will occur. Different soils absorb and hold water at different rates. The amount of water the soil is able to absorb is referred to as its "moisture-holding capacity" and is directly related to the organic matter content of the soil and soil texture. The greater the organic matter content, the more water a soil is able to hold. Soil texture refers to the relative proportion of sand, silt, and clay particles in a particular soil.

Sandy soils are made up of relatively large particles which fit together snugly, creating large pore spaces which are

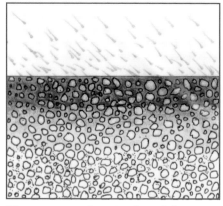

Water acts as a "wetting front," first filling up the pore spaces among the soil particles closest to the surface, and then percolating downward, layer by layer.

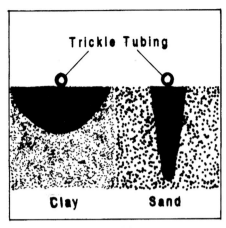

The wetting pattern of drip irrigation depends on the soil. In clay soils, water tends to percolate both laterally and downward, while in sandy soil, it moves primarily downward.

relatively few in number. On a volume basis they have less total pore space in which to hold water than do clay soils. Sandy soils absorb (and lose!) water quickly but have a low water holding capacity. The same volume of water moves further and more rapidly in sandy soils as compared to clay soils. If water is applied as drip irrigation, the wetting pattern is usually deeper but not as wide as in a heavier clay soil. Sandy soils have a fast infiltration rate but will have to be watered more frequently.

Clay soils consist mostly of very tiny particles, which on a volume basis have a larger total pore space than sandier soils, although individual pore size is smaller. Clay soils are able to absorb and hold a great deal of water but have a very slow infiltration rate and are prone to runoff and ponding.

How does this apply to watering or irrigation? The plants themselves will require the same amount of water whether grown in a clay or sandy soil. But plants grown in a sandy soil will have to be watered more frequently to obtain the same volume of water. 2.5 cm (1 in.) of applied water will penetrate to a depth of about 30 cm (12 in.) in a sandy soil and to about 15 cm (6 in.) in a clay soil.

Other Factors Affecting Water Movement

Compaction, layering, salt content, and depth of soil also affect water movement and storage in soils.

A well-granulated soil has more total pore space than a similar soil where the granulation has been destroyed by compaction, leaving fewer macropores and a higher proportion of micropores. Micropores hold water more tightly than macropores, making water less available for plant use and reducing the water-holding capacity of the soil.

Stratification—the layering of soils of different textures—impedes the downward percolation of water. An example would be a layer of clay below a sandy soil, or a layer of sand within a clay soil. The change in texture interrupts and slows capillary action by which water moves. The layer acts as a barrier until a relatively high moisture level has been built up.

Hardpans, often caused by repeated cultivation to the same depth, slow down the rate of water movement into soil and effectively reduce the soil depth from which moisture can be drawn. Both stratification and hardpans may contribute to saturation, oxygen depletion, and death or injury to plants.

Salts increase the strength with which soil water is held by soil particles, thus decreasing the water available to plants. Salts can be buffered to some extent by the addition of generous amounts of organic matter.

Deeper soils will hold more moisture than shallow soils.

The Science of Water and Plants

Water is the major constituent of a plant by weight, making up 80 to 90 percent of annuals and perennials and about 50 percent of trees and shrubs. Plant growth requires enormous quantities of water. About 1,000 g of water must pass through an alfalfa plant to form 1 g of plant material. In a hardwood forest, each tree may transpire 30,000 L (8,000 U.S. gal.) of water per day during the summer. An average-sized tomato plant requires 115 L (30 U.S. gal.) of water in a growing season.

All chemical reactions in plants take place in solutions composed mainly of water. Both photosynthesis and nutrient transport depend on water. Soil nutrients are brought to the root, enter the root, and are carried through the plant in water.

It is the internal water pressure that causes cell walls to stretch and cells to grow. As each of the many thousand cells forming a plant enlarges slightly, we see the overall effect as plant growth. Water within the cell acts in much the same way as air in a balloon. It not only enables plants to grow, it allows them to stand upright. A plant that does not have enough water pressing against its cell walls appears wilted.

How Water Moves Through Plants

Almost 99 percent of the water that enters a plant through its roots exits soon afterward as vapor through tiny holes in the leaves called stomates. During the day, water is almost continually evaporating from the leaves into the surrounding air. This process is called transpiration. On a hot, dry, windy day, the amount of water lost to transpiration can be quite high, requiring large replacement amounts of soil moisture to prevent wilting. A single 15 m (50 ft) silver maple is estimated to use 220 L (60 U.S. gal.) *per hour* during a hot, sunny day.

Transpiration plays a critical role in the function of plants. Its major function is to pull water to the top of even the tallest trees. Water is drawn through many thousands of cells called xylem vessels. These can be thought of as bottomless barrels stacked end to end to form long, narrow pipelines running from the roots to the leaves. Water molecules within this xylem pipeline are like links in a chain. Each time one link (or water molecule) evaporates from the leaf at the top of the tree, it pulls the chain upward by another molecule. Because of water's strong tendency to hold together in drops, it takes less energy to pull the entire chain upward by one link than it would to break it. In order to get water to the leaves, the plant *must* lose water through evaporation. If the soil is unable to supply enough water to maintain the chain, guard cells close the stomates, preventing further water loss.

A second major function of transpiration is cooling. As water evaporates from a leaf into the surrounding air it removes heat from the plant. This cooling is similar to that which a swimmer feels after emerging from a pool. A summer breeze feels far cooler on wet skin than on dry, because water evaporating from the skin removes large quantities of heat. Under hot conditions, plants rely heavily on evaporative cooling. The effectiveness of this method is obvious when you consider the temperature difference of a lawn and an adjacent sidewalk on a hot day.

Photosynthesis: Relating Food Manufacture to Water

Stomate closure reduces moisture loss but also cuts off the plant's supply of carbon dioxide, preventing photosynthesis, the process by which plants manufacture sugar (in effect feeding themselves). During the day, as long as adequate water is available, the stomates remain open and photosynthesis occurs. At night, with no sunlight to power photosynthesis, the stomates close to conserve water. Since photosynthesis is the primary means by which plants generate their food supply, frequent stoppages can lead to an overall decrease in plant growth. This is one of the main reasons why a plant growing under drought conditions will be smaller than a similar one with an abundant water supply.

Water and Roots

Water passing through a cell membrane always moves from an area of higher water purity to an area of lower water purity. Because plant cells contain sugars, salts, and other dissolved substances, the water in soil is usually more pure than the water in a plant. Therefore the relatively pure water from the soil diffuses through the thin wall of the root cell and moves into the less pure water of the root.

A high level of salts, particularly potassium salts, is present in the sap of the root, encouraging the diffusion of water from the soil into the root. This is why plants find life difficult on salt-laden—or saline—soils. Water in these soils is so highly concentrated with salts that the more pure water in the root flows out into the less pure water of the soil, and the plant suffers a water deficit, causing wilting and often death.

Garden Practices that Conserve Water

The first step in reducing water use is the wise choice of plant material. Nature should be your guide. Select plants that are found naturally in the same environment as your garden. A birch tree from a cool, moist river valley will almost certainly decline and die on an arid site without considerable supplemental water. A drought-tolerant green ash from further up the slope of the same river valley will survive much more successfully in a dry garden.

When watering, always water deeply and thoroughly—to the depth of the root system and beyond. Roots will only grow where soil is moist. They will not extend into dry soil. Frequent shallow watering confines roots to the upper level of the soil, leaving plants shallow-rooted and prone to rapid drying between waterings.

Enhanced root growth allows greater water uptake. Phosphorus (the percentage of which is indicated by the second number on the fertilizer label) stimulates healthy root growth. A spring application of a fertilizer such as 16–20–0 or 11–48–0 applied at the rate of 2 kg/100 m² (4 lb/1,000 ft²) will promote root growth.

Be aware of competition from aggressive, shallow-rooted plants with extensive, fibrous root systems. Lawns, ground covers, and herbaceous weeds are particularly competitive and rob valuable soil moisture, especially from newly planted trees. On the other side of the coin, the shallow, far-reaching roots of poplar, Manitoba maple, Siberian elm, and spruce effectively compete for moisture intended for a nearby lawn, vegetable garden, or flower bed.

Concrete, pavement, and large buildings increase air temperatures and limit water availability. Buildings may also funnel wind, often greatly increasing its velocity. Trees and shrubs in highly urbanized settings will lose more water than trees in natural, parklike settings.

Designing for Water Conservation

Several aspects of design lend themselves to water conservation: developing irrigation zones, shaping irrigated areas to conform to sprinkler patterns, grading to prevent runoff, and encouraging water catchment.

"Like laundry on a clothesline": The environment influences plant water use

Most water taken up by the plant is lost through evaporation, and as with wet laundry on a clothesline, factors in the environment will speed or slow the rate of drying that occurs.

Shade reduces the water needs of a plant by lowering the surrounding air temperature. The shaded side of a tree loses about 25 percent less water than the sunny side. A forest tree shaded by many neighboring trees loses considerably less water than a lone tree standing in full sun and exposed to wind. But while the forest tree may lose less water, its roots must compete with neighboring trees for available soil moisture to replenish water losses.

Humidity affects water use. The humidity level over large areas of concrete is significantly lower than the humidity over a lawn or surrounding other living plants. In dry air, water evaporates more readily and plants dry more quickly. Plants increase the humidity immediately around them by releasing water through transpiration. In a dense tree canopy, water lost through transpiration will humidify the air, slowing the rate of water loss from other leaves.

Wind greatly increases the rate of evaporation from leaves. Like laundry on a clothesline, plants exposed to wind dry much faster than those in calm air. By reducing wind velocity, shelterbelts reduce water loss from plants.

Temperature dramatically affects water loss from plants. Plants lose water more quickly on hot days. Water uptake is slowed by low soil temperatures. Evergreens often show dieback due to spring drying. On a hot spring day, the top of a plant may become very warm, causing an increase in transpiration, but the roots remain locked in cold soil and are unable to replenish the water as quickly as it is lost.

Zoning

In conventional landscape design, we consider function, height, color, texture, and season of bloom, but seldom do we think of the water needs of plants except around ponds and streams or in exceptionally hot, dry areas. We often combine plants regardless of their drought tolerance, and will water the entire bed to satisfy the needs of the few plants in it that require the most water. In xeriscape design, plants are first separated into zones according to their water needs, and then arranged with design factors such as height or color in mind.

By grouping plants into zones based on their water needs and then watering them accordingly, irrigation becomes more efficient. Each zone is served by a single type of irrigation and scheduled as a single unit.

Plants are divided into those with low water needs (such as yucca, lilac, and shrub roses), moderate water needs (veronica, little leaf linden, and dogwood), and high water needs (birch, delphinium, and hosta). As well as plant needs, irrigation requirements for each zone should consider soil type (clay, sand, silt, or loam) and its infiltration rate; microclimate, including sun/shade, reflected light and heat, presence of heat-retentive hard surfaces, and shelter/wind; root competition with neighboring trees; and topography—slopes will have a different infiltration rate and need a different irrigation schedule than flat areas. (See p. 20 for detailed information on site analysis.)

Shape and Grade

To avoid compromising aesthetics, professional landscape designers usually develop the design first and then adjust the irrigation system to fit. However, knowing the type of irrigation head or emitter that is appropriate for a particular zone and then shaping the zone to fit the overall delivery pattern of the irrigation device to be used ensures more efficient use of water. By working back and forth between the design and the irrigation system and modifying one or both on paper as you go along, an attractive, water-conserving landscape can be achieved.

Slopes and banks are an invitation to runoff. Conserve water by regrading to direct water toward plantings, terracing, or providing water-catchment areas at the base of slopes. If slopes are part of a design (see sidebar on p. 24), the soil on the slope should be amended to improve water percolation and water applied slowly enough to prevent runoff. Small depressions, called swales, at midslope or at the base can be used to catch and redirect runoff water to where it can be used. Aerating sloped grassy areas increases water percolation.

Ensure that the grade slopes away from buildings and

does not lead to water in your basement or a neighbor's. Be aware of local bylaws concerning the legalities of water movement across adjacent properties.

Water Catchment

Water catchment means catching water—usually rainfall—which might otherwise be lost and directing it toward plantings or holding it for later use.

The most obvious source of water catchment is our roofs. A 100 m² (1,000 ft²) roof will catch an estimated 630 L (165 U.S. gal.) of water in the course of a 0.06 mm (1/4 in.) rain. But as long as it is not going into our basement, most of us never think about where that water might be useful.

A number of catchment options or combinations are available. By using plastic adapters, downspouts can be extended to nearby plantings. Cobblestone or brick swales (sometimes called dry stream beds) can also direct water from downspouts to planting beds.

Downspouts can funnel water into rain barrels or holding tanks for later use. These plastic or metal containers should be placed on a firm, level base and be equipped with a lockable lid, screened inlets to exclude birds and animals, and an overflow mechanism to direct excess water away from house foundations. A bottom spigot to which a hose can be attached facilitates use. Drain rain barrels prior to freeze-up in the fall.

If catchment is to be from a relatively large area of roof, a combination of roof and a slightly sloped driveway or parking area, or a basement sump-pump, it might better take the form of a landscaped holding pond lined with vinyl, concrete, or clay. Water can be delivered to plantings as needed by gravity or a pump.

By slightly sloping driveways, patios, and walkways toward landscape areas, you can cause water to run off onto adjacent lawns or beds rather than flowing directly to the street and storm sewers, or simply puddling and then evaporating from the hard surface.

Bowl-shaped depressions around individual trees and shrubs ensure that irrigation and rain water are directed toward root systems rather than lost as runoff to adjacent nonplanted soil.

Our grandparents used oak barrels to catch rainwater from roofs. There are now a wide range of metal and plastic containers available for this purpose.

Delivering Water to Plants

Scheduling

Scheduling irrigation involves knowing the water needs of plants, the infiltration rate of the soil in which they are growing, and the microclimate in which they are situated.

Ideally, it means filling the entire root zone with water and allowing the soil to partially dry out prior to the next watering. Plants are generally more tolerant of moderate drought than prolonged saturation because saturation limits oxygen availability to the roots, effectively suffocating them.

While the cliché for automated irrigation was once "set it and forget it," such scheduling usually catered to the worst possible scenario in terms of hot, dry weather, and operated at that timing and duration throughout the growing season regardless of actual need. We have all seen public and private sprinkler systems going at full tilt in the midst of a torrential downpour and have shaken our heads in wonder at technology overriding common sense.

Automated systems can be far more wasteful of water than human "hose draggers." Timers and control panels can be both complicated and intimidating, and many people are reluctant to make adjustments and fine tune them once they have been set by the installer.

A far better approach is to explain your irrigation philosophy and needs to a professional irrigation specialist and install a system that is both adaptable and user friendly. Some controls allow you to adapt to seasonal variations by overriding the programmed amount so as to deliver less or more water. Irrigating on an "as needed" basis is the most efficient manner of scheduling in terms of water use.

How much water?

The amount of water needed by a particular plant will depend on: the type of plant, its age, size, and root depth; weather; microclimate; soil; and competition from other plants. Small plants with shallow root systems will need to be watered more often but for shorter durations than will larger, deeper-rooted plants. As plants grow, irrigation can be less frequent but for longer periods of time. The larger the area of moist soil, the less danger of stress if watering is delayed for some reason. With established plants, begin by watering once a week and decrease (or less often, increase) the frequency of irrigation based on observation of the plants.

How do I know when to irrigate again?

Knowing when to water can be determined by the feel of the soil. If the soil is too dry to form a ball when a handful is firmly squeezed, you've waited too long to water. If it is moist enough to form a ball but is somewhat crumbly, it's time to irrigate. If it forms a durable ball and is slick, there is no need to irrigate yet.

Water before signs of moisture stress are evident. Wilt, color change (as the soil dries out, lawns change from green to dull green to blue-grey to grey), leaf roll-up, burning of leaf tips and margins, or in extreme situations, leaf drop are all signals that plants are in need of water. By the time these symptoms are evident, damage will already have occurred.

Ultimately, water scheduling should be based on your cumulative experience with your plants and soil.

Moisture sensors and rain shut-off devices can be used to override preset timers and automatically turn on or off irrigation systems. Soil moisture sensors such as tensiometers and gypsum blocks work best if installed in each zone. They indicate the amount of moisture available to plants and, coupled with automatic on and off valves, determine scheduling. You will need to correlate soil moisture levels with plant needs within each zone to determine at what percent soil moisture the system should be turned on or off. Soil moisture sensors tend to be expensive, may need periodic replacement, and may not be 100 percent reliable.

Automatic rain sensors are designed to override preset scheduling so that irrigation does not take place during rainfall. When a predetermined amount of water accumulates in a collector cup, the system is shut off. Once the collector cup is empty, preset scheduling resumes.

The best time to water...
The optimum time to water is early morning, when it is calm, cool, and relative humidity is high. Little water is lost to evaporation. Plants dry quickly once the sun rises, reducing the risk of foliage diseases, such as powdery mildew, which proliferate rapidly under moist conditions. It is also a nonpeak time for domestic water use, so municipal water facilities are less likely to be overtaxed. Ideally, water should be applied to the soil, where it can be absorbed by plant roots, rather than to the foliage. If you do not opt for an automated system, installing a timer on a garden hose and sprinkler is well worth the effort.

Trees and Shrubs Are Not Lawns

Watering a lawn does not mean that the trees within a lawn are being adequately watered! Remember, a maple tree can use over 200 L (50 U.S. gal.) of water per hour.

Regardless of their drought tolerance, trees and shrubs will need regular watering from planting time to establishment—usually two or three growing seasons. Dig bowl-shaped depressions around newly planted trees and shrubs to direct water toward the plants' roots rather than onto adjacent soil. Applying an organic mulch of 10 to 15 cm (4–6 in.) reduces water loss to surface evaporation. Water—or check to see if water is needed—twice a week during their first month and once a week for the remainder of that season.

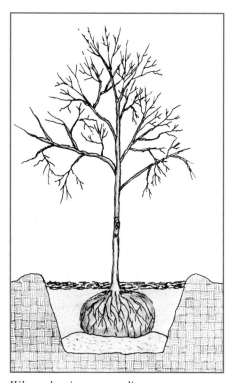

When planting a tree, dig a generous hole, amend it with organic matter, and spread the roots over this "cushion" of amended soil. Fill the planting hole with amended soil and tamp it well, leaving a slight "bowl" or depression to catch water. Water it to the depth of its root system and into the soil below. Mulch the soil surface.

During the second and third season, water deeply twice a month or as needed.

Mature trees should be watered at their drip line rather than at their trunk. The drip line is the soil area below the furthest extent of the tree's branches. Feeder roots—those which absorb water and nutrients—usually end just beyond the drip line and are usually within the upper 40 cm (16 in.) of soil. Set a soaker hose under the drip line and leave it on until the top 40 cm (16 in.) of the soil is moist.

Discontinue watering in late September or early October, when deciduous trees begin to drop their leaves. This is your signal that the trees are beginning to harden off for winter in response to progressively shorter days and colder temperatures. Continuous watering or the application of fertilizer in late fall may slow the hardening of some plants, leaving them vulnerable to winter kill. Once all of the leaves have fallen, give them several deep waterings prior to freeze-up. The object is to allow them to harden off, yet enter winter dormancy with as much water as possible in their tissue and the surrounding soil. This reduces vulnerability to late winter and early spring desiccation.

Irrigation Systems

How you water your plants can vary from a hand-held watering can or hose, to a hose with a sprinkler, to a fully automated underground irrigation system. Watering with a watering can involves time and patience to be done properly. It is really appropriate only for containers or small beds.

Hose Dragging and Portable Sprinklers

Many of us are hose draggers. We use a hose with one or more types of portable sprinklers and move them around as needed. While it may not be as convenient and involves more time and labor, there are a number of advantages to a "manual portable system." It's certainly less costly. And because hauling out a hose takes more effort than turning on a valve or flipping a switch, we usually don't do it unless we feel it's necessary, thereby saving both water and money. A hose is also flexible (unless it's vinyl and it's early April). If we alter our landscape it does not necessitate excavating and redesigning an irrigation system.

As with any type of irrigation, portable sprinklers should provide uniform coverage—the area immediately adjacent to the sprinkler should receive the same amount of water as the area at its farthest extent. The delivery rate of the sprinkler (called the precipitation rate) should not exceed the infiltration rate of the soil. These rates, which will be influenced by water pressure, are usually marked on the sprinkler or its packaging: "2.5" indicates that the sprinkler delivers 2.5 in. of water per hour. Sprinklers that cover a small area usually have a higher precipitation rate than sprinklers that cover a larger area. They necessitate more frequent moving but water more deeply in a given period.

Portable sprinklers vary in their coverage and rates of precipitation. To ensure complete and even distribution, the amount of water should be measured at several locations during irrigation. Place a number of containers (of the same shape and size) throughout the area to be watered. Variations of up to 20 percent are tolerable without harming plants. Remember, the pressure of your water system can vary as much as 15 or 20 psi over an evening of watering on a hot summer day.

Automated Underground Irrigation Systems

Designing and installing a fully automated underground irrigation system involves a lot of homework and a professional installer who is sensitive to your philosophy of water use. Most irrigation companies are willing to work with homeowners to design an effective and efficient underground irrigation system.

Many choices and combinations of timers, controls, pipes, and sprinkler heads are now available. While automated systems are convenient and save time, they are more expensive than other types, and their installation requires excavation. Their efficiency, in terms of water savings, is related to their design, scheduling of water delivery, and monitoring and maintenance during operation. Underground systems for smaller landscapes may be manually activated. Properly installed, an underground system will provide uniform coverage of the area being watered.

Components

At their most basic, these systems consist of a pressurized water source, an optional timer or control panel, control valves, underground pipes, and sprinkler heads or drip emitters. The controller or timer is a clock that opens and closes electrically operated valves on designated days for specified durations. Each zone can be scheduled differently to meet the needs of plants within that zone.

Sprinkler heads are either static and set at their operating height, or of the "pop-up" variety, which automatically lift up when in use, then return to their "seat," out of the way of mowers and people, when not in use. Pop-up heads operate

Types of portable sprinklers

Impulse or impact sprinklers are usually considered the most efficient in terms of uniformity of coverage. They are available in a range of precipitation rates. Balanced coverage is obtained by moving the sprinkler to a number of locations and overlapping coverage.

Revolving sprinklers have rotating arms moved by water pressure. If not well designed they do not provide uniform coverage. High pressure creates a poor distribution pattern. Low pressure may not provide sufficient force for rotation.

Fixed sprinklers shoot water through a pattern of holes on their top. They are variable in quality ranging from excellent (a small metal design with no moving parts) to poor (low-quality plastics that leak and distribute most of the water close to the sprinkler). Consumer information on uniformity of coverage is seldom available.

Oscillating sprinklers move back and forth, covering a square or rectangular area. They often deliver more water at the far ends of their pattern where they pause to reverse direction. Some have a pulsating feature designed to reduce this.

like a spring-loaded pipe. In the absence of water pressure, the spring pulls the nozzle down. When water is turned on, the pressure of the water pushes the nozzle up.

The design of a sprinkler system is based on precipitation rates. This is the amount of water that a system delivers at any point in the irrigated area. It is measured in inches per hour. Manufacturers' rates do not take into account evaporation, wind loss, or runoff.

Sprinklers are about 85 percent efficient, in that 15 percent of the water dispersed is never absorbed by plants. Sprinkler heads distribute water through pressure. They should be spaced according to their rated performance, matching their delivery rate of water to the infiltration rate of the soil. If water pressure is low, you may need more heads to irrigate the same area. On a square meter basis, it is cheaper to install a few sprinkler heads that cover a larger area than it is to install a larger number of sprinklers, each of which covers a smaller area.

Sprinkler heads should deliver water as close to the ground as possible to reduce evaporation losses and wind deflection. Spray heads normally have a trajectory of 23° to 30°. The lower end of this range reduces wind drift and evaporation. Within each zone, heads operating from the same valve should be of the same type and apply the same amount of water on the area they cover. For example, a full circle spray head would apply 11 L (3 U.S. gal.) per minute on a 4.5-m (15 ft) radius circle. A matching spray head that covers only a half circle should apply 5.5 L (1.5 U.S. gal.) per minute because the area of coverage is one half that of the full circle.

Regardless of whether they are stationary or pop-up, sprinkler heads are of several types: fan spray, rotary stream spray, or bubbler.

Fan spray heads
Fan spray heads emit fine sheets or fans of water. In lawns, they are usually set to pop up about 10 cm (4 in.), allowing clearance over long grass. In beds, sprinklers can pop up as high as 30 cm (12 in.), or nozzles can be set on fixed risers at whatever height is most practical for a particular type of plant. These heads are most efficient for annuals, perennials, ground covers, and lawns. They operate at 20 to 30 psi and cover a radius of 1.5 to 5 m (5–16 ft). They are one of the most flexible and efficient systems for small landscape areas.

Fan sprays have no moving parts and cover the entire area to be watered simultaneously. They distribute a fine, uniform spray of water droplets, but because the holes are smaller, their nozzles plug easily. They have a fixed spray pattern. Nozzles are calibrated to provide uniform coverage when different spray patterns from different nozzles are combined

Fan spray heads

Advantages:
- parts are readily available at low cost
- wide selection of nozzles
- operate at low pressure
- reduced spray distance ensures greater control in smaller landscapes

Disadvantages:
- debris may block nozzle
- precipitation rate is fairly high, which may cause runoff on slopes and puddling on heavier soils that have a slower infiltration capacity
- under high pressure, the spray may break up, causing excessive wind drift and misting
- under low pressures, the spray distance may be reduced, resulting in incomplete coverage
- because it requires many heads, the system is more expensive to install

within a single zone. Variable arcs are available so spray patterns can be adjusted for proper coverage of awkward angles. Precipitation rates vary from 4 to 7.5 cm (1.5–3 in.) per hour.

Rotary Stream Sprays

These heads are useful in large, open lawn areas on acreages, farmyards, parks, and golf courses. Water pressure (30 to 80 psi) is used to power an impact (sometimes called impulse or gear-driven) mechanism, which delivers single or multiple streams of water from a rotating sprinkler head. Its range is usually 9 to 18 m (30–60 ft) but can be reduced to 6 m (20 ft) or extended to 34 m (110 ft). Where full or part circle coverage is combined in one zone, nozzles should be selected to provide balanced coverage. Precipitation rates (5–20 mm per hour/0.2–0.8 in. per hour) are somewhat low because water is spread over a larger area.

Bubblers

Bubblers deliver water to a smaller area simultaneously. This type of head is best suited for tree wells, shrub beds, and mixed planting beds of ground covers, annuals, perennials, and shrubs. Bubblers have a range of up to 1.5 m (5 ft) and can apply from 2–7.5 L (0.5–2 U.S. gal.) per minute. Runoff may occur if they are left on too long or if the soil within the planting bed has not been prepared properly to maximize infiltration.

Maintenance

Maintenance means observation. Overhead systems should be checked after installation and then monthly during the growing season: Within each zone, do sprinkler heads pop up and then return to their seat? Are any heads broken or blocked? Is the spray pattern uniform? Is pressure too high, creating fog or mist instead of drops? Is pressure too low, so that coverage is not complete? Are there slow leaks, usually indicated by a higher than normal water bill or localized wet or "lush" areas showing algae growth? Is the duration of the irrigation sufficient to water the soil to an adequate depth to satisfy the needs of plants within each zone (an amount that may change through the growing season with weather changes)? Is the spray pattern covering the proper areas?

   Also look at excess evaporation due to high trajectory angles of sprinklers. Is there runoff, overspray into nontarget areas, or excessive watering below the root zones of plants? Do delivery rates exceed infiltration rates? Once problems have been pinpointed, make adjustments to the system to improve water efficiency.

Drip Irrigation

Drip irrigation systems (also called trickle, microirrigation, low-flow, or low-volume irrigation) apply water slowly and

Rotary stream sprays

Advantages:
• economical system for area covered
• fewer materials required for installation
• slower precipitation rates result in less runoff

Disadvantages:
• high pressure can cause some heads to rotate fast, causing misting or reducing coverage
• low pressure prevents heads from rotating, reducing coverage and causing pop-up problems
• strong winds elongate spray patterns
• longer operating time required to obtain necessary precipitation

Bubblers

Advantages:
• useful for tree wells, shrub beds, and mixed plantings in the small landscape

Disadvantages:
• runoff or puddling if left on too long
• require thorough bed preparation

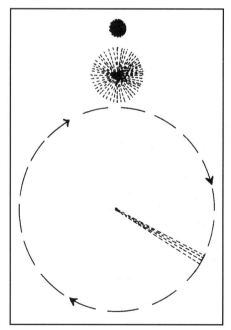

Bubblers (top) and fan sprays (center) cover the entire area to be irrigated simultaneously, but a fan spray is capable of covering a larger area. Rotary stream sprays (bottom) cover an even larger area on a rotating basis.

Drip irrigation

Advantages
• easy and relatively inexpensive to install, and require less excavation than underground systems
• less water is needed since very little is lost to evaporation, wind, or runoff, and none is applied to unplanted or weedy areas or hard surfaces
• energy savings due to lower pumping costs and lower pressure
• because of the low flow rates, soil is seldom saturated to the exclusion of oxygen
• results in fewer weeds, reducing maintenance and pesticide use
• soluble fertilizer can be applied through the lines
• plant stress is reduced
• damage to plants by water impact is eliminated
• fewer disease problems because the foliage remains dry
• because only the soil immediately surrounding each plant is wet, drip irrigation does not interfere with other gardening tasks

Disadvantages
• design information is not as well prepared by the industry as it is for sprinklers; product inconsistency coupled with a low level of industry knowledge about these systems has been a problem in the past
• because you can't actually "see" what's happening below the wetted surface, you may initially lack confidence in the system; digging a few times to check the depth of water infiltration is reassuring
• the system requires a filtration system since emitters are easily clogged with fine soil, organic particles, and algae
• most systems require pressure regulation
• lateral lines are vulnerable to damage from machinery, hoeing, birds, and animals
• emitters must be checked regularly to ensure that they are working
• unlike spray systems, drip systems can not be used for cooling plants, frost control, or washing down foliage
• there is potential for salt accumulation at the edge of the wetted area

under low pressure to the root zone of each plant, maintaining near optimum levels of soil moisture.

Drip systems are close to 100 percent efficient, in that almost all of the water is delivered to the root zone of the plant. But they are not suited to the entire landscape—certainly not lawns, ground covers, or most flower beds. They work extremely well where nonspreading plants are grown in rows (although for design purposes, these rows may be curved). Drip irrigation is most often seen in vegetable gardens, young shelterbelts or tree plantings, with fruit such as strawberries and raspberries, and orchards.

Components
Drip systems are composed of a head or control system, a main delivery line, and lateral lines with emitters.

The head
The head consists of a control station with a pressure regulator, filter, back flow preventer, and control valve. Optional timers and fertilizer injectors are available. Water flows into the head, where it is measured, filtered, treated if needed, and regulated through pressure and timing. Timers rather than meters are generally used to control the amount of water delivered through the system. Soil or organic particles must be removed by filtering to prevent blockage of the emitters. Because emitters are designed to operate at a specific pressure, pressure regulators are used to reduce household water pressure to a rate that is compatible with non–pressure compensating emitters. Many self-compensating emitters are on the market, but high pressure on the lateral line can cause the connections to come apart.

Main line
A main line, usually buried and constructed of polyethylene plastic pipe, carries water under pressure from the head to the lateral lines, which branch from it and have control valves for each zone.

Lateral lines
Lateral lines are designed in conjunction with the emitters selected for a specific project. They are often covered with a mulch, for aesthetic reasons, to prevent vandalism, and to protect the tubing from deterioration caused by ultraviolet light. If the system is more permanent, they are buried at least 30 cm (12 in.) deep.

Emitters
Each emitter along the lateral lines should provide the same amount of water, plus or minus 10 percent. This is done by supplying water at a set pressure (pressure regulating) or lowering the pressure to a specified range at each emitter (pressure compensating). Each lateral line is designed to have

a specific "allowed length of run." This may be up to 120 m (400 ft) and is the length within which emitters will deliver a uniform amount of water. Changes in elevation will affect the length of run. If there is a slope greater than 2 percent, or rolling terrain, pressure compensating emitters are recommended. If used across slopes, place the emitters on the upper side of the plants.

Emitters deliver 2 to 15 L (0.5–4.0 U.S. gal.) of water per hour and are usually placed next to individual plants along the lateral lines. Water emitted from the line moves by capillary action beneath the soil surface. The actual size of the wetted area of soil is determined by the soil texture, the delivery rate of the emitter, and the duration of irrigation.

If salts are present in the soil, water released from an emitter generally moves the salts away from the plant toward the perimeter of the wetted area.

Conventionally, drip irrigation is scheduled more frequently than irrigation with overhead systems, and wets a relatively small volume of soil, which plants deplete rather quickly. Scheduling drip irrigation so that it is less frequent but wets a larger volume of soil encourages deeper rooting.

To prevent clogging, most emitters have a flushing action when the system is turned on or pressurized. As the pressure starts to climb, a spurt of water from the emitter flushes particles from the outlet.

There are two main types of emitters: line source, which is manufactured with a series of regularly spaced outlets punched along a pipe; and point source, which is punched where required at the time the system is installed.

Line source emitters are used primarily for vegetable rows in a garden or for mass plantings of similar plants. The emitters are installed in the line during the manufacturing process. There are three general types: biwalled or twin-walled tapes, with evenly spaced, laser-drilled holes; hardwall tubing or pipe, with externally mounted button emitters at regular intervals; and hardwall tubing or pipe with in-line emitters.

Biwalled or twin-walled tapes consist of two parallel tubes. Water moves along the entire length of the larger-diameter tube with periodic openings into the secondary tube. At closer spacings along the secondary tube are openings (emitters) that distribute water to the soil. The step-down process of moving from a larger to a smaller diameter tube restricts the flow and results in a more uniform delivery of water from the beginning to the end of the tape.

These tapes vary in thickness from 4 to 25 ml. Emitter spacing is at 15, 23, 46, 61, or 91 cm (6, 9, 18, 24, or 36 in.). Tapes are less expensive than hardwall tubing, and their durability is related to the thickness of their walls. The heavier types will last four to six years, while the thinnest is

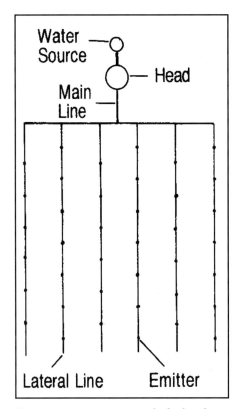

Drip systems are composed of a head or control system, a main delivery line, and lateral lines with emitters. They are useful in irrigating orchards, vegetable gardens, shelterbelts or tree plantings, and small fruit such as strawberries and raspberries.

usually good for only one growing season. Tapes are generally more vulnerable to punctures and bird and mouse damage.

Hardwall tubing or pipe is more expensive than biwalled tape but more durable. It usually lasts 10 years on the soil surface and somewhat longer if buried. It can be purchased without emitters, with externally mounted button emitters, or with in-line emitters. These emitters are pressure compensated and allow a consistent distribution over the full length of a lateral line. Through emitter design, the water pressure is reduced using mechanical diaphragms, friction loss, or fluid dynamics. Because increased pressure is adjusted in the emitter, the delivery rate of water remains almost uniform along the entire line.

Point source emitters are single- or multiple-outlet emitters that are inserted into the lateral lines at the site when the drip system is installed. Pressure-compensating emitters are placed along the line to correspond with the location of the plants or areas to be irrigated. Point source emitters are more flexible in that more can be added as the plants grow and need more water. Single or multiple tubes (sometimes called spaghetti tubing) can be attached to the emitter and direct water to the "point" of use: the plant. Although emitters can be buried, the tubing outlet (where the water emerges) should be under a mulch or at the soil surface. Access sleeves are available for locating and easily servicing buried single or multiple emitters. These sleeves resemble vertical plastic pipes and are fitted over the emitter and its tubing.

Emitters are rated in liters (gallons) of water per hour, with normal rates of 2, 4, or 8 liters (0.5, 1, or 2 gal.) per hour. They are available in single outlet units or as multiple units with up to eight outlets.

Maintenance

Lateral lines should be flushed out immediately after installation or any repairs to the system, prior to the first irrigation each spring, monthly during the growing season, and at the end of each season to remove any accumulated sediment. Remove the clamp at the end of each lateral line and turn on the water for 5 to 10 minutes until all particles have been flushed out.

Other Options: Soaker Hoses and Porous Pipe

Soaker hoses are long tubes of rubber or plastic with rows of tiny holes. They are connected to a garden hose and laid on the soil surface along the side of plant rows with the holes facing up or down. Facing the holes down reduces evaporation losses considerably but also limits the area that is wetted.

Soaker hoses

Advantages
- excellent for drip line of mature trees
- portable

Disadvantages
- subject to wind losses if facing up
- limited area is irrigated if facing down
- limited length for even delivery
- variations in hole size
- easily damaged

If facing downward, they may be covered with mulch.

Soaker hoses deliver water fairly equally along their length provided they are no longer than 15 m (50 ft). Although cheaper than drip, they are not considered as efficient because it has been difficult to control hole sizes in manufacture and variations are common, although the use of lasers has made newer products more reliable. Soaker hoses are portable but may be left in place indefinitely. The thin plastic types are easily damaged.

Composite rubber porous pipe is a type of subsurface irrigation that was developed in the 1970s for crop use. Rubber chips are bonded together to form a hose with numerous holes along its length. Lines are buried 15 to 30 cm (6–12 in.) below the soil surface and water moves down through the soil by capillary action similar to line source emitters.

Composite rubber porous pipe

Advantages
• similar to those of drip irrigation

Disadvantages
• a tendency to underwater
• clogging
• root intrusion
• animal damage
• because the entire system is hidden it is more difficult to monitor than other types of irrigation, and problems only become evident as plants start to wilt and die
• the bonding or rubber can break down and change flow rates
• variations in chip sizes and material densities cause variations in hole sizes and lead to uneven watering

he three most obvious benefits of mulching are water conservation, weed control, and soil improvement.

Chapter 5

Mulch

Imitating Nature

A perennial bed mulched with 10 cm (4 in.) of grass clippings and topped with a thin layer of coarse peat moss which serves merely to improve its appearance.

Sara Williams

A careful look at the floor of a northern coniferous forest, an aspen bluff, or our native grasslands should tell you a lot about mulching, not only about the product, but the about process as well. For centuries, plants have been dropping leaves, twigs, and branches onto the soil below them. These form a layer of undecayed and decaying organic matter, eventually rotting and returning nutrients to the soil for reuse by other plants, as well as improving the soil structure. In the process, they conserve moisture by insulating the soil against temperature extremes and by limiting weed seedling germination by excluding light and forming a physical barrier.

In contrast, traditional gardening has had a perception that bare soil is best, with not a single leaf allowed to fall onto a tree or shrub bed.

Many values related to our landscape linger from agricultural practices of a previous era. But while in agriculture change is economically imperative, these practices continue unchallenged in our gardens: "black dirt" tilled within an inch of its life continues to be seen as a virtue. It's time we looked at some of these practices with an eye to what's actually going on rather than what our neighbors might think.

Mulch protects plant roots from heat, cold, and drought, keeps fruit clean, enriches the soil, and controls weeds. It has other functions as well. It is derived from the Middle English word *molsh* or the German *molsch,* meaning soft or rotten, a reference to decaying organic matter.

Mulching is an integral part of the recycling process. In mulching, we use organic materials, formerly regarded as waste and sent to the landfill, to safeguard soil and water.

Why Mulch?

The three most obvious benefits of mulching are water conservation, weed control, and soil improvement. But what appears to be a simple process on the surface is really an intricate recycling of nutrients.

Water Conservation

There are many ways in which a mulch conserves water. Weed suppression is one. Weeds compete with other plants for water. If weeds are controlled by mulch, more water is available to landscape plants.

Organic mulches cool the soil, lowering temperatures at a 2.5 cm (1 in.) depth by as much as 6° to 8°C (11°–14°F). Cooler soils result in less evaporation. In a study at Cornell University, soil moisture percentages in mulched plots were approximately twice as high as in unmulched plots. In another study, a 5 cm (2 in.) layer of pine needles reduced evaporation by 65 percent compared to an unmulched soil. If the mulch layer itself absorbs moisture, it more than compensates for this in its reduction of evaporation of water from the soil.

Soil under a mulch is generally softer because it is protected from compaction and water impact. This increases water percolation and decreases runoff. By protecting the soil from wind, evaporation is further reduced. It may be that less leaching occurs because the movement of water through the soil is slower since the mulch reduces the initial impact of rain or irrigation.

The surface of a planting bed mulched with a coarse-textured material is usually raised by 5 or 10 cm (2–4 in.). In many cases this increased height and rougher texture is sufficient to act as a snow trap. Not only does the mulch trap snow, insulating the plants over winter, but snow melt provides added moisture in the spring.

Weed Control

Weeds compete with landscape plants for space, light, nutrients, and water. If you were to carefully examine the top several centimeters (few inches) of soil, you would find thousands of weed seeds waiting to germinate. Their require-

A cautionary note

The mulch layer will also prevent self-seeding annuals, biennials, and perennials from perpetuating themselves.

ments are usually moisture, warmth, and light. The mulch layer prevents germination by excluding light. If perchance weeds do germinate, the physical barrier formed by the mulch makes emergence almost impossible. Likewise, weed seeds that blow onto the surface of the mulch would find it difficult to root through the mulch into the soil below.

Controlling weeds by mulching avoids the root damage to plants that cultivation—either by tiller or hoe—so often inflicts. Damaged roots result in weaker plants that are less able to absorb water and soil nutrients. Woody plants such as poplar or the mayday tree respond to root damage by suckering. Mulching suppresses weeds without damaging roots or stimulating unwanted suckering. It is also a more environmentally friendly practice than the use of herbicides.

Soil Improvement and Conservation

A mulched soil is far less prone to erosion and the loss of valuable topsoil. Crusting of the soil surface caused by the impact of water droplets impedes seedling emergence and water percolation. Crusting causes runoff; mulch allows slow and steady percolation.

Mulch maintains more even soil moisture, making heavy soils less prone to the cracking—and root tearing—that occurs as the soil dries.

As the mulch layer decays it adds organic matter to the soil, releasing nutrients and improving soil aggregation. This results in better aeration as well as water- and nutrient-holding ability.

With less moisture and temperature fluctuation and added organic matter, microbial activity within the soil is stimulated, resulting in greater nutrient availability and enhanced plant growth.

The mulch layer acts as a cushion, preventing compaction of heavier soils as we go about our garden chores. (It also cushions falling fruit, in many cases preventing bruising.)

Temperature Modification

A mulch layer insulates the soil below, moderating temperature extremes and preventing sudden temperature swings. By cooling the soil surface during the hot days of summer, mulches encourage healthy roots and prevent root injury caused by excessively high soil temperatures.

In spring and fall, mulches reduce the freeze-thaw cycles of heavy soils which cause heaving of young plants and root injury to others. Mulching is especially beneficial to evergreens, which lose water through transpiration 12 months of the year. Mulching postpones hard freezing of the soil in fall, so trees can withdraw water from the soil for a longer period,

"Dust mulches"

Earlier in this century it was believed that a finely tilled surface would interrupt capillary action—the movement of water through the small pore spaces among the soil particles—thus reducing surface evaporation. This practice led to increased wind erosion and loss of precious organic matter from the soil and is no longer recommended.

possibly reducing winter desiccation and browning. (The downside of this practise is that it may delay acclimation and the onset of dormancy, resulting in winter injury.) Mulching keeps the soil cooler in early spring, preventing premature emergence of spring bulbs, which might be nipped by frost.

Reduced Water Splash

Mulch absorbs water and almost entirely eliminates mud and water splash. This has the obvious effect of keeping flowers or strawberries clean and more aesthetically pleasing. Less obviously, it greatly reduces soil-borne diseases, preventing much of the splashing that spreads fungal spores and bacteria.

Design Functions

In a subtle manner, mulches add color and texture to our yards. Because they are so diverse, they can be used on a wide range of landscapes from the natural to the very formal. They unify planting beds, especially when the plants themselves are young, small and seemingly widely spaced within the bed. They let the world know that, indeed, this is a bed and should be walked around rather than through. They make flower beds and vegetable gardens more accessible in wet weather.

Mulching materials such as post peelings and bark chips can also serve as a ground cover for utility areas or be used to form garden paths or walkways. Used around individual specimen trees on a lawn, mulch keeps mowers at a safe distance, protecting the tree trunks from damage incurred by overzealous operators.

From a design point of view, it is more pleasing to use coarser mulches around larger plants and finer mulches around smaller plants.

Problems with Mulch

There are problems associated with mulch. As Kathleen K. Meserve observed in an article written over 40 years ago, "in the case of mulch, the price is mice." This is particularly true in rural or newer suburban areas. Many mulches make an excellent home in which mice can procreate and raise families. Most damage occurs under the snow in winter when other food supplies are limited. The mice girdle the bark and cambium layer of trees and shrubs. Warfarin-coated grain, available from most rural municipalities, can be placed in bait stations which are accessible to rodents but inaccessible to other wildlife and family pets. When using straw or other materials around trees, keep it at least 20 cm (8 in.) from the trunk.

Fire is another hazard in extensively mulched beds, particularly if using straw, evergreen needles or cones, or peat moss.

Fresh sawdust, straw, or grass clippings may cause a temporary nitrogen deficiency because the soil bacteria that break down these products use nitrogen as a source of energy. Once decayed, nitrogen is again released for plant use.

My own experience with using these materials as a mulch is that they break down very slowly under our arid prairie conditions and seldom if ever cause a nitrogen deficiency. To be on the safe side, you may wish to spread 0.5 kg (1 lb) of nitrogen fertilizer per 50 kg (100 lb) of mulch on the soil surface prior to applying the mulch. Hardwood chips from deciduous trees decompose more slowly than straw, decreasing the potential for nitrogen deficiency.

Slugs prefer a dark, moist, cool environment, and life under many mulches is ideal. If slugs have been a problem in your flower beds or vegetable garden, make a concerted effort to get rid of them before mulching. (Not an easy task!)

If the mulch layer is too deep—over 10 or 12 cm (4–5 in.)—it may cause an oxygen depletion in the soil atmosphere. This is more likely to affect shallow-rooted trees in poorly drained or heavy soils which are prone to waterlogging. The use of mulch on poorly drained sites may worsen the problem. Correcting drainage problems or using the area as a bog garden or water catchment area are alternatives to consider.

Fine-textured mulches such as peat moss should only be used as a cosmetic dressing over materials such as grass clippings. Applied in this manner they will not act as a wick, drawing moisture from the soil below.

There is also the question of the toxicity of wood products. It is well known that black walnut trees produce an allelopathic substance called juglone, which inhibits the growth of nearby plants. *Thuja plicata*, western red cedar, is not recommended for use as wood chips, but is not normally grown on the prairies. None of the woody plants grown on the prairies are likely to have allelopathic effects. (See p. 38.)

Acidification is usually not a problem on our alkaline soils.

Applying and Maintaining a Mulch

Preparation

Prior to applying any mulch, ensure that the area is relatively smooth and weed free, especially of perennial weeds such as dandelion, thistle, and perennial grasses. A mulch layer of 10 to 15 cm (4–6 in.) will not kill these weeds. Spot-spray them with a translocated herbicide such as glyphosate, or eliminate them by solarization (described in chapter 6).

When to Mulch

Mulch can be applied at almost any time through the growing season when it is available. Although the majority of mulches are maintained on a permanent basis, there are some instances where mulches are seasonal.

A **summer mulch** is applied to annual beds and vegetable gardens once the soil has warmed to about 20°C (68°F) and root growth is active. Its main function is to suppress weeds and conserve water. At the end of the growing season it is either composted elsewhere or incorporated into the soil.

A **winter mulch** is used to protect perennial plants from temperature variations through the winter as well as desiccation from drying winter winds. It is applied over strawberries and roses just prior to freeze-up. It is removed in spring as soon as plant growth resumes, often being placed on the soil around these plants to conserve moisture, control weeds, and prevent mud splash on flowers or fruit during the growing season.

How Deep?

The depth and evenness of the mulch layer is critical. A minimum of 10 cm (4 in.) is recommended. Less than this depth will not work! A more shallow layer may conserve some water and mitigate some temperature change, but will not suppress weeds. It is much better to mulch a smaller area to the recommended depth than to mulch a larger area at less than the recommended depth and be disappointed with the results.

A depth greater than 12.5 or 15 cm (5–6 in.) may inhibit the gas exchange between the soil atmosphere and the air above, resulting in oxygen depletion and injury to plant roots. More is not necessarily better!

If using organic material over plastic or a woven fabric, use 8 cm (3 in.) in order to exclude sunlight (these materials deteriorate under ultraviolet rays), provide a cushion against wear and tear, and in public spaces, hide the underlying material from potential vandalism. One cubic meter (1 yd³) of most materials, spread 10 cm (4 in.) deep, will cover about 7.5 m² (80 ft²). Apply mulches carefully around low herbaceous plants, taking care not to smother them.

Water and Mulch

Before applying mulch, ensure that the plants within the bed are watered to a depth of 30 to 45 cm (12–18 in.) depending

Selecting a mulch: An overview

Vegetable gardens
plastic, straw, grass clippings

Annual flower beds
grass clippings overlaid with coarse peat moss, incorporated at end of growing season

Shrub and tree beds
wood chips, coarse bark, evergreen needles and cones, flax shives, post peelings

Perennial beds
grass clippings overlaid with coarse peat moss

on the depth of their feeder roots. Apply the mulch layer and water again so that the mulch is thoroughly moist. Deeper but less frequent watering is the key.

Mulch Renewal

Planting beds that are permanently mulched will need topping up every few years. The timing of this will depend on the type, depth, and durability of the mulch used. All organic mulches will eventually decay. Although this necessitates replacement, this is not a bad thing because nutrients and organic matter are added to the soil below. Unless the bed is to be totally renovated, new mulch is simply placed on top of the original layer. The old mulch is not incorporated into the soil.

Types of Mulches

What makes a good mulch? Some of the characteristics of a good mulch are ready availability, low or no cost, and ease of application. It also helps if they are not easily blown about by wind, add organic matter to the soil, and are free of weeds, insects, disease, or materials harmful to plants.

Mulches are usually classified as organic or inorganic. Many of the organic mulches are by-products of local industries which might otherwise end up in the landfill. Their availability varies from one geographic area to another. While sea hay, spent hops, and cocoa hulls are not readily available in the prairie region, we still have much to choose from. Grass clippings are free for the taking, as are leaves. Post peelings (waste material in the production of fence posts) are free, but there is a cost in transportation. Decorative bark is costly.

Inorganic mulches are manufactured products, and usually have a cost associated with them.

Organic mulches

Organic mulches include grass clippings, wood products, straw, peat moss, and even newspapers. All of these will have to be renewed periodically—more often than inorganic mulches. But all of them add nutrients to the soil and improve the soil structure as they decay. They usually keep the soil cooler and are more conserving of water than inorganic mulches.

Grass clippings
Grass clippings are the universal mulch: readily available, free, and fairly easy to apply. Commonly heard objections to their use include their smell, the introduction of grass into

planting beds, 2,4–D contamination, and their appearance.

If used as soon as they are raked or bagged, there is no smell associated with grass clippings. When left in plastic bags they heat and begin to decompose anaerobically, in much the same way as silage, and with much the same smell. Although it is often recommended that they be allowed to dry on cement surfaces in 2.5 cm (1 in.) layers prior to use, this is probably unnecessary.

If lawns are mowed when the grass is 7.5 to 10 cm (3–4 in.) in height, no lawn grass seeds should be introduced. What may be introduced is annual bluegrass (*Poa annua*), which is considered a weed and is able to colonize lawns and flower and produce seed at very low heights. By watering deeply but less frequently and overseeding bare patches in your lawn with recommended cultivars in early spring, you can eliminate annual bluegrass in your lawn.

The broadleaf herbicide 2,4–D should only be applied as a blanket application to a lawn if the entire lawn is infested with weeds. By spot spraying individual weeds as they appear, contamination of the lawn and environment is reduced. Clippings should be composted for the first three mowings after the application of 2,4–D, after which they may safely be used as mulch. 2,4–D breaks down within 30 days after application.

Apply grass clippings loosely to a depth of 10 cm (4 in.). If you find the appearance of grass clippings on flower beds displeasing, top-dress with a few centimeters (1 in.) of coarse peat moss. Remember, it is the grass clippings that are doing the work. The thin layer of peat moss is merely cosmetic.

Coarse sphagnum peat moss

Peat moss is partially decayed sphagnum moss found in northern peat bogs. It can be costly, coarser grades are sometimes difficult to find, and if used over large areas, it could constitute a fire hazard. But it is excellent when used as a thin top-dressing over grass clippings in annual or perennial flower beds. Peat moss is attractive, lightweight, and weed- and insect-free. It is best moistened prior to application and wetted again after application. If allowed to dry out completely, it may initially resist rewetting. A 100 dm^3 (3.8 ft^3) bale will cover 50 m^2 (150 ft^2) to a 2.5 cm (1 in.) depth.

Shredded bark or post peelings

Post peelings are a by-product of fence posts. Posts are run through a debarker, which removes the bark in thick strips. Peelings are usually free for the taking but may be a long way from a particular garden. They are coarse-textured, suitable for tree and shrub beds, garden paths, and utility areas. They have an attractive color and smell, and are slow to break down. Once applied to the soil surface, the pieces hold

---

Elm chips as mulch

Dutch elm disease is caused by a fungus that is spread from one tree to another by the elm bark beetle. In order for the elm bark beetle to lay its eggs, branches must be dead or dying and have their bark intact. "Brood galleries" are constructed immediately under the bark.

Elm bark beetles find elm trees by smell. Although they will be attracted to chipped elm wood and may hover around it, it is highly unlikely that they will be able to raise young on elm chipper debris used as mulch as long as the chips are small.

In Manitoba, it is recommended that elm chips not be used in areas where Dutch elm disease is a problem because of concerns about attracting the beetles into these areas. In Saskatchewan, elm bark chips must be burned or buried and cannot be used as mulch.

While it is generally assumed that using elm chips as a mulch outside of elm areas will not encourage the spread of Dutch elm disease, check your current provincial regulations prior to using elm chips as mulch.

A group of evergreens growing with lower branches intact in an informal, mulched, curved border. The mulch controls weeds, conserves moisture, and makes mowing easier.

together and do not blow, allow free water percolation, and resist compaction.

Decorative bark

This is a more chunky material, usually brownish-red in color, and dried prior to bagging. It is produced specifically for the landscape industry and can be expensive if used over large areas. Decorative bark resists compaction and blowing and allows free water percolation. It is used in tree-shrub beds where appearance is important, often over woven landscape cloth.

Chipper debris

For many decades, material pruned from trees was sent to dumps or landfills. Because of the escalating cost of maintaining these sites and the associated increased user fees, most tree prunings are now being chipped and either composted or used as mulch. Chips are usually free for the hauling from municipal pruning crews, utility companies (which routinely prune under their lines or along their easements), or private pruning companies.

The texture and composition and attractiveness of wood chips varies depending on the species and size of the material being pruned and the time of year. In summer, chipper debris includes leaves. In winter it does not. Christmas trees are often chipped at municipal sites, and these mulches will likely include tinsel! Chipper debris is used in tree-shrub beds as well as shelterbelt plantings.

As a mulch it is coarse-textured, allows free water percolation, interlocks, and does not blow or scatter. It weathers to a grey color over time. Durability is related to the size of the chips and the depth of application, but it generally lasts three to seven years under dry prairie conditions.

Sawdust and wood shavings

Sawdust and wood shavings are free from sawmills, lumber mills, retail lumber stores, and local high school or community college shop teachers. They are widely available and used to mulch small fruit, trees, shrubs, vegetables, row crops, hardy spring bulbs such as tulips and daffodils, and gladioli. They compact and decompose relatively quickly. With minimal soil contact, breakdown is slow and nitrogen depletion generally not a problem. They improve the soil as they decompose. If spread over wide areas, they may constitute a fire hazard.

Evergreen needles and cones

There is a pervasive and perverse tendency to attempt to

grow lawns under evergreens. Lower branches are removed to allow head space for the mower operator, mutilating once graceful conifers, topsoil is brought in, and still the grass fails.

Grass was never meant to grow under evergreens. Think about our coniferous forests: the forest floor is carpeted with cones and needles, mulching the soil, retaining moisture and supplying nutrients.

Why not emulate nature and allow your own evergreens to grow with lower branches intact and a natural mulch of their own cones and needles? If the soil surface under your evergreens is bare, begin by covering it with any of the recommended mulches. Recycled chipped Christmas trees are a good start. Then let the cones and needles fall! They look good, do not compact, allow free water percolation, and decompose slowly.

Straw

Wheat, rye, oat, barley, and flax straw are widely available and inexpensive. They are used with coarse-textured plants or where appearance is not important: small bush fruits, orchards, vegetables, shelterbelts, and newly planted trees. Straw allows good water percolation, conserves water, and cools the soil, buffering it from day/night temperature changes. It is often used as a winter mulch to protect strawberries and tender roses. If shredded, it is fine for use on flower beds. Flax straw is particularly durable and will need renewal less often than other straws. Hay is generally considered more weedy, but has been used successfully on shelterbelts to conserve moisture. Woven straw mats are used to control erosion on seeded or planted banks or slopes and have now largely replaced jute or burlap.

Problems associated with the use of straw include mice, increased fire risk, the introduction of grain as weeds, and sometimes a temporary nitrogen depletion.

Flax shives

Flax shives are a by-product of flax straw used in the production of paper. Shives form a dense mat, preventing weed germination by light exclusion. They are an excellent mulch for perennial beds and tree-shrub borders. Apply flax shives to a depth of 10 cm (4 in.), keeping it 10 cm (4 in.) away from tree trunks to discourage rodent damage to trunks.

Mowed leaves

Bagged every autumn by zealous gardeners, leaves are a readily available mulch that all

A natural mulch of evergreen cones and needles under evergreens is attractive, conserves moisture, and controls weeds.

too often ends up in the landfill. If leaves are falling thickly over your lawn, simply shred them with your lawn mower and rake them onto adjacent tree and shrub beds, the vegetable garden, annual flower beds, and perennial borders to a depth of 20 to 25 cm (8–10 in.). By spring they will have all but disappeared.

Newspapers

Although less aesthetically pleasing, heavy layers of newspapers have been used as a mulch where appearance doesn't matter. They should be wetted or weighed down with rocks to keep them in place. Avoid using color sections, which may contain inks made of toxic heavy metals that can enter the food chain.

Inorganic Mulches

Inorganic mulches, such as plastic sheeting, landscape cloth, and rock, are more durable than organic mulches, but are usually manufactured with nonrenewable materials and do not benefit the soil.

Plastic

Plastic (polyethylene) is among the cheapest of the inorganic mulches. It is usually available in rolls. In landscape applications it is almost always covered with a more attractive organic mulch to protect it from ultraviolet light, wear, and potential vandalism. Because they are not in direct contact with the soil, these organic mulches last longer but never contribute to the soil. The use of UV-resistant plastic is recommended.

Plastic mulches control weeds and allow for air exchange between the soil atmosphere and the air above, but do not permit water penetration except through the openings of planting holes. Plants mulched with plastic are best irrigated with a drip system.

Tomatoes, peppers, eggplants, cucumbers, squash, melon, and sweet corn respond well to all types of plastic mulch, usually producing earlier crops with higher yields, cleaner fruit, and less disease.

Clear plastic mulches create a greenhouse effect, resulting in very high soil temperatures during hot, sunny weather. Some degree of soil warming promotes root growth of heat-loving plants, but during prolonged periods of extremely hot weather, soil temperatures under clear plastic mulch may rise to injurious levels.

Black plastic is less effective than clear plastic for soil warming, but it has the advantage of also controlling weed growth. It is laid over level, weed-free soil. Slits are made at appropriate intervals and vegetable seedlings planted into the soil through the slits. Drip irrigation lines are laid with emitters serving each plant. Although water does not penetrate it, soil moisture below the plastic is retained.

Landscape cloth

Sometimes referred to as "geotextiles," these fabrics are made of woven or bonded polypropylene or nonwoven polyester. Woven fabrics allow for water, fertilizer, and air penetration, reduce surface evaporation, and block weeds. They are stronger and more durable than plastic sheeting, but more costly. Like plastic, they are usually covered with a decorative organic mulch when used in a landscape situation. Nonwoven polyester fabrics last longer and are more resistant to chemical and temperature degradation than polypropylene, but are also more expensive.

Before applying these fabrics, grade the area so that it is level, and remove any weeds. The fabric is laid over the soil and slits are cut where plants are to be placed. Once planted,

---

Mulching shelterbelts and young trees: A special application

For many years the accepted practice for keeping shelterbelts weed free has been tillage, either by machinery or hand hoeing. Both are labor-intensive, and are often carried out too close to the young trees and at too great a depth. The net result is damaged roots, suckering, and excessive evaporation due to the depth of tillage. Herbicides are also used to control weeds, but sometimes damage trees.

Using mulch to control weeds in newly planted shelterbelts has advantages over both tilling and herbicides. It is more environmentally friendly and has the added benefits of trapping moisture while minimizing evapotranspiration, and reducing wind erosion and soil crusting.

Mulches recommended for shelterbelt trees include plastic rolls, individual sheet mulches, wood chips, and flax shives.

Individual sheet mulches

Individual sheet mulches are made of porous plastic, fabric pad, straw glued to paper, or recycled paper coated with wax. They vary in size, but a minimum of 60 x 60 cm (2 x 2 ft) is recommended. They are porous, allow water to reach the soil, and are effective in controlling weeds. Lightweight and easy to apply, most contain ultraviolet inhibitors and last about three years—when the trees are taller than surrounding weeds and are able to compete for light, space, nutrients, and moisture. They are more expensive than herbicide applications but less likely to damage trees.

Mow weeds prior to planting trees to reduce rodent habitat and make tree planting and mulch application easier. The mulch is applied as soon as young trees are planted. Secure with rocks or staples. Using clods of soil is not recommended because they eventually crumble, providing a site for weed colonization.

Roll mulches

Black plastic roll mulches are used for shelterbelt and wildlife plantings. Like sheet mulches, they prevent weed seed germination by blocking light, conserve moisture, and prevent soil erosion, but are impermeable to water.

Areas to be planted should be level, weed free, and without clods so the plastic can be laid flat. Available in 450 m (1,500 ft) rolls, they usually contain an ultraviolet inhibitor, and are laid in place over the newly planted trees with a mechanical applicator. The tree seedlings are then pulled through slits cut in the plastic. Seedlings should not be allowed to rub against the plastic. The plastic is pinned to the soil at each tree with staples or a rock. The edges of the plastic sheet are secured with soil rolled onto them by the mechanical applicator.

Permeable woven plastic rolls of 100 m (300 ft) and 150 m (500 ft) are also available but are more expensive. They contain ultraviolet inhibitors, are very durable, and are permeable to water. They are applied the same way as the plastic rolls.

Wood chips or chipper debris

Wood chips prevent weed germination by excluding light, maintain a cool soil temperature, and reduce water evaporation from the soil. They are free but may not be available in all locations.

Wood chips should be applied to a depth of 10 cm (4 in.) and kept 10 cm (4 in.) from the tree trunk to discourage rodent damage. It is generally recommended that they be allowed to age for six weeks prior to use. This allows time for decomposition, alleviating any potential for a nitrogen deficiency, or the release of ammonia or other volatile organic acids which might injure the trees' lower leaves.

Flax shives

Flax shives are a by-product of flax straw used in the production of paper. They form a dense mat, preventing weed germination by light exclusion, and conserve soil moisture. Apply to a depth of 10 cm (4 in.), keeping shives 10 cm (4 in.) from tree trunks.

a minimum of 5 cm (2 in.) of organic mulch should be placed over the fabric to improve its appearance, reduce wear, and protect it from ultraviolet light and vandalism. Any weeds that penetrate the fabric should be spot-killed with glyphosate.

Rocks and gravel
Rocks and gravel are available in many sizes and colors. Larger rocks may be used in rock gardens or as a structural part of the landscape, and rounded, river-washed cobbles make attractive dry stream beds. The use of crushed rock and gravel as mulch, however, is generally discouraged. Although long-lasting, they are costly in terms of the energy input required to mine, crush, and transport them, and they should be considered a nonrenewable resource. They are often used over plastic sheeting, but if weeds germinate within the rock mulch, removing them is hard on the knuckles. They reflect heat and light, raising temperatures and providing a rather inhospitable microclimate for most plants as well as people. Rocks do not improve the soil, and limestone chips may raise the pH of soils. Smaller rock aggregates are more mobile than generally believed, moving with foot traffic as well as lawn mowers. Rocks are often used in xeriscaping, but their presence is more indicative of a "zeroscape" than a "xeriscape."

ome areas of your lawn are there simply by default. They are seldom walked on unless you are behind a mower.

Chapter 6

Lawns

Less Is Better

Lawns are among our landscape's biggest consumers of water. To look good, our traditional lawn grasses must have more water than is available through natural participation in the form of rain and snow. In the United States, it is estimated that 50 percent of household water is used on the landscape, and the vast majority of this is applied to lawns.

Lawns occupy the largest amount of space in our landscape. This is very much a North American phenomena and is associated with our concept of space and low population.

Historically, lawns were once natural meadows used as public space, or "commons," in towns and villages in Europe—a place where livestock could be grazed and fairs and meetings held. In the 18th and 19th centuries, lawns surrounded the homes of rural gentry and were cropped short by sheep. The invention of the lawn mower in the 1830s made lawns maintainable even for the urban middle class.

More recently, lawns have become almost a suburban status symbol justifying the overuse of pesticides. This quest for perfection motivates some of us to overapply water, fertilizer, and pesticides in their care.

Benefits of Lawns

Lawns are a resilient, comfortable, and safe place for play and leisure. As a design component in the landscape, they unify the yard and set off flower beds and mixed borders. They provide that perception of space and openness so dear to the prairie dweller. They reduce dust, glare, and air pollution, and help control erosion and runoff. Irrigated lawns may reduce fire danger.

Grass lowers summer air and surface temperatures through transpiration. As water inside the plant evaporates through the tiny openings in the leaf surface called stomates, it changes to vapor. Every gram of water that does this extracts 540 calories of heat from the plant's surface, cooling the atmosphere around it.

That long sward of green lawn is also psychologically therapeutic, giving us a sense of quiet, of calmness, and of well-being.

The Downside

Conventional lawns must be watered. The costs involved in watering include the cost of the water itself as well as the equipment used to deliver it. This equipment may vary from a hose with a manually attached sprinkler to an elaborate automated underground irrigation system.

Lawns are costly to establish and to maintain over the many decades of their life. Mowing involves equipment and its maintenance, as well as gas and oil or electricity. Fertilizers and pesticides are generally applied (often at higher rates than needed). Nutrients and chemicals applied to the lawn often end up polluting waterways and aquifers.

Finally, we invest a lot of time in the establishment and maintenance of our lawns, but few of us consider mowing a labor of love.

Rethinking Lawns

Function

Take a second look at the amount of turf you have and consider what you actually do with it. Survey the lawn areas of your landscape. What is the function of each area? How is each area used by your household?

The intimate

Some of your lawn area is indeed used for leisure. You sit on it, lie on it, a toddler toddles on it, a teenager sunbathes. . . . Your contact is generally of an intimate nature. This area of lawn should be left as conventional lawn, but perhaps redefined to fit the shape of your irrigation system so as to conserve water.

Some parts of your lawn may be so intensively used that they may be better converted to "hard surfaces"—unplanted areas such as decks or patios. These can withstand heavy amounts of human traffic and need no water, fertilizer, or mowing. These areas are usually immediately adjacent to the house. Could some of your lawn area be converted to hard surface area?

The hardly-used-at-all

Other areas of your lawn are there simply by default. They are seldom walked on unless you are behind a mower. These are usually peripheral to the area of more intense use and may consist of odd strips or difficult-to-reach corners. Long, narrow areas between the street and the sidewalk or between the sidewalk and the driveway are almost never used as lawn. These are easily replaced with lower maintenance drought-tolerant ground covers.

The visual sward

Many areas of a conventional lawn are seen but not actually used. Their function is almost purely visual. Entire front lawns could easily be converted to beds of drought-tolerant ground covers, flowers, shrubs, and ornamental grasses to provide color, texture, and form. They would become much more interesting and, once established, involve less maintenance.

In rural areas, on farms and acreages, large areas of lawn are there only as a visual sward of green. They are usually composed of rough bunch-type grasses and were never intended to be walked or sat upon. They are never watered or fertilized and are mowed only as needed. These may be left as they are or overseeded with more recently developed low-maintenance cultivars. They may be visually broken up by mass plantings of drought-tolerant perennials, ornamental grasses, or tree-shrub borders (see p. 23).

Options

If your household makes little or no use of the existing lawn, there are several options to consider. You may want to retain a conventional lawn but reduce its area to that which is actually used. Reshape the portion of the lawn that is retained so that it conforms to the pattern of a standard sprinkler, thereby reducing water wastage. Or retain the entire lawn but discontinue watering it during the heat of the summer and accept summer browning. Alternatively, the lawn can be eliminated entirely.

Retain, but...

Size and location

Consider the size and location of your existing lawn. It should be placed where it will be used as a lawn. This may be close to a patio, deck, or back door. It may be under a tree that provides shade. It may be next to a swimming pool, swing set, or sand box—wherever the members of your household sit, lie down, and recreate, where they go barefoot and are actually in intimate contact with the lawn.

The size of your lawn will depend on household use. Observing your family at play and at leisure over a period of several weeks during the summer will determine this.

Shape

Regardless of whether the sprinkler head that delivers water to your lawn is part of an underground system or attached to the end of the hose, consider the shape of its delivery pattern. To use water more efficiently, shape your lawn to coincide with the shape in which your water is delivered (or how it will be delivered if you are installing a new irrigation system). Outline the shape of your proposed lawn with a garden hose. Then set up the sprinkler you will be using and modify the shape of the lawn until it coincides with the delivery pattern of your sprinkler.

Round, square, and oval lawn areas are generally more conserving of water. The more rectangular the lawn area, the less efficient is the irrigation and the greater the loss of water. A California study concluded that lawns with the same area need increasingly more water as their perimeter increases.

This does not mean that the lawn itself must be square or circular. Adjacent flower and shrub beds can soften the geometry while still ensuring that the area as a whole is water efficient.

Accept summer browning

Our conventional lawns are composed of cool-season grasses, which grow most actively at a temperature range of 16° to 24°C (60°–75°F). If temperatures rise above 24°C (75°F) and there is insufficient water, they cease growth and enter dormancy. While they may appear brown and lifeless, they are not dead, though they certainly lack the appeal of a lush, green lawn.

Refraining from irrigating and accepting summer browning involves a greater tolerance for seasonal changes than most of us have. It may necessitate developing a fairly thick skin to pressure from more conventional neighbors.

Replace with...

Drought-tolerant alternatives

Small areas of lawn in odd corners and long, narrow grassed strips are easily replaced with drought-tolerant annuals, perennials, ornamental grasses, and ground covers. Larger areas of lawn can be replaced with layered mixed borders. (For ideas on the development of such borders, consult chapter 2; for selection of plants, see chapter 7.)

Lawns adjacent to large expanses of reflective aluminum or white siding, white stucco, or cement are particularly susceptible to drought stress caused by reflected heat and light. Nor are these spaces conducive to leisure activities. They are better planted with drought-tolerant ground covers.

Hard surfaces

Some areas of a conventional lawn can be replaced with hard surfaces. Although wooden decks require upkeep, they remain a popular choice. Patios should also be considered. Crushed gravel, sand, or organic mulches such as post peelings can also be used for paths. Avoid large areas of cement or asphalt, which absorb heat or reflect light and aggravate drought conditions.

Drought-tolerant grasses

Substitute drought-tolerant grasses for those large expanses of conventional lawn that are seen from a distance but seldom used. Drought-tolerant grasses are usually bunch-type grasses, which form small clumps with spaces between. These spaces are less evident if the lawn is seeded thickly and mowed regularly at 15 cm (6 in.). In smaller urban yards this may not be easy, since many conventional mowers cut at a maximum height of 10 cm (4 in.) The ride-on mowers used by most rural dwellers have a higher maximum cutting height.

In large rural yards the conventional lawn and the "distant" lawn can be separated by gently curving borders of massed drought-tolerant perennials or ornamental grasses (see chapter 2). The difference between the two types of lawns is not likely to be noticed (at least not by "a man riding by on a fast horse").

Water-Conserving Practices

Establishment

The vast majority of lawn problems can be traced to poor soil preparation during the establishment of the lawn. Most of these are related to insufficient topsoil or organic matter, poor grading, or persistent perennial weeds.

The importance of proper site and soil preparation cannot

Overseeding rather than renovating

Sometimes it is easier to overseed an existing lawn with a more drought-tolerant species rather than to totally renovate. This procedure involves mowing the lawn as short as possible, removing thatch and other debris, top-dressing with 1 cm (½ in.) of soil well amended with organic matter, and overseeding at up to twice the normal seeding rate with a drought-tolerant grass species. The grass seed is raked in, rolled so that it is in firm contact with the soil, and kept moist for several weeks. This is not a foolproof method, and germination and establishment is seldom 100 percent. Because watering also encourages the growth of the original sod, the new grass may have difficulty rooting through the old sod and into the soil below.

be overemphasized. The benefits of good site preparation include water conservation and lower maintenance inputs—including your time—during the lifetime of the lawn.

If you are establishing or renovating a small area of lawn using grasses that will be irrigated, the following water-conserving practises are particularly important. If you are dealing with large areas of lawn that will not be irrigated, some of these practises will not be practical.

Removal of debris

If the site has been the scene of recent construction, remove (rather than bury) all building materials. When simply covered, these materials may cause problems with water percolation or be toxic to plants. They may also lead to subsequent sinking and settling of the soil and disturbance of the final grade. They may limit the depth of rooting of the lawn, causing heat- and drought-stress.

Weed control

Weeds rob lawns of moisture and nutrients, shade and crowd out lawn grass, and may harbor disease and insects. Use only purchased topsoil that has been "screened" to remove rhi-

Options for removing an existing lawn

If your lawn is in poor condition because of poor site preparation or you decide to use a more drought-tolerant species, you must first remove the existing lawn. Some methods involve the use of herbicides, others do not. Some are more labor intensive than others. Some are (almost!) instant, while others involve an entire growing season. Regardless of which method you use, try to retain and incorporate existing organic matter.

Physical removal

Sod is cut to a depth of 5 cm (2 in.) with a mechanical sod cutter or a sharp spade, removed, and either composted or used elsewhere. The disadvantages of this method are that it is very labor intensive and that organic matter—the old turf—is permanently removed from the site. Because the finished grade is reduced by several centimeters (a few inches), topsoil will have to be added, costing additional time, labor, and expense.

Turning sod upside-down

Turning the sod upside-down in place retains organic matter but is labor intensive. It takes several weeks to kill the sod and there is no assurance that the kill will be fully effective. Some subsequent weeding will be necessary.

Cultivation

Repeated rototilling while keeping the area fallow for a growing season retains the old sod but takes time. It also breaks down soil structure and encourages the loss of organic matter.

Soil solarization

Water the lawn deeply to moisten the soil (moist soil conducts heat more readily than dry soil) and encourage fast, succulent

growth. Then cover the area with clear plastic, anchoring its edges with rocks, bricks, or soil to hold it tight against the soil. Leave the plastic in place until the grass is dead—about three to six weeks. The intense heat generated underneath the plastic kills vegetation. This method works best during the heat of the summer when daytime temperatures are above 30°C (85°F) for a week or two. It is less effective during cooler spring and fall weather.

Herbicides

Herbicides containing the chemical glyphosate (sold under trade names such as Roundup, Sidekick, Clear-it, and Erase) are registered for home use. Follow label instructions, especially mixing rates and the optimum temperature and leaf stage at which the product should be applied. These products are most effective when the lawn is actively growing. Allow two weeks from the time of application until the lawn is dead. Incorporate the dead sod into the soil. Glyphosate becomes inactive with contact with the soil. New plantings can be carried out immediately after the dead sod has been incorporated.

Mulching

If you plan to replace existing lawn areas with ground covers such as junipers or daylilies, simply dig generous-sized planting holes into the existing sod. Amend the soil within these planting holes and water well after planting. Apply a mulch layer of 10 to 15 cm (4–6 in.) over the remaining lawn. The mulch layer will kill most (but not necessarily all) of the grass. Grass emerging from the mulch can be killed by spot applications of glyphosate or hand-digging.

zomes of quack grass and other perennial weeds. If you are establishing a lawn on existing soil, there are several options for the control of perennial weeds. All of these are more effective if you first water the soil well to encourage the emergence and growth of weed seeds, roots, or rhizomes present within the soil. After the weeds have emerged:

Spray the weeds with a chemical herbicide containing glyphosate (sold under trade names of Roundup, Side Kick, Clear-it, and Erase). Follow label directions for mixing and timing of application. Once the weeds are dead (generally within 14 days), incorporate them into the existing soil as long as no seed heads are present. They constitute organic matter, which should not be wasted.

Cover the area with clear plastic for about six weeks during the heat of midsummer. The excessive heat generated through this process (called solarization) kills almost all vegetation. Once weeds are dead, and as long as viable seed heads are not being reintroduced, incorporate them into the soil.

Hand dig or rototill the area three or four times during the growing season, watering well between tilling, to encourage all perennial weed rhizomes or seeds to grow. Avoid unnecessary cultivation, especially when the soil is wet.

Grading

Prior to spreading topsoil, establish the final grade of the subsoil. Soil should be sloped at about 2 degrees away from buildings, driveways, sidewalks, and patios. This ensures that excess rain or irrigation water flows away from foundations and walkways and that ice does not form on hard surfaces.

Steep slopes are awkward for sitting and other forms of human leisure and are difficult surfaces on which to establish a lawn. Mowing, fertilizing, watering, and weeding are also difficult or dangerous. If slopes cannot be eliminated, it is better that the area be terraced and planted with alternative ground cover material.

If the lawn is to be sodded, the final grade, once topsoil has been spread, should be 2 cm (3/4 in.) lower than adjacent hard surfaces so that the sod will be level with sidewalks and driveways.

Topsoil

It is beneficial to remove and stockpile existing topsoil prior to establishing the grade. A minimum of 10 to 15 cm (4–6 in.) of topsoil containing at least 5 percent organic matter is recommended. More is almost always better. Prior to spreading the topsoil, rototill the subsoil so that differences in soil texture do not form an artificial layer that impedes water percolation or root penetration. Apply half of the topsoil and rototill, then apply the second half and rototill again. The object is to have a gradation between the topsoil and subsoil to prevent the formation of a "perched water table," caused by the layering of two distinctly different soil types.

Organic matter

Incorporate 6 to 10 cm (2–4 in.) of organic matter—well-rotted manure, compost, peat moss, or spent mushroom compost (see chapter 3)—into the topsoil to improve its nutrient- and water-holding ability. This is an important practise that can make a big difference. Some communities in the United States with chronic water shortages have imposed bylaws setting out the minimum amount of organic matter—usually 5 percent—that must be incorporated before conventional high–water using lawns may be established.

Soak to settle

Before seeding or sodding, if there is no rain, water the area thoroughly over a few weeks to ensure final settling of the soil and encourage remaining weeds to germinate so that they can be controlled before the lawn is seeded or sodded.

Maintenance: Inputs from a Xeriscape Perspective

By applying as many of the principles of xeriscape as possible during the establishment stage, water can be conserved even with a conventional lawn. Make appropriate decisions about the size, shape, and location of your lawn. Grade it properly. Amend the soil with generous amounts of organic matter.

The way you subsequently water, mow, fertilize, and weed also makes a difference.

Water

Water plays a role in hundreds of physiological and biochemical processes that take place within plants. All nutrients—other than carbon dioxide, which is taken from the air—enter the plant through the roots in soluble form in the soil water.

To maintain a lush, green appearance, conventional Kentucky bluegrass lawns need a minimum of 2.5 cm (1 in.) of water per week in spring and fall and up to 4 cm (1.5 in.) during the heat of the summer. If this is not provided by rainfall it must be supplied through irrigation.

Delay watering your lawn until the top several centimeters (few inches) of soil moisture from spring melt has dried out. During the growing season, water only when the soil surface has begun to dry out. At each watering, the soil should be moist to a depth of 20 centimeters or more (8 in.). Ideally this will be several centimeters (a few inches) below the root zone of the lawn.

Deep root development is one of the major factors in

Seeding versus sodding

There are advantages and disadvantages to both methods of lawn establishment. Site and soil preparation are identical.

Seeding

Seeding allows greater choice over the type of grass to be used. Although cheaper than sodding, it takes considerably longer and involves a much higher degree of labor over an extended establishment period. Use high-quality seed. Canada No. 1 grass seed allows only 0.5 percent weed seed on a weight basis and requires that the seed be 85 percent pure and have a germination rate of 70 percent. Denser seeding rates result in thicker lawns sooner.

Sow grass seed when conditions are most favorable for its germination and least favorable for germination of weed seeds. Weed seeds germinate readily in spring when cultivation has brought them close to the soil surface, and light, moisture, and temperature conditions are optimal for their growth. Cool-season grasses are best sown in mid to late summer. There is less weed competition, and six to eight weeks remain for establishment prior to the onset of winter. Because natural rainfall is at its lowest at this time of year, irrigation is usually necessary during the establishment period.

Seeding rates are usually given as a range. Use higher rates: if you are unable to water; on slopes, banks, or areas prone to erosion; or if you want an established lawn as quickly as possible.

To determine the amount of seed needed, divide the number of square meters in the area to be seeded by 100, and multiply by the seeding rate. Seeding rates are given by genus or species later in this chapter.

If using several species or cultivars, mix seeds together prior to spreading. Use a Cyclone-type bag spreader or a push-type centrifugal or drop spreader. For more uniform distribution, divide the amount of seed you need in half, set your spreader at the lowest possible setting, and spread half of the seed in a north-south direction and the other half in an east-west direction. Use a roller to ensure that the seed is in firm contact with the soil.

Care after seeding is critical. Young grass seedlings are very sensitive to heat and drought and should never be allowed to dry out. Even moisture is especially critical during hot, dry, windy weather.

Watering seedlings is quite different from watering an established lawn. It should be frequent and light, with little pressure and fine droplets. As the root system penetrates deeper so should the depth of irrigation. The frequency of irrigation is gradually decreased as the depth of irrigation is increased.

Mowing stimulates tillering and rhizome production, increasing the density of the lawn. Mow a newly seeded lawn to 6 cm (2.5 in.) when the grass reaches 10 cm (4 in.) in height. By leaving the grass slightly higher, you will provide a greater leaf surface area for food (carbohydrates) manufacture through photosynthesis and will enhance rooting. It is particularly important during the establishment period not to weaken the plants by removing more than one-third of the leaf blade at each mowing. Ensure that the blades of your lawn mower are sharp. Do not use a newly seeded lawn until after its second or third mowing.

Wait at least eight weeks after emergence of the grass before controlling broadleaf weeds with a selective herbicide such as 2,4–D. Earlier spraying may injure grass seedlings.

Sodding

Sod produces an almost instant lawn. It immediately reduces erosion and runoff and involves much less fuss and maintenance during establishment than seeding. It is, however, more expensive and your choice of grass is more limited.

Site preparation is the same. If slopes and other difficult sites are to be grassed, sod is preferred to seeding.

Sodding can be carried out through most of the growing season as long as rooting can occur prior to freeze-up. More water will be needed during the heat of midsummer. If possible, select a sod grown in the same soil texture as that in your yard. This will ensure better water percolation and faster root penetration of the sod into the soil.

Good-quality sod will have been grown from seed under irrigation. It is dense, weed free, and holds together when handled. Sod pieces should be uniform in size and thickness. 2 cm (3/4 in.) sod establishes more quickly than thicker sod. Sod should be harvested, delivered, and laid within 24 to 30 hours. If left in piles it is very vulnerable to heating and drying. Upon delivery, place sod in the shade, cover it with a tarp, and lay it as quickly as possible.

Rake and moisten the soil just prior to sodding. Do not lay sod on dry, crusted soil. A minimum of 15 cm (6 in.) of topsoil is recommended for sodding. A high-phosphorus fertilizer such as 10–51–0, 11–48–0, or 16–20–0 should be incorporated into the upper 5 cm (2 in.) of soil prior to sodding so that phosphorus is readily available to ensure good root development.

Begin sodding at a building or sidewalk or along a straight line created by a taunt string. Lay the sod in brickwork fashion. Sod should be laid perpendicular to slopes, starting at the bottom and working upward. Roll after laying to eliminate any unevenness of the soil and to put the sod in firm contact with the soil. Water thoroughly—through the sod and 15 cm (6 in.) into the topsoil below. Sod  has a very limited root system and is very vulnerable to drying out. To quote Dennis McKernan of Olds College in Olds, Alberta, sod "is a transplanted plant that has had most of its roots cut off in the harvesting process." If allowed to dry out, sod pieces contract and leave gaps which must then be hand-filled with soil, a laborious process.

The relationship between root and top growth

It's important to understand the relationship between root- and top-growth. Short grass blades mean a smaller area capable of photosynthesizing and producing food for the plant. Mowing too short reduces vigor by reducing the ability of the plant to manufacture food. If food manufacture is limited, the root system, which depends on the leaves for its sustenance, will be reduced. As mowing height is lowered, root mass becomes smaller. A small root system limits the plant's ability to take up water and soil nutrients, making it more vulnerable to the stresses of heat, drought, cold, or heavy wear. Higher-cut grass is more tolerant of stress, especially during the heat of summer.

drought tolerance, regardless of grass species. This is accomplished through deep and thorough soil preparation and deep, infrequent watering. Water is initially absorbed near the soil surface and then at progressively greater depths as water percolates into the soil. Watering deeply but less frequently discourages warm-season weeds and annual bluegrass, which thrive on shallow but frequent irrigation.

If you decide to retain a fairly large lawn, separate it into irrigation zones according to water needs. Areas requiring more water include those with heavy use and associated wear, ones adjacent to large masses of cement or reflective siding, and those in competition with the root systems of trees. Where turf density is low, there is a greater loss of water from the soil surface through evaporation. Lawns on slopes or banks, especially those with a south- or west-facing exposure, will also require more water, but irrigation will have to be interrupted to prevent runoff. Lawns in the shade of buildings will require less water.

Irrigation systems can apply water at a faster rate than can be absorbed into the soil. The result is runoff onto sidewalks and streets. Time irrigation so that what is applied can be absorbed. Some soils will require an interrupted schedule with 15 minutes on and 30 minutes off for efficient absorption. Water during the coolest time of the day when winds are calm, usually in the early morning from 1 a.m. to 7 a.m.

Excessive watering after applying fertilizer or pesticides may cause them to leach below the root zone of the grass and contaminate the water table. Depending on soil type, only 10 mm (^{1}/2 in.) or less of water is needed to bring these products into the root zone where they will be used.

Mowing

From a human perspective, we mow our lawns because they are more comfortable to sit on at 7.5 cm (3 in.) than at 30 cm (12 in.). Culturally, our perception of a lawn is a short green sward rather than a hayfield or a meadow.

Mowing the lawn makes it thicker because mowing removes hormones in the expanding leaf that would otherwise inhibit additional shoots from being initiated from the crown.

Taller grass shades and cools the soil surface, reducing moisture loss caused by evaporation. The height of the grass, coupled with its increased density, reduces weed seed germination, which conserves still more water and reduces herbicide use. Grass grown in the shade will especially benefit from a higher cut. The increased leaf area compensates for the lack of direct sunlight falling on the leaf surface.

The recommended height to which conventional lawns should be cut is 5 cm (2 in.), with mowing recommended when the lawn reaches 7.5 cm (3 in.) in height, thus reducing the blade height by one-third. By waiting until the lawn is about 12 cm (4.5 in.) in height and cutting to 7.5 cm (3 in.), you are still only removing one-third of the grass blade.

Keep the blades of the mower sharp. Dull blades produce a ragged cut, increasing the cut surface area of the leaf and associated moisture loss. The cut surface turns an unsightly grey-green. The opportunity for disease entry is also increased.

Mowing patterns should be changed regularly to reduce wear patterns.

Fertilizers/Pesticides

Fertilizer is used to compensate for wear—use of the lawn—and tear—mowing of the lawn. Each mowing removes nutrients. Returning clippings to the lawn recycles nutrients, reducing fertilizer requirements by as much as 15 percent. It is estimated that nitrogen inputs can be reduced by as much as 0.5 kg/100 m^2 (1 lb/1,000 ft^2) per year. Use a mulching mower to cut clippings into smaller pieces, which decompose faster and are less likely to contribute to a thick thatch layer. Over time, as clippings are recycled within the lawn, fertilizer requirements will continue to decrease somewhat.

Poor fertility leads to low lawn density and more weeds. Increasing fertility and mowing height produces more shade on the soil surface, reducing weed seed germination and the need for herbicide use.

Overfertilizing may lead to excessive growth, fertilizer "burn," and the leaching of nutrients with associated water contamination.

Heavy nitrogen applications stimulate shoot growth at the expense of the root system, leaving the root system less

2,4–D

If you use 2,4–D (a herbicide used to control broadleaf weeds in lawns), allow three mowings before applying the grass clippings as mulch. These clippings may be safely composted. Trials in Saskatoon and elsewhere have indicated that 2,4–D will break down within 30 days when properly composted.

Fertilizer formulations

Fertilizers are commonly sold as quick-release granules, slow-release granules, or in liquid formulations.

Highly soluble granular forms of nitrogen such as urea and ammonium nitrate are economical and quick-acting and remain effective within a wide temperature range. There is a danger of overapplication, with associated burning. These forms of nitrogen readily leach into the soil and may be lost if the lawn is overwatered or subject to heavy rain. They usually remain effective for four to six weeks. Examples are 34–0–0 (ammonium nitrate) and 21–0–0 (ammonium sulfate).

Slow-release granular fertilizers release nutrients slowly over a longer period from a single application of fertilizer, resulting in more even plant growth. Instead of surges of nitrogen followed by possible deficits, the release is slow and steady. These fertilizers release nutrients at a slower rate during cooler weather or under drier soil conditions.

Although more expensive, using a slow-release fertilizer reduces labor as well as the chance of groundwater contamination. Slow release fertilizers may reduce pesticide use because there are fewer growth peaks. The succulent growth associated with growth peaks is more susceptible to disease entry and insect infestations.

These products are usually a combination of slow and quick release nitrogen forms and typically contain sulfur-coated urea (SCU), isobutylidene diurea (IBDU), or organic sources of nutrients such as poultry manure, blood and bone meal, canola meal, or sewage sludge. Organic forms must be broken down to their inorganic forms by microorganisms within the soil before they are available for plant use. They are usually low in actual nitrogen. Because of our cool prairie spring conditions, it may not be advantageous to use a formulation with more than 50 percent of the nitrogen in slow-release form.

Turf adjacent to water bodies should be fertilized with slow release fertilizers to lessen chances of contamination from runoff or leaching.

Liquid fertilizer is the most expensive formulation, and because nutrients are in a water-soluble form, they tend to be very susceptible to leaching into the groundwater. A few of these are less prone to leaching.

capable of supplying water and dissolved nutrients to the top growth. Grass is then very vulnerable to heat- and drought-stress and accompanying wilt. Lawn grasses grown with deep but less frequent irrigation and lower nitrogen levels are less prone to wilting.

Grass Species

Conventional lawns—those which are irrigated, fertilized, and regularly mowed—are composed of rhizome-forming grasses which knit together to form a sod. On the prairies, lawns are usually a mixture of Kentucky bluegrass and creeping red fescue. More recently, some turf specialists are recommending the replacement of Kentucky bluegrass with chewings fescue because of its lower demand for water, fertilizer, and pesticides.

Nonirrigated lawns—those found on most farmyards and acreages—are composed of bunch grasses such as wheat-grasses and sheep fescue. These have a clumpy growth habit and never form a true knitted sod.

With either type of lawn, a mixture of two or more species and a few cultivars within each of these species is recommended rather than a monoculture of one grass species. Visually, they are not that different, but it's important to follow the adage of not putting all of your eggs in one basket. If drought, cold, or pestilence knock out one species or cultivar, you will still have a lawn.

Cool-season versus warm-season grasses

Most prairie grasses are categorized as cool-season grasses. They grow best (and are bright green) in spring and fall when daytime temperatures range from 16° to 24°C (60°–75°F) and soil temperatures are low. During the heat and drought of midsummer they respond by decreasing leaf growth and becoming dormant. Although the crown of the plant remains alive, they "go brown." Watering allows the turf to remain green through the summer. The growth cycle of cool-season grasses peaks in spring (May and early June), producing lush top growth as well as root growth, and again in September and October. Root growth remains active as long as soil temperatures are above freezing.

Warm-season grasses break dormancy when temperatures rise above 10°C (50°F) and flourish during the heat of mid-summer when temperatures are between 27° and 35°C (80°–95°F). They become dormant in fall when temperatures fall below 10°C (50°F). They are usually less hardy and few survive the –40°C (–40°F) winter temperatures common on the prairies.

While most conventional lawn grasses (right) are rhizomatous and soon knit together to form a continuous sod, many of the low-maintenance grasses (left) are bunch grasses, which remain individual, tuft-like plants.

Bunch versus sod-forming grasses

While most conventional lawn grasses are rhizomatous and soon knit together to form a continuous sod, many of the low-maintenance grasses are bunch grasses, which remain individual, tuft-like plants. While they thicken and spread over time, they do not form a sod. If seeded thickly at the time of establishment and mowed regularly, they fill in more quickly.

Sod-forming grasses recover from damage, wear, and tear more quickly due to their rhizomatous nature. Bunch grasses are much slower to recover because they have fewer growing points.

"Miracle" dryland grasses are sometimes marketed as substitutes for conventional lawn areas. Many of these are bunch grasses and do not provide a comfortable surface for a human body. If your intention is to lie down or walk barefoot on your lawn, you're better off with the conventional sod-forming grasses.

High-Maintenance, Irrigated Lawns

A conventional prairie lawn is almost always composed of Kentucky bluegrass and creeping red fescue. Together these form an ideal lawn on which to sit, play, or walk. They also have excellent recuperative potential—if damaged by heavy wear, disease, or drought, they recover quickly. But these lawns are only maintained by significant inputs of water and fertilizer and regular mowing.

Kentucky bluegrass (*Poa pratensis*) was introduced to North America from Europe during the Colonial era. Deep green, fine textured, and long lived, it is a cool-season grass that spreads by tillers—by sending up new shoots closely adjacent to the original clump—and rhizomes. It forms a dense, hard-wearing sod with roots typically to 15 cm (6 in.) below the soil and occasionally to 25 cm (10 in.). Most cultivars have good spring and fall color. Some cultivars become brown during extended hot, dry periods but green up when watered. Tiller production and root growth are stimulated by shorter days and cooler temperatures. They generally stand heavy wear and recover quickly.

Kentucky bluegrass does poorly in shade and under conditions of drought or poor fertility. Under high humidity, many cultivars are prone to powdery mildew. Kentucky bluegrass requires high inputs of water, fertilizer, and mowing to look good and wear well. A blend of several cultivars should be used.

Seeding rate: 0.5–0.7 kg/100 m² (1–1.5 lb/1,000 ft²)

Creeping red fescue (*Festuca rubra* var. *rubra*), also native to Europe, is a low-growing, fine-textured, medium to dark

Recommended cultivars of Kentucky bluegrass

'Adelphi' (1972) is dense, low growing, and dark green, with good heat tolerance and disease resistance. It looks good under conditions of low maintenance and has excellent low-temperature color retention and spring green-up. It establishes quickly.

'Banff' is a dwarf cultivar with good all-season color, and is resistant to both powdery mildew and snow mold. It is very winter hardy.

'Baron' (1970) is a dark green, dwarf cultivar with high density. It establishes quickly and has good disease resistance, except for susceptibility to snow mold.

'Birka' (1968) is a medium- to fine-textured, medium–dark green dwarf cultivar. It is shade tolerant, resistant to powdery mildew, and responds well under low-maintenance conditions.

'Nugget' (1965) is dense and low growing. It was developed in Alaska and is resistant to powdery mildew and snow mold. It is somewhat shade tolerant but has poor low-temperature color retention and spring green-up, and poor heat tolerance. It is very wear tolerant.

'Park' (1975) is a blend of 15 selected strains from Minnesota. It germinates quickly, with good seedling vigor, and has a rapid establishment rate. Its fertility requirements are low, but it is susceptible to snow mold.

'Ram I' is a low growing, dark green cultivar of medium texture. It is resistant to powdery mildew and has good spring green-up.

'Touchdown' has excellent spring green-up, is very wear tolerant, and is resistant to powdery mildew.

'Washington' has proven itself an excellent low-maintenance grass in various trials. It is aggressive during establishment, has a wide blade, and good drought tolerance.

green grass with narrow, stiff blades. It can be mowed at 7.5 cm (3 in.). It spreads by tillering and rhizomes. Its root system is dense and fibrous. It has good "wear resistance" and stands up well to foot traffic and use. It is tolerant of shade, low fertility, and drought. It does not tolerate wet soils or excessive nitrogen and discolors in hot or dry weather. Seed germinates within two weeks.

Creeping red fescue blends well with Kentucky bluegrass, but requires only 20 percent of the nitrogen needed by Kentucky bluegrass. It is believed to have a weak allelopathic effect, exuding compounds from its root system that may inhibit the germination and/or growth of some other plants (but apparently not chickweed!).

Seeding rate: 1.6–2.0 kg/100 m^2 (3.5–4.5 lb/1,000 ft^2)

Low-Maintenance, Nonirrigated Lawns

Low-maintenance grasses are those species and cultivars that persist with few inputs, requiring little water, fertilizer, or mowing. Instead of being smooth and soft, they tend to be clumpy, lumpy, and rather harsh on the human hide. One does not walk barefoot on them. They are usually mowed at 7.5 to 15 cm (3–6 in.)—somewhat higher than conventional lawn grasses—and removal of 40 percent of the leaf blade is considered acceptable. These grasses are best viewed from a distance but fit in nicely with the xeriscape concept. Once established, they require only occasional mowing and almost no irrigation, fertilizer, or pesticides.

Fescues (*Festuca* spp.)
Although fescues are considered bunch grasses, many of the newer cultivars have been selected because they lack this characteristic. They are slow to establish, but once established may have extensive root systems. Fescues have low water and fertility needs and are adaptable to many soil types.

Seeding rate: 1.6–2.0 kg/100 m^2 (3.5–4.5 lb/1,000 ft^2)

Chewings fescue (*Festuca rubra* var. *commutata*) is native to Europe and has narrow, dark blue-green leaves. It can be mixed with creeping red fescue and Kentucky bluegrass in conventional lawns, and cut as low as 5 cm (2 in.). It reproduces by tillering, has good shade- and drought-tolerance, and is also adapted to infertile, acid soils. It is believed to be weakly allelopathic, exuding a compound from its roots that inhibits the germination and/or growth of other plants. Chewings fescue and creeping red fescue make a good blend, similar in height to a conventional lawn but requiring less water, fertilizer, and mowing.

Sheep fescue (*Festuca ovina*) is strongly clumping and blue-green in color, has good drought tolerance, and is

From Manual of Plant Species Suitability for Reclamation in Alberta.

Sheep fescue
(*Festuca ovina*)

widely adaptive: from dry to moist soils and from basic to acidic. It is indigenous to both Europe and North America. 'Nakiska' is a newer cultivar with a less clumpy habit.

Hard fescue (*Festuca ovina* var. *duriuscula*), native to Europe, has a mature height of 15 to 25 cm (6–10 in.), with wider blades and a more greyish green color than other fescues. It is slow growing and slow to establish, but once established forms a low ground cover that is competitive with weeds. Growth slows down but does not stop during the heat of the summer. It is both drought- and shade-tolerant. Newer cultivars seem less clumpy and many contain endophtyes—genetically built-in biological controls against insects and disease.

Canada bluegrass (*Poa compressa*)
Shorter growing (10-30 cm/4–12 in.) and coarser than Kentucky bluegrass, Canada bluegrass is blue-green in color and has a wide adaptation from moist to dry, infertile soils and from acid to basic. Native to western Eurasia, it may be native or introduced to North America. Although it has a fibrous root system with extensive rhizomes, its growth habit is clumpy. It has good wear and stress tolerance, and is drought tolerant and disease resistant.

'Canon' and 'Reubens' are less clumpy to nonclumpy, with a 10 cm (4 in.) mowing height. They require far fewer inputs than Kentucky bluegrass. 'Reubens' tolerates acid soils and has early spring green-up.

Seeding rate: 0.5–1 kg/100 m² (1–2 lb/1,000 ft²)

Wheatgrasses (*Agropyron* spp.)
Although very drought tolerant, wheatgrasses show a strong clumping habit and are less dense than other grasses.

Seeding rate: 1.4–2.3 kg/100 m² (3-5 lb/1,000 ft²)

Crested wheatgrass (*Agropyron cristatum*, syn. *A. pectiniforme*) is native to Siberia but has become naturalized in some areas of North America. It is a clumping bunch grass with excellent drought tolerance and a height of 20 to 40 cm (8–16 in.). Some cultivars are lower growing. The species seeds readily and if allowed to set seed will become invasive once established, particularly if planted near or among native grass species.

'Fairway' crested wheatgrass remains one of the best grasses for nonirrigated lawns. Its leaves are green and somewhat wider than those of Kentucky bluegrass. Native to the cold, dry regions of Siberia, it is shorter, denser, and finer stemmed than the species, as well as slower growing. It is an upright bunch grass with an extensive and deep fibrous root system. It has a good germination and establishment rate and propagates naturally by seed. Drought tolerant, cold hardy,

> **Recommended hard fescue cultivars:**
>
> 'Spartan' is dark blue with a 7.5 to 15 cm (3–6 in.) mowing height that blends in well with bluegrasses. Once established, it is aggressive and competitive with weeds.
>
> 'Aurora' is dark blue-green and fine textured with a 7.5 to 15 cm (3–6 in.) mowing height and good drought tolerance.
>
> 'Biljart' (Netherlands, 1963) is dense, deep green, very fine textured, tufted, and drought resistant, and is considered one of the best turf-type hard fescue cultivars.
>
> 'Durar' (1949) is more clumpy but both drought resistant and shade tolerant.
>
> 'Reliant' is another good low-maintenance cultivar.

Crested wheatgrass (*Agropyron cristatum*, syn. *A. pectiniforme*)

From Manual of Plant Species Suitability for Reclamation in Alberta.

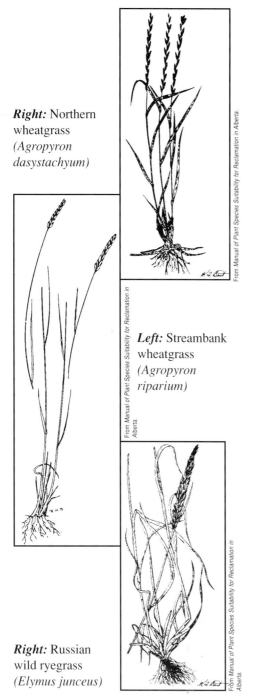

Right: Northern wheatgrass *(Agropyron dasystachyum)*

From Manual of Plant Species Suitability for Reclamation in Alberta.

Left: Streambank wheatgrass *(Agropyron riparium)*

From Manual of Plant Species Suitability for Reclamation in Alberta.

Right: Russian wild ryegrass *(Elymus junceus)*

From Manual of Plant Species Suitability for Reclamation in Alberta.

and tolerant of mowing, it is adapted to a wide range of soils. It becomes brown during hot, dry periods. Very competitive with weeds and useful in erosion control, it is invasive and should not be mixed with native species.

Northern wheatgrass *(Agropyron dasystachyum)*, a native species, is relatively low growing at 20 to 30 cm (8–12 in.), with a strong spreading habit and extensive rhizomes. It establishes quickly and is well adapted to slopes, banks, and sandy soils. Greyish green in color, it has a clumpy appearance. The cultivar 'Elbee' has excellent drought tolerance.

Streambank wheatgrass *(Agropyron riparium)* is a dryland species used in pure stands or in mixtures with small amounts of Kentucky bluegrass. Native to North America, including western Canada, it is a low-growing, sod-forming grass, with narrow leaves and stems 30 to 80 cm (12–30 in.) high. It has vigorous rhizomes, is long-lived, and colonizes both by seed and its spreading root system. It flourishes on well-drained soils, withstands mowing, and is highly competitive with weeds under dryland conditions. Long recommended for farm lawns, it is establishes quickly with good germination and seedling vigor.

Russian wild ryegrass *(Elymus junceus)*

This dryland grass species is used in pure stands or in mixtures with small amounts of Kentucky bluegrass. Native to western Siberia, it is used primarily as a pasture grass, a reclamation species, and for sand dune stabilization. It is a tall (1 m/3–4 ft), densely tufted bunch grass with a deep root system, and is easily propagated by seeds, reseeding itself naturally if left unmowed. It is adapted to light, heavy, and alkaline soils and has a high salinity tolerance. Intolerant of shade, it tolerates traffic, is not as invasive of adjacent areas as crested wheatgrass. It is considered one of the best grasses for nonirrigated farmyards and lawns. Many of the improved cultivars lack seedling vigor and may take two to three years to become established. An exception is 'Cabree,' which has outstanding seedling vigor. Other cultivars include 'Mayak,' 'Sawki,' 'Swift,' and 'Piper.'
Seeding rate: 2.3 kg/100 m^2 (5 lb/1,000 ft^2)

Native Grasses

Native grasses come in many colors and textures and together form a mosaic rather than a uniform swath. They change through the seasons as conditions of temperature and precipitation change. Once established, native grasses will perform well if allowed to grow to maturity. Most do not tolerate the intensive use we give our conventional lawns. These grasses have generally been used in low-maintenance situations where their primary function is visual.

Native grasses should be kept separate from traditional lawn and pasture grasses, with which they will seldom successfully compete, especially during the establishment stages. Bromegrass and crested wheatgrasses are particularly aggressive and will choke out native grasses, which are much slower to establish. Mixing aggressive agronomic and nonaggressive native species is seldom successful.

Although much more readily available than it was a decade ago, native grass seed may still be difficult to obtain and relatively expensive. It is strongly recommended that local seed sources be used as a plant will be better adapted to the region in which they are growing than the same species from a more distant location. (See list of suppliers in chapter 9.)

Blue grama *(Bouteloua gracilis)* came out as one of the top grasses in recent low-maintenance trials conducted in southern Alberta by the Prairie Turfgrass Research Centre in Olds, Alberta. Although a densely tufted bunch grass of up to 20 cm (8 in.) in height, blue grama will form a sod cover in about a year if mowed monthly through the summer. The narrow, grey-green leaves are curly. It has excellent heat and drought tolerance, but poor shade tolerance. It is well adapted to both clay and sandy soils and is an important range species.

Other native grasses being used in restoration projects or for nonirrigated spaces include: needle and thread grass *(Stipa comata)*, tufted hair grass *(Deschampsia caespitosa)*, big bluestem *(Andropogon gerardi)*, little bluestem *(Schizachyrium scoparius)*, and western *(Agropyron smithii)* and northern wheatgrass *(Agropyron dasystachyum)*.

The following native grasses can be utilized as ornamental grasses: little bluestem *(Schizachyrium scoparius)*, big bluestem *(Andropogon gerardi)*, switch grass *(Panicum virgatum)*, tufted hair grass *(Deschampsia caespitosa)*, fringed brome *(Bromus kalmii)*, Indian rice grass *(Oryzopsis hymenoides)*, sheep fescue *(Festuca ovina)*, common reed grass *(Phragmites communis)*, and Canada wild rye *(Elymus canadensis)*.

Smooth bromegrass *(Bromus inermis)* is no longer recommended for nonirrigated areas (or irrigated lawns) because of its aggressive nature. Brome grass is an open, coarse-textured, cool-season grass that is drought tolerant and requires little fertility. Native to Europe, Siberia, and China, it spreads by rhizomes and seed and has an extensive root system. It is intolerant of close mowing, not resilient to wear, and becomes brown during extended drought. Extremely invasive and naturalizing quickly, it is very competitive with native species.

Prairie Turfgrass Research Centre drought-tolerant selections

Twenty-five grasses were evaluated over three summers by the Prairie Turfgrass Research Centre in Olds, Alberta. Trials were established to determine: how quickly these grasses established from seeding; their ability to withstand drought; their mature height; and their competitiveness with weeds.

The results of these trials indicated that blue grama grass, 'Elbee' northern wheatgrass, 'Spartan' hard fescue, and 'Fairway' crested wheatgrass exhibited the best of these characteristics. These grasses combined low mowing height, drought tolerance, and competitiveness with weeds. There was, of course, a consistent relationship between the ability of a grass to establish itself quickly from seed and its ability to compete with weeds.

Further Reading

Lawns

Turfgrass Science and Culture, by James B. Beard (Prentice-Hall, New Jersey, 1973).

Great Plains Turfgrass Manual, by Dennis McKernan (LifeWorks, Olds, Alberta, 1994).

Part 2

Xeriscape Plants

any drought-tolerant plants have been part of prairie gardens for years, but until now we may have thought of them only as attractive plants.

Chapter 7

Ornamentals

For the xeriscape

Appropriate Plant Selection

A plentiful palette

Prairie gardeners have an incredibly large variety of hardy, drought-tolerant plants to choose from. Many of these may have been part of our gardens for years, but until now we may have thought of them only as attractive plants rather than as drought tolerant.

What Makes a Plant Drought Tolerant?

Most plants avoid drought by growing only where there is adequate moisture to sustain their needs. Marsh species are not found on dry hills, and plants that grow on dry hills are not found in deserts.

Within their range of adaptability, plants avoid drought by either enhancing their uptake of limited soil moisture or conserving the water within their tissue.

A major factor determining the amount of water absorbed by a plant is the depth and concentration of its root system. Plants that have deep tap roots in combination with shallow surface roots, such as Scots pine, are able to capture moisture from light rains as well as water from lower in the soil profile.

Grasses often form very dense roots through which little water is able to pass. By developing highly fibrous root systems, they collect a large amount of soil moisture before it can penetrate into the soil and be used by more deeply rooted species.

Almost all of the water leaving a plant is lost through the tiny openings in the leaves called stomates. Trees such as green ash, which are able to close their stomates at the first sign of drought, are more drought tolerant than those that cannot, such as trembling aspen.

Plants with small, thick leaves lose water more slowly than plants with large, thin leaves. This is because smaller leaves have less surface area from which water can evaporate. This gives pussytoes an edge over large-leafed elephant ears (*Ligularia* spp.) in times of drought.

Small hairs or scales on a leaf surface are effective in reflecting light, shading the leaf surface, and reducing air movement directly over the leaf—in effect, acting as a microscopic shelterbelt. These hairs, called "trichomes," often give the plant a silver appearance. Silver- or grey-leafed plants such as wolf willow or *Artemisia* are often more drought tolerant than their green counterparts.

Succulents, such as hens and chicks and sedum, store water in their thick, fleshy leaves. This allows them to survive conditions of extreme water stress. As well, they open their stomates for entry of carbon dioxide only during the cool of night. A modification of normal photosynthesis permits these plants to take in and absorb carbon dioxide at night for use in photosynthesis the following day.

Bulbs are able to withstand drought through a combination of avoidance and water storage. Growth and flowering of the more drought-tolerant bulbs often occurs during spring and fall, when temperatures are cooler and soil moisture levels usually greater. They avoid growth during hot, dry summers. With others, the bulb itself acts as a storage organ for both nutrients and moisture. That's why it is so critical not to remove the leaves of lilies, tulips, and their kin until the foliage has yellowed and fallen naturally. The leaves photosynthesize and provide food for the bulb—energy that is for the most part funneled into next year's flowers. These bulbs are purchased and planted as dormant bulbs in the fall and flower the following season.

Reducing Maintenance

For ease of maintenance, it's essential to place plants where they will grow well. Trying to fight nature results in weakened plants that are more vulnerable to disease and insect problems and might ultimately die and need replacement.

In choosing plant materials, know the site preferences of each plant and place it accordingly. Does a particular plant perform best in sun or shade? Peonies require full sun. If your yard has mature trees that cast dense shade, they may never bloom. Canada violets do well in a shady location.

Moisture requirements are also critical. Scots pine, golden currant, and Russian olive are all quite drought tolerant. Willow and birch are "wet site species." They require even moisture and fare poorly under drought.

Wind is another factor. Hydrangeas demand a sheltered site out of the wind. Caragana does not.

Soil pH also affects how plants perform. Most prairie soils are basic, or alkaline, with a pH above 7.0. Plants like blueberries and azaleas require a more acidic soil, with a pH between 4.5 and 5.5. They simply will not grow in basic soils.

Further reading

Annuals for the Prairies, by Edgar W. Toop (University of Alberta, University of Saskatchewan, Lone Pine Publishing, 1993).

Dictionary of Plant Names, by Allen J. Combes (Timber Press, Portland, Oregon, 1985).

Flowers and Plants: An international lexicon with biographical notes, by Robert Shosteck (Quadrangle, The New York Times Book Company, 1974).

Horticultural Horizons, by Frank Leith Skinner (Manitoba Department of Agriculture, 1966).

Hortus Third, Liberty Hyde Bailey Hortorium (Macmillan, New York, 1976).

Manual of Plant Species Suitability for Reclamation in Alberta, Hardy BBT Limited (Alberta Land Conservation and Reclamation Council, 1989).

Perennials for the Prairies, by Edgar W. Toop and Sara Williams (University of Alberta, University of Saskatchewan, 1991).

Stearn's Dictionary of Plant Names for Gardeners, by William T. Stearn (Cassell Publishers Limited, London, 1996).

Trees and Shrubs for the Northern Plains, by Donald G. Hoag (North Dakota Institute for Regional Studies, 1965).

Wildflowers Across the Prairies, by F. R. Vance, J. R. Jowsey, and J. S. McLean (Western Producer Prairie Books, Saskatoon, 1984).

Woody Ornamentals for the Prairies, by Hugh Knowles (University of Alberta, 1989).

Wyman's Gardening Encyclopedia, by Donald Wyman (Macmillan, New York, 1986).

Ornamental Plant Descriptions

Trees & Shrubs   97

Perennials   131

Vines   160

Bulbs   165

Annuals   168

Native Plants   190

ψ *Acer ginnala* (ginnala maple, Amur maple)

The ginnala maple is native to China, Japan, Siberia, and Manchuria. The species name is possibly from the Greek *ginnos* (a small mule), referring to the plant's size and toughness.

Fast growing, ginnala maple is classified as either a large shrub or, if pruned to a single trunk, a small, rounded tree of about 5 m (15 ft) in height. The flowers, produced in May, are greenish-white and inconspicuous. Leaves are three-lobed, with the middle lobe longer than the side lobes. The leaf veins and petioles are red. Fall color varies from yellow to orange to red, becoming bright scarlet at its best. The paired, winged seed pods, or samaras, are bright red, ripening to a straw color.

Culture: Ginnala maple prefers well-drained soils with a pH below 7.0 and full sunlight, although it will tolerate partial shade. It will have better growth with protection from wind. It is susceptible to lime-induced chlorosis (see p. 34).

Use: Use in smaller urban yards or massed in larger spaces, as an informal hedge, and for screening. Seeds are retained into winter and are a treat for grosbeaks and other birds.

Fall color

ψ *Acer negundo* (Manitoba maple, box elder)

Manitoba maples are native to the prairies and have been used extensively as shelterbelt, shade, and boulevard trees. They are fast growing, attaining a height of 10 to 13 m (30–40 ft) or more during their 60-year life span. Their leaves resemble those of ash—compound with three to seven irregularly lobed leaflets—rather than classic maple leaves. Autumn color is yellow. Male and female flowers are on separate trees; only female trees produce seeds. The female flower is greenish-yellow in drooping clusters. The male flower is a dense, red tassel. Flowers appear before the leaves. The seed pods are winged and V-shaped and persist into winter.

Culture: Manitoba maples are adapted to full sun and a wide range of soils. They will not do well in shade. Problems include a relatively weak structure that is prone to breakage; sensitivity to 2,4–D (they are considered an "indicator plant" to its presence); and their attractiveness to aphids, which excrete "honeydew" onto decks, picnic tables, and vehicles. They are also beloved by cankerworms and red and black box elder bugs. If wounded, the tree may produce an abundance of watersprouts from the base of the trunk.

Use: Excellent in shelterbelts, farmsteads, or acreages, they cannot be recommended for smaller urban lots due to their size and undesirable characteristics. They are excellent for tree houses and climbing, provide food and cover for a wide variety of birds, and may be tapped for maple syrup.

Fall color

Left: fall color

Sara Williams

Brian Baldwin

Department of Horticulture Science, University of Saskatchewan

ѱ *Amelanchier alnifolia* (saskatoon berry)

The species name, *alnifolia,* means alder leaf and refers to the alder-like leaves. A native shrub well known for its sweet, edible fruit, the saskatoon also has ornamental flowers and attractive fall color. It shows tremendous variation in form. Heights generally range from 2.5 to 4.5 m (8–15 ft), with a spread of 1 to 2 m (4–6 ft). Dense, erect clusters of fragrant white flowers are produced in May, followed by edible, dark blue berries in midsummer. Used by Indigenous Peoples and early European settlers, saskatoon berries have become a major commercial fruit crop on the prairies in the last decade.

Cultivars include 'Honeywood,' 'Northline,' 'Pembina,' 'Smoky,' and 'Thiessen.' 'Altaglow' is a white-fruited saskatoon, columnar in form, with outstanding fall color varying from gold to purple.

Culture: Saskatoons grow in a wide range of soils, in sun or partial shade. They are less fruitful in shade. They are drought tolerant once established. If grown within a few kilometers of junipers, they may become infected with saskatoon-juniper rust, especially following warm, rainy springs. This fungal disease is characterized by orange lesions on the leaves and fruit of the saskatoon plants.

Use: Saskatoons are excellent as part of an informal shrub border, as a small specimen tree, or a tree grouping. They are widely used in shelterbelts, providing cover and food for birds. The edible berries are a bonus!

Brian Porter

Amorpha canescens (leadplant)

The genus name is derived from the Greek word *amorphos,* meaning shapeless or deformed, and describes the one-petalled flower. The species name, *canescens,* means ashy-grey, a reference to the leaves. The common name arose from the mistaken belief that the presence of this shrub indicated lead deposits in the soil. Native to Canada as well as the American Midwest, it is about 1 m (3 ft) in height, with grey, compound leaves with up to 45 leaflets. Small, blue flowers on 15 cm (6 in.) spikes are produced in July.

Culture: It grows well in poor, dry soils in full sun, and can become invasive.

Use: Because of its suckering habit, it is useful for naturalizing, stabilizing soil, and roadside plantings.

Amorpha fruticosa (false indigo)

A member of the pea family, false indigo is native to the Prairies. The common name alludes to its use as a blue dye. A shrub of 1 to 1.5 m (3–5 ft), it is initially mound-like but may become leggy and somewhat sprawling with age. It has long, compound leaves and 15 cm (6 in.) spikes of small blue or purple flowers. Its overall texture is very fine.

Culture: False indigo is well adapted to dry, sunny locations. In partial shade, it flowers less and is somewhat more sprawling.

Use: Because of its form, it is not often seen in the well-manicured landscape. It is useful in a more rural, naturalized setting. It is a nectar plant for butterflies.

Brian Baldwin

Ψ Arctostaphylos uva-ursi (bearberry, kinnikinnick)

Both the common and botanical names refer to the reputed love of bears for the fruit. An evergreen, woody ground cover native to the prairies, bearberry forms a prostrate mat about 15 cm (6 in.) in height. Its thick, glossy green leaves usually turn bronzy green in winter. The pink-and-white flowers are urn-shaped. The fruit is bright scarlet, 1 cm (less than 0.5 in.) in diameter, and persists through the winter. 'Vancouver Jade' has fragrant, dark pink flowers and spreads more readily.

Culture: Usually found on dry, sandy slopes, it grows in full sun or light shade on well-drained, acid or alkaline soil.

Use: This excellent ground cover fits in well in a perennial border or rock garden. The berries are eaten by birds.

Sara Williams

Ψ Caragana spp. (caragana, pea shrub)

First introduced to western Canada from Siberia in the 1880s, caragana is native to Russia, Siberia, Mongolia, and China. It is well adapted to prairie conditions and is still used extensively in hedging and farm shelterbelts. The pinnately-compound leaves give the plant a fine-textured appearance. A member of the pea family, its yellow, pea-like flowers are borne profusely in June, followed by long, pea-like pods, which split open audibly during the hot days of August.

Common caragana (*C. arborescens*) is often seen in shelterbelts and was once used extensively as hedging. About 4.5 m (15 ft) in height, it is upright and spreading, becoming leggy with age if not rejuvenated. The species itself can hardly be considered ornamental, although some of its cultivars are.

Recommended cultivars: • *C. arborescens* 'Lorbergii' (fern-leafed

'Sutherland' caragana

Brian Baldwin

Ornamentals • 99

Above: weeping caragana
Left: pygmy caragana
Below: globe caragana

Sara Williams

Brian Baldwin

Brian Baldwin

caragana) is a mutant, about 2 m (6 ft) in height, with extremely fine-textured leaves resembling those of the asparagus fern. It is commonly grafted onto a "standard" stem of caragana 'Sutherland' and may be oddly attractive as a feature plant in the smaller landscape. • *C. arborescens* 'Pendula' (weeping caragana) has normal caragana foliage but a weeping habit. It too is often grafted onto a standard. On its own roots it is useful as a ground cover, particularly on a bank or slope. Its twisted stems are attractive in winter. • *C. arborescens* 'Sutherland' ('Sutherland' caragana) is compact, with a narrow, upright, columnar form of 3 to 3.5 m (10–12 ft). It can be used as a screen or where a vertical accent is needed. It does not tend to sucker. • *C. arborescens* 'Walker' ('Walker' caragana) is both weeping and fine-leaved and is therefore of greater value. It is useful on its own roots as a ground cover or cascading over a retaining wall. • *C. frutex* 'Globosa' (globe caragana) is 1 m (3–4 ft), compact, and carries its foliage right to the base. It does not flower. In the formal landscape it is used as a low hedge, or even a substitute for boxwood (*Buxus sempervirens*), which is not hardy. • *C. pygmaea* (pygmy caragana) is fine-textured and mound-shaped to about 1 m (3 ft) and does not sucker. It is spiny and hence valuable as an impenetrable low hedge, informal or trimmed.

Culture: Caraganas are salt tolerant and do well in full sun on well-drained soils but do not tolerate flooding. Seeds germinate readily in cultivated garden areas and naturalize in adjacent bush or woods. Suckers arising from the rootstock onto which cultivars have been grafted should be removed. Caraganas are sometimes attacked by blister beetles.

Use: Depending on the selection, caraganas may be utilized as feature plants, high or low hedges, screening, ground covers, or in shelterbelts. They are excellent for "traffic control," and provide cover for wildlife. Because of their size and tendency to sucker and self-seed, only a few are suitable for smaller yards.

B. J. Godwin

Corylus cornuta (beaked hazelnut)

Corylus, the Greek name for this plant, is derived from the word *korys*, meaning helmet. *Cornuta* means horned. Both describe the small, edible nut; it is covered with bracts (the husk) that resemble a helmet and come to a point, or horn. The hybrid 'Kerr' has a larger nut. Native to the dry thickets and woods of the prairies, these shrubs are about 2 m (6.5 ft) in height with an upright, spreading form. The flowers, borne in April, are rather inconspicuous. Male and female flowers occur on the same plant, but pollen from a different plant is required to produce nuts. Leaves turn yellow in autumn.

Culture: Plant in full sun or partial shade on well-drained soil. It spreads by suckering.

Use: Useful as a wildlife planting and for naturalizing. The nuts are eaten by blue jays, bears, and squirrels.

ψ *Cotoneaster* spp. (cotoneaster)

The genus name is from the Latin *cotoneum,* meaning quince, and refers to the quince-like appearance of the fruit. Native to Asia, cotoneasters are a variable group of shrubs with small leaves, some of which turn scarlet red in the fall, and red or dark blue berries. They range from low ground covers to taller shrubs.

Hedge cotoneaster *(Cotoneaster lucidus)* is one of the best hedges available to prairie gardeners and is noted for its compact form and small, dark green leaves which turn a brilliant orange-red in the fall if grown in full sun. Shaded plants are more yellow. The species name *lucidus* means shiny and refers to the lustrous leaves. Untrimmed, hedge cotoneaster can attain a height of up to 3 m (9 ft). The flowers are small and inconspicuous, the fruit dark blue to black. It may need renewal pruning every 10 to 15 years. This involves cutting it to ground level in early spring prior to leaf emergence.

Cotoneaster integerrimus (European red-berried cotoneaster) is 1 to 2 m (4–6 ft) in height, more open and branched, and less suited to a formal hedge. It is excellent in an informal shrub border or as an untrimmed hedge. Its blue-green foliage is not as glossy, nor does it have the outstanding fall color of the hedge cotoneaster; it turns a straw yellow. Red berries are produced in late summer.

Cotoneaster adpressus (creeping cotoneaster) is a prostrate plant of less than 0.3 m (1 ft) with red berries. It is useful as a ground cover but is not dependably hardy on the prairies. *C. horizontalis pepursila* is a hardier creeping type. The cultivar 'Praecox,' often sold as *C. adpressus,* is similar but larger, with more arching branches. It is native to central China.

Cotoneaster submultiflorus and *C. tomentosus* are used as informal plantings.

Culture: Cotoneasters prefer open, sunny locations and well-drained soils. They are susceptible to fireblight, silver leaf, and, in mid to late summer, pear slug.

Use: Depending on the species, cotoneasters are utilized as formal hedges, informal shrub borders, or as ground covers. They are valued both for their fruit color and fall foliage and provide food and cover for birds.

European red-berried cotoneaster

Hedge cotoneaster in fall.

Hawthorn in flower.

Brian Porter

Hawthorn in fruit.

J. G. N. Davidson

ψ *Crataegus* spp. (hawthorn)

Large shrubs or small trees somewhat resembling a crabapple in fruit and form, hawthorns are attractive in spring when in flower and in late summer and fall when in fruit. The fruit is generally red and about 1 cm (0.5 in.) in diameter. The common name is a combination of the word *haw,* meaning a hedge or enclosure, for which they are commonly used in England, and *thorn,* referring to the nature of their armament. Leaves are highly variable among species. Because species hybridize easily, identification is often difficult.

• *Crataegus arnoldiana* ('Arnold' hawthorn) is about 3.5 m (12 ft) in height and makes an attractive small tree with shiny leaves, single white flowers, and large, scarlet fruit. It can be pruned to a single trunk. • *C. chlorosarca* is a small tree with a pyramidal growth habit, mostly lacking thorns, with black fruit, native to Asia. • *C. chrysocarpa* (round-leaved or fireberry hawthorn) is the most common native species, with dark green, glossy leaves and red-orange berries. Three m (10 ft) in height, it has white flowers and thorns. • *C. columbiana* (Columbian hawthorn) is native to the Cypress Hills of Alberta and Saskatchewan, 3.5 m (12 ft) in height, with white flowers, dark red fruit, and well armed with stout thorns up to 6 cm (2.5 in.) in length. • *Crataegus crus-galli* (cockspur hawthorn) is a native hawthorn with white flowers and bright red fruit retained over much of the winter. Both the common and botanical names refer to the similarity of the long thorns to the spurs of a rooster. It is up to 5 m (15 ft) in height, with a distinctive and attractive horizontal branching habit. The bright green, glossy leaves show resistance to rust. In a sunny exposure, the foliage has good fall color ranging from orange to scarlet. *C. crus-galli* var. *inermis* (thornless cockspur hawthorn) is similar but lacks thorns. • 'Snowbird' is a thornless hybrid (*C. oxyacantha* x *C. succulenta*) from Agriculture Canada's Research Centre at Morden, Manitoba. It has double white flowers and is 3 to 3.5 m (10–12 ft) in height. It may require a sheltered location in zone 2b. It is resistant to cedar-apple rust.

Culture: Hawthorns do well in full sun on a variety of soils as long as drainage is adequate. They may occasionally be infected with pear slug or fireblight. Cedar-apple rust is the most serious problem.

Use: Hawthorn's size, flowers, and fruit make it an excellent but underused tree in the small urban yard or grouped in larger spaces. It is used in shelterbelt plantings. It provides nesting sites and food for birds.

Cytisus pilosa 'Vancouver Gold' ('Vancouver Gold' broom)

Broom was once used to sweep floors in Scotland, hence the common name. *Cytisus* is from the Greek name for this shrub, *kytisos*. *Pilosa* means covered with long, soft hairs. The species is native to Europe. 'Vancouver Gold' is only 8 cm (3 in.), with a compact growth habit. It has bright green stems covered with a profusion of bright yellow, pea-like flowers in spring. The fruit that follows is a flat pod.

Culture: Plant in dry, infertile soil in full sun. Once established, it resents disturbance and is not easily transplanted. On the prairies it is best placed in a well-protected location.

Use: Excellent in a mixed or shrub border or in a rock garden.

Brian Baldwin

Ψ *Elaeagnus angustifolia* (Russian olive)

Elaeagnus was a name once applied to the genus willow. *Angustifolia* means narrow-leafed. Russian olive is native to Europe and Asia. A large shrub or graceful, fine-textured tree, it ranges in height from 4.5 to 7.5 m (15–25 ft). Leaves, twigs, flowers, and fruit are all covered in minute grey scales, giving the tree a silvery appearance. The long, narrow leaves are retained over winter, giving it a permanent hoar-frosted appearance. The yellow-and-silver flowers, borne in early June, are highly fragrant but inconspicuous and are followed by inedible olives. Thorny and non-thorny forms are available.

Culture: Russian olives tolerate saline soil, but not poor drainage. They do best in full sun. Some clones may suffer from winter injury.

Use: These trees are used as specimen or shade trees, screen plantings, and in shelterbelts. The silver foliage contrasts well with evergreens. The olives are eaten by birds.

Brian Baldwin

Sara Williams

Ψ *Elaeagnus commutata* (wolf willow, silverberry)

Native to the prairies, wolf willow casts its sweet scent along fence lines in May. An upright and sometimes leggy shrub of up to 2.5 m (8 ft), it suckers freely, forming thickets. The branches and leaves are covered with silvery scales. The tubular flowers are inconspicuous, silver outside and yellow inside. They have four petals and are extremely fragrant. The small, silver fruit is dry and mealy. 'Zempin' is an improved cultivar.

Culture: Plant in full sun in a variety of soils. It is saline tolerant.

Brian Baldwin

Use: Wolf willow is used for wildlife plantings, naturalization, reclamation, and on banks and slopes to control erosion. It provides food and cover for birds and is a bee nectar source. Grafted onto Russian olive rootstock (to prevent suckering), it is useful in a shrub border, especially if planted where one can smell the scent in spring.

Brian Baldwin

ψ *Fraxinus pensylvanica* **var.** *subintegerrima* **(green ash)**

Green ash is native to Manitoba and Saskatchewan. Fast growing and long lived, it reaches 20 m (60 ft) in height, with an upright, oval form. Fall color is an attractive gold. Each of its pinnately compound leaves has five to nine leaflets. Male and female flowers are borne on separate trees. Single-seeded samaras produced by female trees are retained through the winter and eaten by birds. It has a deep, fibrous root system which is able to tap subsoil moisture. Prominent frost cracks on the main trunk are common but seldom damaging.

'Patmore' is a male clone from Manitoba that leafs out earlier in the spring than most other green ash and retains its foliage longer into the fall. 'Marshall's Seedless' is similar.

Culture: Green ash do well in full sun or partial shade in a variety of soils. They are occasionally attacked by cankerworms, lygus bugs, leaf-rollers, and, in female trees, gall mites.

Use: Excellent as shade or boulevard trees and in shelterbelts.

Sara Williams

Genista tinctoria **(dyer's greenweed, broom)**

Native to Europe and western Asia, broom was introduced into commerce in the early 1600s as a dye plant. A low, upright shrub of 1 m (3 ft), it has bright yellow, pea-like flowers in June and equally bright green leaves. Both the tiny leaves and the bright green branches photosynthesize. It is a member of the pea family and is used to produce a yellow dye, hence the common and botanical names. *Tinctoria* means used in dyeing. 'Rossica' is a vigorous cultivar.

Culture: Broom is well-adapted to infertile, well-drained soils and performs best in full sun. It is difficult to move once established.

Use: This is a useful replacement for forsythia in areas of the prairies where deep snow cover is not dependable. It is easily incorporated into an informal shrub bed, a perennial border, mixed border, or rock garden.

Ψ *Halimodendron halodendron* (Siberian salt tree, salt bush)

The genus name means tree of the sea shore. The species name is a combination of *halo* (salt) and *dendron* (a tree). The names say it all: a tree that grows along the Siberian coast, well accustomed to the salt spray of the sea. A member of the pea family and related to caragana, the salt tree has fine-textured silver leaves and spines, and forms a 2 to 3 m (6–9 ft), upright, spreading, and somewhat leggy shrub. The leaves are pinnately compound, each with four sessile leaflets and the terminal leaflet modified to form of a spine. In autumn the leaflets fall, but the central spine-tipped vein remains on the tree. The pale lilac flowers are pea-like, appear in midsummer, and are quite ornamental. They are followed by a brownish yellow pod. The pods remain on the tree through winter. The salt tree suckers profusely but may be grafted onto *Caragana arborescens* to reduce suckering.

Culture: The Siberian salt tree will grow on any well-drained soil in full sun. It is salt tolerant.

Use: This is a good plant for naturalization, reclamation on dry soils, or highway plantings where winter salt spray would damage most other woody plants.

Ψ *Hippophae rhamnoides* (sea buckthorn)

Both the botanical and common names make reference to this plant's resemblance to the common buckthorn *(Rhamnus).* A large, upright shrub of 3.5 m (12 ft), sea buckthorn is native to Europe and Asia. The flowers are small, yellow, and inconspicuous. It has narrow, silver leaves and twigs which terminate in sharp thorns. The bright orange fruit is held closely to the branches and persists over winter. The fruit is 6 to 10 mm (0.25–0.4 in.) in diameter and is high in vitamin C. It is planted extensively in Russian shelterbelts and processed as a juice and pulp because of the vitamin C content. Plants with fewer thorns are being selected to make harvesting less difficult.

Culture: Sea buckthorn is both drought- and saline-tolerant and should be grown in full sun. It is dioecious, so both male and female plants (1 male:7 female) are needed if the attractive fruit are to be produced. It suckers if the roots are disturbed.

Use: This is an excellent shrub for farmyards, acreages, or shelterbelts. Its suckering habit precludes its use in a smaller urban setting. It has excellent winter landscape value because of the retained fruit and is useful as a wildlife planting. Magpies eat the berries. It provides good cover and nesting sites for small songbirds. The fruit is used for jelly.

'Depressa Aurea'

'Dunvegan Blue'

Rocky Mountain juniper

Brian Baldwin

Sara Williams

Sara Williams

ψ *Juniperus* spp. (juniper)

Junipers are among the most drought tolerant of the ever-greens. The leaves are scale-, awl-, or needle-like. The male cones are very small and inconspicuous. Female cones mature to become dark blue, berry-like fruit with a waxy, powdery coating, or "bloom." The fragrant fruit is used to flavor gin and a Norwegian beer, but is believed to be poisonous to livestock. Many species and cultivars exist, varying from ground covers to columnar forms of 3.5 to 4.5 m (12–15 ft).

Juniperus communis (common juniper) is native to much of North America, Europe, and Asia. Extremely variable in form and height, on the prairies it is usually about 1 m (3 ft) and tends to turn purple in cooler fall weather. It has sharp, awl-shaped needles with a white band down the center of the upper side. The needles are arranged in whorls of three. Indigenous peoples used the fruit both decoratively and as an insect repellent. Early settlers used them as a coffee substitute. 'Depressa Aurea' is a selection with golden yellow foliage equal or superior to the better known 'Golden Pfitzer' (*Juniperus* x *media* 'Pfitzerana') and less prone to winter browning.

Juniperus horizontalis (creeping juniper) is native to the Canadian prairies and is generally 15 to 30 cm (6–12 in.) high. The leaves are scale- or awl-like. Cultivars include 'Bar Harbour' (grey-green), 'Blue Chip' (bright blue), 'Waukegan' (blue turning purple in fall), 'Dunvegan Blue' (silver blue), 'Prince of Wales' (bright green), 'Hughes' (blue), 'Andorra' (light green turning purple in fall, with a more upright form), and 'Wapiti' (green turning purple in fall).

Juniperus sabina (savin juniper) is native to Europe, but many selections have proven hardy on the prairies. It has arching foliage which is typically vase-shaped and 0.5 to 1.5 m (2–5 ft) in height. The scale-like leaves are not prickly, and their bright green color is retained through winter. 'Arcadia' is bright green and 0.5 to 1 m (2–3 ft); 'Skandia' is more compact at 30 cm (12 in.) in height, with bright green foliage, resistant to saskatoon-juniper rust; 'Tamariscifolia' is 45 to 60 cm (18–24 in.) in height and mound-shaped; 'Youngstown' has feathery foliage and turns purple in fall; 'Calgary Carpet' is bright green, compact, and horizontal in habit.

Juniperus scopulorum (Rocky Mountain juniper) is native to Canada. It varies in form from pyramidal to columnar and attains heights from 3.5 to 6 m (12–20 ft). *Scopulorum* means growing on rocks or cliffs and refers to its native habitat. The foliage is green, silver, or blue-grey. Among the denser selections offered are 'Blue Heaven,' 'Grizzly Bear,' and 'Medora.' Most are susceptible to saskatoon-juniper rust.

Culture: Junipers prefer a well-drained soil and require full sun to maintain a dense form. This is especially true of blue-grey selections. They will usually perform well on southern and western exposures where cedars will not. Unfortunately, many (especially *J. communis* and *J. scopulorum)* are alternate hosts for saskatoon-juniper rust. Branches infected with rust should be removed by pruning as soon as rust is noticed.

Use: Depending on their size and form, junipers are used as foundation plantings, screening, massed as ground covers or understories, to hold difficult slopes or banks, or in a rock garden. The berry-like cones add to their landscape value. They provide cover and food for birds, which often act as dispersal agents for the seed.

Larix sibirica (Siberian larch)

As the name implies, this species is native to Siberia and northeast Russia and is much better adapted to dry conditions than our own tamarack *(Larix laricina)*. It is a large, fast-growing tree, up to 18 m (60 ft) in height, that retains a pyramidal form throughout its life. The branches arch gracefully down, turning up at their tips. It has soft, bright green, flexible needles. On new growth, the needles are single and spirally arranged along the branch. On older growth, they are in dense clusters on short pegs. Like other larches, the Siberian larch is deciduous, loosing its needles in the fall. In spring, new growth is early and a lovely soft green. The fall color is an outstanding golden yellow. The male cones look like catkins and wither once the pollen is shed. The female cones resemble small wooden roses and persist on the naked branches throughout the winter. They mature in one season.

Culture: Plant on most well-drained soils in full sun.

Use: Because of its size, the Siberian larch is well suited as a specimen tree in larger urban yards, acreages, and farm plantings. It is used in shelterbelts, where it establishes quickly. The fall color contrasts well with evergreens.

Fall color

Ψ *Lonicera* spp. (honeysuckle)

A fast-growing shrub of 2.5 to 3.5 m (9–12 ft), honeysuckles are valued for their flowers (usually pink, but also white, yellow, or red) and their berries (mostly red, but also orange, white, or blue). The flowers are produced in pairs in the leaf axils in June and July. The bark is thin and peeling.

Unfortunately, in the past decade some species have been devastated by infestations of an aphid causing abnormal purplish tip growth resembling a witch's broom, dieback,

Brian Baldwin

Above and left (detail): Tartarian honeysuckle in flower *Below:* sweetberry honeysuckle

Brian Baldwin

Hugh Skinner

and eventual death. The following honeysuckles have shown resistance to this insect: • The Amur honeysuckle *(L. maackii)* is 2.5 to 3 m (8–10 ft) in height, with white flowers and dark red fruit that matures a bit later than most, providing longer fall landscape value. The branches form a horizontal pattern that is quite attractive. It was introduced from Asia via Lautaret, France, by Skinner's Nursery in Manitoba in 1929. • 'Cameo' is a resistant seedling selected at Boughen Nurseries in Valley River, Manitoba. It has white flowers, shiny leaves, and is about 2.5 m (8 ft) in height. • 'Clavey's Dwarf' *(L. tatarica* x *L. xylosteum)* has yellow flowers, grey-green leaves, a very dense form, and is about 1 m (3 ft) in height. It is very useful as a low hedge but seldom flowers or fruits and has little winter landscape value. • 'Flamingo,' also from Boughen's, is similar to 'Cameo,' but with pink flowers followed by red berries, which are retained into winter. • *L. tatarica* 'Arnold Red' is attractive, 2.5 m (8 ft), with deep pink flowers and red berries. • 'Miniglobe' has the same parentage as 'Clavey's Dwarf' and is similar. It is 0.5 m (2 ft) in height and is useful for massing. • The sweetberry honeysuckle *(L. caerulea* var. *edulis)* is an edible-fruited species. The cultivar 'George Bugnet' is an upright shrub of 1.5 to 2 m (5–6.5 ft) with cream to yellow flowers and pairs of blue fruit. • 'Sunstar,' a seedling selected by Sunstar Nurseries in Edmonton in 1988, is 2.5 m (8 ft) in height, with white flowers and red fruit.

Culture: Honeysuckles are tough, drought-tolerant shrubs, well adapted to prairie conditions. They do best in full sun or partial shade on well-drained soils.

Use: The taller honeysuckles are useful on larger lots, acreages, or farmyards as informal hedging, in shrub borders, screenings, and shelterbelts. They do not lend themselves to small urban settings or more formal landscapes. The dwarf honeysuckles are used for low hedging and for massing. Honeysuckle is a nectar plant for butterflies, and the fruit is eaten by birds and other wildlife.

Malus spp. (crabapple)

Small, dense, low-headed trees of up to 7.5 m (25 ft), flowering crabapples are ideally suited to the smaller urban landscape. Relatively fast growing, their life span is about 40 years. Flowers are white, pink, or red; leaves range from green to purple. By definition, the fruit of crabapples is 4 cm (1.5 in.) or less in diameter. Those termed "rosyblooms" *(Malus* x *astringens)* have pink to red flowers and purplish leaves.

The Siberian crabapple *(M. baccata)* is about 7.5 m (25 ft) with white flowers. Although somewhat susceptible to fireblight, the white flowers contrast well with the rosyblooms. It has been used to impart hardiness to many of the ornamental crabapple cultivars. Recommended are: • 'Arctic Dawn,' a large, very hardy tree with pink flowers. • 'Gary,' 6 m (20 ft), with arching branches and a profusion of bright rose-pink flowers. The red leaves it produces in spring turn bronze-green by midsummer. Fruit is retained over winter. • 'Hopa,' 7.5 m (25 ft), has nearly red flowers with white at the base of each petal, and red-green leaves. Fruit drop at maturity may cause a litter problem. • 'Kerr,' which has white flowers and edible fruit. • 'Kelsey,' 6 m (20 ft), with semi-double, purple-red flowers. Its dark red spring foliage turns to copper green by summer. It bears little or no fruit. • 'Red Splendor,' with light pink flowers followed by small, scarlet fruit, which is retained over winter. • 'Rudolph,' 6 m (20 ft), has a round form. A profuse bloomer, with red buds turning to pink flowers, it is very winter hardy. • 'Selkirk,' a rosybloom with pink flowers and bright red fruit. • Snowcap, a white-flowering cultivar. • 'Strathmore,' with pink flowers, a narrow, upright form, bronze-purple foliage, and fruit suitable for jelly. • 'Thunderchild,' which has pink flowers, purple leaves, and small, red fruit.

Culture: Once established, crabapples do well on the prairies, especially in more sheltered sites. They prefer a deeper soil with adequate drainage and full sun. Select cultivars (such as 'Thunderchild') that are resistant to fireblight.

Use: Flowering crabapples are excellent trees for smaller yards, and when grouped are equally suited to a more expansive landscape. They are used as boulevard trees, for screening, in shelterbelts, and as wildlife plantings, where they provide cover and are an excellent winter food source for waxwings and other fruit-eating birds.

Above: *Malus* 'Snowcap' *Right:* a selection of seedling rosyblooms

Philadelphus lewisii 'Waterton' ('Waterton' mockorange)

Philadelphus is from the Greek phrase for brotherly love, after an Egyptian pharaoh by that name. The species name honors Captain Meriwether Lewis of the Lewis and Clark Expedition. Native to the Waterton Lakes National Park, this erect and spreading shrub of 2 to 2.5 m (7–8 ft) produces a profusion of single, white flowers on arching branches in June. Their fragrance resembles orange blossoms (thus the common name) Because the flower buds are formed in the fall, buds may be killed above the snow line on plants in unsheltered locations.

Culture: Plant in full sun in a range of soils. Water regularly for the first five years or until established. Once the root system is developed it is quite drought tolerant.

Use: Use in a mixed border or an informal tree-shrub border.

Brian Baldwin

Brian Baldwin

Brian Baldwin

Physocarpus opulifolius (common ninebark)

An upright, spreading shrub of 2 to 3 m (6.5–10 ft) with arching branches, ninebark is native to North America from Quebec to Virginia. The common name alludes to the cinnamon-brown bark, which peels to reveal a number of layers (though not necessarily nine). The genus name is from the Greek words *physa*, meaning bladder, and *karpos*, fruit, a reference to the attractive, inflated, red pods produced in late summer. The species name, *opulifolius*, refers to the resemblance of its leaves to those of *Viburnum opulus*. The greenish white flowers bloom in June. 'Dart's Gold' is a smaller, compact cultivar with golden foliage. 'Luteus' has greenish-yellow leaves in which the yellow is most pronounced in early spring.

Culture: Drought tolerant, they perform best if grown in full sun on well-drained soils. In shade, the yellow foliage of golden ninebark is much less pronounced. They are subject to chlorosis in soils with a high pH.

Use: Plant in a mixed border, mass, use as foundation plantings, and in informal tree-shrub borders.

Picea glauca var. *densata* (Black Hills spruce)

Picea is from the Latin word for pitch pine, which is derived from *pix*, meaning pitch or resin. The species name means glaucous, referring to the dull greyish blue needles. *Densata* means dense and describes its form. Black Hills spruce, a variety of white spruce, was introduced by the Black Hills Nursery of South Dakota in 1920. It is a denser and more compact form of white spruce with a narrow pyramidal form, and is better adapted to prairie conditions than the species. It makes rapid growth while young, and has short, blue-green needles.

Culture: Plant in full sun on a range of soils. It is resistant to winter desiccation and is drought tolerant.

Brian Porter

Use: Black Hills spruce can be used as a specimen tree or as a grouping, as screen plantings, and in shelterbelts. It provides food and cover for birds.

Ψ *Picea pungens* (Colorado spruce)

Pungens means sharp-pointed, a reference to the extremely sharp needles. A large (to 18 m/60 ft) and somewhat formal evergreen, spruces can live over 100 years. They have a pyramidal form and needles that vary from green to blue-grey. Native to the Rocky Mountains, those sold as "blue spruce" are usually budded or grafted selections and therefore somewhat more expensive than those propagated from seed. The root system is shallow, spreading, and close to the soil surface, making it difficult to grow other plants or a lawn under a spruce.

Spruce needles are four-sided (square in cross-section) and feel "bumpy" when rolled between your fingers. They are singly and spirally arranged on the branches. Newer growth always appears brighter and more deeply colored because of the waxy coating, or bloom, on the needle surface. This is eventually worn away by the action of wind, rain, and grit.

Branches are arranged in whorls with a single whorl produced each year. New growth ceases by early summer.

Male cones are small, yellow, and located on the lower branches. Once they have shed their pollen in spring, they disintegrate. The female cones are much larger and on the ends of branches in the upper part of the tree. They mature, disperse seeds, and fall within a year.

Among the recommended selections are: • 'Glauca Globosa,' a dwarf spruce of 1 m (3 ft) with a round, spreading form) • *Picea pungens* var. *pumila,* which is very similar • 'Hoopsi,' smaller, with a dense, narrow pyramidal form and silver-blue foliage • 'Koster,' which has pendulous branches with bright blue needles • 'Moerheim,' which has a narrow pyramidal form and compact, blue needles, with an almost tiered effect • 'Morden Blue,' which is the same color as 'Koster' but is more dense and pyramidal in form.

Culture: Fully hardy and adaptable to a wide range of soils, the Colorado spruce is drought tolerant but seems to perform better on heavier soils. They require full sun. In sheltered locations they are sometimes infested with spider mites. Cooley spruce gall aphid and spruce budworm are occasionally a problem.

Prune spruce as little as possible, allowing the lower branches to extend to the ground. To control weeds, mulch with grass clippings, chopped straw, or leaves, and allow needles and cones to fall. Tilling damages roots as well as lower branches.

Dwarf Colorado spruce (*Picea pungens* var. *pumila)*

Colorado spruce

Use: Consider the mature height and width of spruce before planting it. It is among the larger trees planted on the prairies and is better suited to an expansive landscape. Spruce are used as screening, specimen trees, and in shelterbelts. They provide food (seeds) and excellent winter cover for birds.

Pinus spp. (pine)

Pines grow naturally on light, sandy soils and are well suited to the prairie xeriscape. Their needles, in bundles of two, three, or five, are roughly triangular in cross-section and arranged spirally on the whorled branches. Male and female cones are on the same tree. The male cones are found on young shoots at the base of the tree and disintegrate after releasing pollen. When transplanting pines, ensure that the root ball is left intact. Exposing the fine, fibrous roots to air and sun more often than not dooms the transplant to failure.

Pines provide cover and food for birds.

Louis Lenz

Ψ *Pinus banksiana* (jack pine)

The species name honors Sir Joseph Banks, a British horticulturist. Native to our northern forests, the jack pine is the most widely distributed pine in Canada. To the early European settlers and modern farmers alike, jack pines signaled poor soil and unproductive farmland. When grown in the open, they are typically gnarled and twisted, with a broad, open form like a Group of Seven painting. In the forest, they are taller and straighter due to competition with other trees for light. They reach up to 12 m (40 ft) and can live 150 years.

Needles are sharp-pointed, dark green to yellowish-green, and in bundles of two, but splayed apart within the bundle. The cones have no prickles. Most remain closed and will persist on the tree for 10 to 20 years until triggered to open by the heat of fire. The root system is wide spreading and fairly deep, usually with a tap root.

Culture: They tolerate poor, sandy, or gravelly soils as long as drainage is adequate and they receive full sun.

Use: Jack pines are useful in naturalization on poor soils. They make an interesting specimen tree where a twisted, gnarled appearance is wanted, but other pines are usually favored for landscape use.

Pinus cembra (Swiss stone pine)

The species name, *cembra*, is from the Italian name for this tree. Native to the European Alps and into Asia, it has a narrow, upright, columnar to pyramidal form, reaching a height of 12 m (40 ft). Needles are in bundles of five and very soft, long, and resistant to sunscald injury in early spring. The bark is smooth and light grey. Relatively slow growing, Swiss stone pine is extremely hardy, very attractive, trouble-free, and sadly underused.

Culture: Plant in full sun and well-drained soil.

Use: Excellent in a tree-shrub border or as a specimen tree.

Ψ *Pinus contorta* var. *latifolia* (lodgepole pine)

The species name, *contorta*, means twisted and may be a reference to the gnarled branches or the twisted needles. It is native to the Rockies and Cypress Hills, and the common name refers to the use of the long, straight trunk in teepees and lodges by Indigenous peoples, who also used the resin for waterproofing canoes, baskets, and moccasins.

Exceeding 20 m (65 ft) in height, it has a life span of up to 200 years. The needles are dark green to yellow-green, in parallel bundles of two, twisted, and sharp-pointed. The scales of the cones have sharp, fragile bristles, or points. The cones persist on the tree for 10 to 20 years. The root system consists of a tap root and spreading lateral roots.

Culture: Plant in full sun on a wide range of soils.

Use: Useful for screening, as a specimen tree, and in shelterbelts.

Ψ *Pinus flexilis* (limber pine)

Both the botanical and common names indicate the flexible nature of the young branches. Native to British Columbia, Alberta, and North Dakota, it reaches only 9 m (30 ft) and is often multi-trunked. Although moderately slow growing, it can live for several hundred years. The bark is light grey and very smooth. The needles are blue-green and in bundles of five. The cones mature in winter, when they open to release seeds.

Culture: Adapted to dry, rocky, exposed sites, limber pines will grow in full sunlight on a variety of soils as long as drainage is adequate.

Use: They are excellent as specimen trees, especially in smaller yards where a larger conifer would be overwhelming.

Sara Williams

Sara Williams

ψ *Pinus mugo* (mugo pine)

The species name, *mugo,* is from an old name used in the Tyrol Mountains of Austria, one of the areas to which it is native. Mugo pines are quite variable in height, ranging from less than 1 m (3 ft) to 6 m (20 ft) or more. Their form is also variable, from low and spreading to almost upright. Needles are in bundles of two, and the foliage is bright green. *Pinus mugo* var. *pumilio* is a dwarf form. 'Compacta' is a dense, rounded cultivar of 1 m (3 ft). 'Teeny' is similar.

Culture: Although they do well on a wide range of soils, they will need regular watering until they are established (about five years) and their root system is well developed. After that, they are quite drought tolerant.

Use: Depending on the form, mugo pines can be placed in a mixed border, used in a rock garden, as foundation plantings or mass planted.

Sara Williams

ψ *Pinus ponderosa* (ponderosa pine, bull pine, western yellow pine)

The species name, *ponderosa,* means heavy and refers to the wood. Ponderosa pine is native to British Columbia and southward. It reaches 15 m (50 ft) or taller, with a straight trunk with orange-brown bark and a narrow crown, and will live several hundred years. It has a wide-spreading root system with a deep and massive tap root. The long needles (15 to 20 cm/6–8 in.) are usually in bundles of three, dark green to yellow green, and sharp pointed. Each scale on the pendulous cones ends in a rigid, sharp prickle. They mature in fall and open to release seeds over the winter.

 Pinus ponderosa var. *scopulorum* is a smaller, more compact version of the ponderosa pine. It is native to the Black Hills of South Dakota and is hardy in most of the prairie region. It has shorter needles, a more columnar form, and dark grey bark, and is more appropriate to smaller landscapes.

Culture: Grow in full sun on a wide range of soils.

Use: Ponderosa pines make excellent specimen trees.

Ψ *Pinus sylvestris* (Scots pine)

Scots pine is native from Scotland through Europe and into Russia and Siberia. The species name, *sylvestris*, meaning woods, makes reference to these vast tracks of forest. It is a medium-large (up to 14 m/45 ft), fast-growing conifer, characterized by an attractive, papery, peeling, orange bark. It is dense when young, but the whorled branches become more open and the form more flat-topped with age. In unsheltered locations, the trees sometimes bend with the prevailing winds.

The slightly twisted needles are held in bundles of two, and are usually retained for three to five years. The male cones are yellow and disintegrate after shedding pollen. The female cones mature in their second autumn and release seeds through late winter and early spring. During the first warm days of spring, the cones pop open audibly as the seeds are released. The root systems are moderately deep and wide spreading, particularly on sandy soils.

Culture: Scots pine is adapted to full sun and a wide range of soils, but seems particularly well suited to sandy soils. Trees grown from seed from its northern range are perfectly hardy; those from seed collected from southern Europe and most cultivars are not. Two occasional problems are sapsuckers (a woodpecker that damages the bark with a series of geometrically aligned holes) and borers (insects that bore into the wood, sometimes causing the top of the tree to break off).

Use: Scots pine is useful as a specimen tree in urban or rural settings. Because of its deep tap root, it does not compete with lawns or flower beds as would a spruce. Its open, less geometrical form, lends itself to the more informal landscape. It is used as screening and in shelterbelts.

Ψ *Potentilla fruticosa* (cinquefoil)

Potentilla is from the word *potens,* meaning power, a reference to the ancient medicinal uses of some species. *Illa* means small. Thus we have a small plant of great power—certainly a tough one with a long period of bloom.

Native to the prairies, the species has deep yellow, buttercup-like flowers up to 2.5 cm (1 in.) in diameter, which are borne in small clusters at the ends of branches throughout the summer. The grey-green, compound leaves each have five leaflets (thus the common name, cinquefoil, meaning five leaves). It forms a bushy shrub of 30 to 120 cm (1–4 ft) and grows well on sandy soils.

The hybrids are a group of small (up to 1 m/3 ft) flowering shrubs with white or yellow flowers, although newer cultivars

'Katherine Dykes'

are being selected with pink- and peach-colored flowers. They produce a flush of blooms in June, with less profuse flowering throughout the summer. The bark is loose and shredding.

Among the more dependable cultivars are: • 'Abbotswood,' with large, pure white flowers and a dwarf, spreading habit (60 cm/2 ft high, 90 cm/3 ft wide). It begins blooming earlier than most and continues until late summer. • 'Coronation Triumph,' an upright plant of 1 m (3 ft) with a loose, informal appearance. It is one of the longest-blooming potentillas, with bright green leaves and large yellow flowers. • 'Elizabeth' (syn. 'Sutter's Gold'), a dwarf, bushy shrub to 1 m (3 ft) which blooms in late summer with large (2.5 cm/1 in.), clear yellow flowers. • 'Goldfinger,' with a profusion of large, bright yellow flowers on compact, 0.5 to 1 m (2–3 ft) plants. • 'Katherine Dykes,' slightly smaller (up to 0.5 m/2 ft), with an arching growth habit, pale yellow flowers, and grey-green leaves. • 'Snowbird,' a semi-double white. • 'Yellowbird,' a semi-double, bright golden yellow.

Culture: Under extremely hot, dry conditions spider mites may be problematic. Plant in full sun on well-drained soil. Plants are weaker and less floriferous in shade.

Use: Because of their size and long blooming period, potentillas are useful as foundation plantings, in shrub borders, perennial borders, or a mixed border. They are well suited to informal groupings and massing as ground covers.

Ψ *Prinsepia sinensis* (cherry prinsepia)

An upright and spreading shrub of 1 to 2 m (4–6 ft), cherry prinsepia is characterized by a loose form, arching branches, and stout thorns. The genus was named after James Prinsep (1799–1840). *Sinensis* means of China—it is native to Manchuria. It leafs out very early. The leaves are light green, long, narrow, and lance-shaped. The flowers are small, yellow, and inconspicuous, but are followed by attractive, somewhat flattened, cherry-like, red fruit which is retained over winter.

Culture: Prinsepia is fully hardy and will grow in a variety of soils in full sun or shade. It is drought tolerant and untroubled by disease or insects.

Use: Because of its thorny nature, it is excellent for "traffic control" or as a barrier planting. Leave it in its natural form as part of an informal shrub border. The fruit is sometimes used for jelly, but if left on the plant through winter, it is consumed by birds.

Prunus x *cistena* (cistena cherry, purple-leaved sandcherry)

Professor N. E. Hanson selected this low, multi-stemmed cross of *P. pumila* and *P. cerasifera* 'Atropurpurea' in 1909 at the State Experimental Station in Brookings, South Dakota. It is usually killed back to the snow line but will regrow about a meter (3 ft) each summer. It is used primarily for its attractive, red-purple foliage. Under prairie conditions it may not flower or fruit reliably above the snow line. The pink flowers are small and relatively inconspicuous.

Culture: Plant in full sun in well-drained soil. Plants grown from cuttings on their own roots are preferred to grafted plants.

Use: With its purple leaves, the cistena cherry is an excellent addition to a shrub or mixed border. Its size makes it suitable for a smaller yard, or it can be massed in a more expansive landscape.

Sara Williams

Ψ *Prunus fruticosa* (Mongolian cherry)

Prunus indicates it is of the plum or cherry genus, *fruticosa* its shrubby nature. Native from Europe to Siberia and into Mongolia, Mongolian cherry has been in cultivation for over 300 years. It has an upright, spreading form, up to 1.5 m (5 ft) in height, with dark green, glossy leaves, small, white flowers, and small, bright red, edible, sour cherries.

Culture: Plant in full sun on well-drained soil.

Use: Use as a wildlife planting, massed, or as an underplanting where high ornamental value is not a consideration. Its strong suckering habit precludes its use on smaller properties.

Brian Baldwin

Prunus padus var. *commutata* (mayday tree)

Padus is the Greek name for wild cherry; *commutata* means changed and is used for a species that resembles one already known (in this case *Prunus padus*, the European bird cherry). The mayday tree leafs out early in spring and is usually in full bloom in mid-May, hence the common name. Native to northern Europe and Asia, it is a fast-growing, vigorous tree of up to 9 m (30 ft). It is usually grown as a single trunked, oval-headed tree but is sometimes seen in clump form. The true mayday is said to be non-suckering, but it readily hybridizes with chokecherries (to which it is related), and the

Department of Horticulture Science, University of Saskatchewan

Brian Baldwin

progeny have varied characteristics. The fragrant, white flowers and drooping clusters of edible black fruit are similar. 'Dropmore' has larger flowers.

Culture: Maydays grow on a variety of soils and prefer full sun. They are susceptible to the fungal disease black knot. If the roots are injured through cultivation, they usually sucker.

Use: Use as an ornamental shade tree and in shelterbelts and wildlife plantings. It provides cover and food for birds.

Sara Williams

Sara Williams

'Jumping Pound'

Ψ *Prunus pensylvanica* (pincherry)

The pincherry is native to much of North America, including the Canadian prairies. The species name, *pensylvanica*, refers to Pennsylvania (or William Penn's woods). The common name is a reference to the size of the fruit. Pincherries grow to about 4.5 m (15 ft) and are considered a large shrub or small, round-headed tree. The smooth bark is red brown. The lance-shaped leaves are bright green in summer and turn a bright yellow-orange in fall. Small, white flowers in round clusters are produced in great abundance in May and are followed by clusters of small red cherries, which are excellent in jelly.

Some of the better cultivars are: • 'Jumping Pound,' which reaches 3.5 m (12 ft) and has a lovely weeping form • 'Mary Liss,' which has larger fruit than the species • 'Stockton,' which is double flowering, making it an attractive ornamental.

Culture: Pincherries do well in full sun on well-drained soils. Most sucker freely, but they will sucker much less if mulched. Root disturbance from cultivation encourages suckering.

Use: The improved cultivars are excellent in an informal shrub border and as specimen trees, either singly or in groupings. The species are used in shelterbelts, for naturalization, reclamation, and wildlife plantings. Birds eat the cherries. Branches may be cut and brought indoors in February for winter forcing of blooms.

Ψ *Prunus tenella* (Russian almond)

Tenella means dainty, and this is an apt description of Russian almond in flower. The "almond" of the common name refers to the inedible, flat fruit, which is covered with soft, silky hairs. Native from Europe to Siberia, it is a small shrub up to 1 m (3 ft) in height, with a strong suckering habit. The single flowers are pink and open before the leaves in early May.

Brian Porter

Prunus x *nigrella* 'Muckle' (Muckle plum), a hybrid of the Canada plum *(Prunus nigra)* and *Prunus tenella,* is 3 m (10 ft) in height, with an upright, oval form. The bright red buds produce bright pink, single flowers in spring before the leaves emerge.

Culture: This tough shrub grows on a wide variety of soils in full sun or partial shade, though it is less floriferous in shade.

Use: Although useful in shrub borders, as a ground cover, or as an underplanting below trees, its tendency to sucker precludes its use in a formal or well manicured landscape.

Prunus tomentosa (Nanking cherry)

An upright shrub of 1 to 2 m (4–6 ft), Nanking cherry is native to China and Japan. It produces white to pink flowers in early May prior to the appearance of its dull, wrinkled leaves. The word *tomentosa* describes the velvety hairs that cover both sides of the leaves. The fruit is bright red and 1.5 cm (over a half inch) in diameter. It is not an exceptionally long-lived plant.

Culture: Nanking cherries will grow in various soils in full sun and are drought tolerant once established. Shelter from the wind is beneficial. Two or more plants in close proximity enhance fruit set.

Use: Nanking cherries have ornamental value when in flower and fruit. They are used as specimen shrubs, in mixed borders, and in wildlife plantings. They provide food and cover for birds—and what the birds leave behind makes excellent jam and jelly.

Prunus triloba 'Multiplex' (double flowering plum)

Triloba means three lobed and describes the leaves. 'Multiplex' means much folded, a reference to the double flowers. Native to China and North Korea, it was introduced to Europe in 1855. It is an upright, spreading shrub of 2 to 3 m (6.5–10 ft), with a profusion of double, pink flowers in early spring. It does not fruit. *Prunus triloba* 'Dropmore,' introduced by Skinner's Nursery in 1964, is a very reliable, early-blooming form of 2 m (6.5 ft).

Culture: Place in full sun or light shade on well drained soil. Plants from cuttings grown on their own roots are preferred.

Use: Use in a mixed or shrub border, as an accent plant, or an informal hedge.

Brian Baldwin

Above: 'Schubert' chokecherry; *left:* fruit of 'Schubert' chokecherry; *below:* chokecherry in flower

Brian Baldwin

Sara Williams

ψ *Prunus virginiana* var. *melanocarpa* (chokecherry)

The chokecherry is a large, upright shrub or small tree native to much of temperate North America. Usually found in shrub form, it will reach up to 4.5 m (15 ft) in height and is quite broad due to its tendency to sucker. The fragrant, white flowers are produced in long racemes in May and are followed by clusters of small, black, edible cherries in July and August.

Various cultivars are available: • 'Boughen's Chokeless' has almost non-astringent fruit. • 'Boughen's Yellow' has large, yellow, sweet fruit, as does 'Spearfish.' • 'Copper Schubert' has coppery green leaves that color more quickly than 'Schubert,' and less astringent, red fruit. • 'Garrington' is a compact and pendulous but very productive cultivar. • 'Schubert' is noted for its purple-red foliage. The leaves emerge green in the spring, changing to purple by midsummer. The fruit is blue-black. 'Mini-Schubert' is much smaller and more compact but otherwise similar.

Culture: Hardy and drought-tolerant, chokecherries are adapted to a wide variety of soils and do well in full sun or partial shade. They are susceptible to black knot, a fungal disease that can be partially controlled through pruning.

Use: If pruned to a single trunk, chokecherries make an attractive small tree. On a small property, their tendency to sucker requires control. As a large shrub they are useful in an informal shrub border, for wildlife plantings, and shelterbelts. The fruit makes an excellent jam or syrup. They provide food and cover for birds.

Sara Williams

ψ *Pyrus ussuriensis* (Ussurian pear, Manchurian pear)

Pyrus is the Latin name for pear. The species name refers to the Ussurian Mountains of Manchuria, to which it is native. Trees grown from seed collected by the famous plant explorer E. H. Wilson were introduced to Canada through Skinner's Nursery in 1927. The small (5.5 m/18 ft), low-headed trees have an oval form. Stems are covered with stout thorns (this is not a climbing tree!). The white flowers, produced in early spring, are very fragrant, but the tree does not begin blooming until it is about 10 years of age. The fruit is small and gritty.

Culture: It will grow in a range of soils in full sun.

Use: The Ussurian pear is used in tree-shrub borders or as a specimen tree.

ᴪ *Quercus macrocarpa* (bur oak)

Native to Manitoba and southeast Saskatchewan all the way to the Maritimes, bur oak is a large, attractive, long-lived (about 200 years) tree of 14 m (45 ft) or more. The Latin name for oak is *Quercus*. *Macrocarpa* means large fruit and refers to the size of the acorns. Bur means a clinging seed case, another reference to the fringed or "mossy cup" acorn.

Bur oak has a straight trunk, a high head, and often, branchlets with thick corky ridges. Although it has a long-standing reputation for slow growth, very young trees on sandy soil have put on 30 cm (12 in.) of growth in a single season without supplemental water. Its leaves are typically oak-like, with seven to nine deep lobes, shiny green above and whitish below, with yellow to red fall coloration. It has a deep, wide-spreading root system with a deep taproot.

Culture: Adapted to most of the prairies, the bur oak is drought tolerant once established. The taproot makes it difficult to transplant once it is over 0.5 m (a few feet) high. This is probably the reason why it has not been readily available commercially until recently.

Use: This underused tree is excellent as a shade or specimen tree in a medium or large lot. Because it has a taproot rather than a spreading, shallow root system, it does not compete with nearby lawns or flower beds.

Rhus glabra (smooth sumac)

The genus name is from the Greek *rhous*, which describes the red fruit. *Glabra* means smooth, describing the twigs, leaves, and buds. This leggy, dioecious shrub of 3 to 3.5 m (9–12 ft) suckers freely and soon forms a thicket. Its large, pinnately compound leaves are dark green above and dull green below. The small, red-brown fruit is formed in dense, cone-shaped clusters and is often retained through winter. 'Midi' is about 2 m (6 ft) in height. 'Mini' is 1 m (3 ft).

Rhus trilobata (lemonade sumac, skunkbush) is a low, spreading native shrub of 1 m (3 ft). The leaves are aromatic when crushed and turn purple in the fall. Flowers are small, yellow, unpleasantly scented, and appear before the leaves. The red or orange fruit clusters that follow are sticky and hairy. Both common names refer to the scent of the foliage. The species name, *trilobata*, means three-lobed and describes the leaves.

Culture: Plant on well-drained soils in full sun. They seem to tolerate pollution and poor soils.

Use: These shrubs need space and are not suited to small yards or formal planting. They are adapted to massing, naturalization, reclamation, soil stabilization, and wildlife plantings.

Brian Baldwin

Above: fall color
Left: mass planting of alpine currant in winter

Sara Williams

Ribes alpinum (alpine currant)

Alpine currant is native to Europe from Wales to Russia. The genus name, *Ribes*, is from the Persian or Arabic word for acid-tasting, a reference to the fruit. The species name, *alpinum*, means of the mountains, its native habitat. A ball-shaped shrub of 1 to 2 m (3–6 ft), it has a tidy appearance due to its fine branches, density, and fullness to its base. The small, bright green leaves appear very early in spring.

The inconspicuous yellow flowers are sometimes followed by red berries. It is dioecious, so plants of both sexes must be grown to ensure fruit. Because they are often propagated from cuttings taken from a single plant (and are therefore of the same sex), fruit is seldom produced.

Culture: Alpine currants will grow in a variety of soils in either sun or shade. They appear more compact and dense in full sun and are more floriferous. Spider mites are sometimes a problem, as is powdery mildew.

Use: Reputed to be fairly tolerant of urban air pollution, alpine currants are used as an unclipped hedge, an informal grouping, in a mixed border, as foundation plantings, or massed as a ground cover or an understorey beneath trees. If berries are present, they provide food for birds.

Ψ *Ribes aureum* (golden currant)

The species name, *aureum*, means golden and is a reference to the golden yellow flowers. This native plant is found in the Cypress Hills and elsewhere on the prairies. It reaches 1 to 2 m (4–6 ft), with loose, open, arching branches, often becoming somewhat leggy with age. Like other currants, it lacks prickles. The fragrant, tubular, yellow flowers in late May and June are followed by edible black currants. The tiny, light green leaves are three-lobed, wedge-shaped at their base, and turn an attractive orange-scarlet in the fall. It spreads through suckering.

Culture: Golden currant is adapted to a variety of soils in sun or partial shade. Currant worms often infest the fruit, causing premature drop. Powdery mildew is sometimes a problem.

Use: Plant it where you can take advantage of its fragrance. Its form precludes its use in formal plantings, and its tendency to sucker makes it more useful on larger lots, acreages, and farmyards. It is also used as a wildlife planting, providing food and cover for birds. It is a butterfly nectar plant. The fruit is edible and used for jams and jellies.

Sara Williams

Above: fall color
Left: fruit

Sara Williams

ᴪ *Ribes oxycanthoides* (wild gooseberry)

The species name comes from the Greek: *oxys* means sharp, and *akanthos* thorn. Native to the prairies, the wild goose-berry is a low, spreading shrub of almost 1 m (3 ft), with light green leaves and sharp, slender prickles. The flowers are an inconspicuous yellow-green. The edible fruit is red-purple when ripe. The foliage is bright orange in fall. 'Dwarf Dakota' is a compact cultivar with a spreading form and exceptionally glossy foliage which turns red-bronze in fall.

Culture: Plant in full sun or partial shade on well-drained soil.

Use: Wild gooseberry is used for massing, wildlife plantings, and underplantings.

Hugh Knowles

Rosa spp. (rose)

Many of the shrub roses long grown on the prairies are drought tolerant. Most are large and prickly, and some sucker. Among the native roses are: • *Rosa acicularis* (prickly rose), which is up to 2.5 m (8 ft) high. The species name, *acicularis*, means sharp-pointed and refers to the abundant prickles on younger stems. The rosy pink, highly fragrant flowers occur singly in June and July and are followed by red, long-necked, pear-shaped hips which persist over winter. • ᴪ *Rosa arkansana* (prairie rose) was used in much of the hybridizing work that produced the Parkland series of roses. Flat, pink flowers bloom from June to August. Short (up to 0.5 m/2 ft) and bushy, it usually dies back to ground level each winter. • *Rosa woodsii* (common wild rose or woods rose) is up to 1.5 m (5 ft) in height, with pink flowers produced in small clusters followed by round, red hips. Both the common and species name refer to its habitat, the woods.

Among the more drought-tolerant non-native species and hybrid selections are: • ᴪ Altai rose *(Rosa spinosissima* var. *altaica),* from Asia, an upright, somewhat leggy plant of 1.5 to 2 m (5–6 ft), with large, slightly fragrant, single, white flowers in early June, followed by very large, purple-black hips. It suckers freely and is good for screening or an informal shrub border. • 'Hansa' is a rugosa hybrid with large, highly fragrant, red-purple, double flowers with repeat bloom. The plant is large (2 m/6 ft) and round, with the characteristic handsome, wrinkled, dark green leaves of the rugosa ("rug-osa" means wrinkled). • ᴪ 'Hazeldean' is a double yellow rose that blooms in June and is resistant to blackspot. It is about 1.5 m (5 ft) in height and suckers freely. • 'Marie Bugnet' is 0.5 to 1 m (2–3 ft), with fragrant, white flowers. • 'Morden Centennial,' one of the Parkland series of roses, is 1.5 m (5 ft) in height, with fully double, large, pink flowers

Brian Baldwin

Sara Williams

Top: 'Morden Centennial' *Middle:* fall color of prickly rose *Left:* woods rose

Sara Williams

Above:
red-leafed rose
Left:
'Therese Bugnet'

Sara Williams

Sara Williams

Brian Baldwin

Brian Baldwin

borne singly and in clusters. It blooms on both old and new wood throughout the summer, but will stop blooming after the first flush if hips are allowed to form. • 'Prairie Youth,' a Morden introduction, is a little over 2 m (7 ft), with arching branches and clusters of salmon pink flowers. • Ψ *Rosa rubrifolia* (red-leafed rose) is an upright, 2 m (6 ft) shrub rose with arching branches and reddish purple stems and leaves. The flowers are single and pink and the red hips are retained through the winter. • 'Therese Bugnet' is a tall rose with large, deep pink, very fragrant, double flowers. Another rugosa hybrid, it has recurrent bloom and does not sucker.

Culture: These roses grow best in full sun in a rich, organic soil. They will perform better with mulching, protection from wind, and with even moisture during establishment.

Use: Shrub roses are used as ornamentals, for naturalization, reclamation, in shelterbelts, and in wildlife plantings, where they provide food and excellent nesting cover for birds and serve as butterfly nectar plants. The larger shrub roses and those that sucker are suitable for a natural hedge or an informal shrub border. Shorter, non-suckering types can be planted in smaller urban yards where any other rose would be used, where they work well in a mixed border. Their hips provide fall and winter landscape value and are used in jelly.

Ψ *Sambucus racemosa* (European red elder)

Native from Europe to western Asia, elders are tall, loose shrubs with arching branches, 2 to 3 m (7 to 10 ft). Creamy flowers in flat terminal clusters are followed by dense clusters of small, scarlet berries. They have finely divided, pinnately compound leaves, each with three to seven coarse-toothed, dark green leaflets. Fast-growing, red elders are capable of putting on 0.5 to 1 m (2–3 ft) of growth per year. Occasionally, they may suffer the same degree of dieback, which usually shows up the following spring. Golden-leafed cultivars and dwarf forms are also available. Larger types may be pruned to a single trunk to form a small tree.

Culture: Elders will grow in a range of soils in full sun or partial shade, but will bloom less in shade. All golden-leaved types require full sun to develop golden coloration. When dieback occurs there may be considerable maintenance in pruning the pithy stems in spring, but vigorous new growth usually occurs. Elders may be cut to near ground level every five or six years in spring to control size and encourage vigorous young growth.

Use: As shrubs, they are best used in informal plantings or for naturalizing, screening, and wildlife plantings. As a small tree, elders are well placed in a smaller urban setting. They provide food and cover for birds and are a butterfly nectar plant.

Ψ *Shepherdia argentea* (silver buffaloberry)

The genus was named to honor John Shepherd (1764–1836), curator of the Liverpool Botanic Garden. The species name, *argentea*, refers to the silvery leaves and stems. The fruit was used by Native peoples to flavor buffalo meat, hence the common name. Buffaloberry is a large native shrub of 3.5 m (12 ft) that often forms dense thickets. Branchlets grow almost perpendicular to the branches and terminate as stout thorns. The leaves are strap-shaped. The creamy white, inconspicuous flowers bloom in May, and are followed by clusters of red—or sometimes orange or yellow—berries in midsummer. Because it is dioecious, plants of both sexes must be in close proximity to ensure fruit.

Only 1 m (3 ft) in height and round and upright in form, *Shepherdia canadensis* (russet buffaloberry) is also native to the prairies. It has grey-green leaves with a brown underside. The yellow flowers are followed by red to orange fruit.

Culture: Buffaloberry will grow on any well-drained soil in full sun and is saline tolerant. Russet buffaloberry may be grown in partial shade.

Use: Because of its size and tendency to sucker, silver buffaloberry is best used as an informal planting on a larger lot, for screening or as a barrier planing. It is used extensively for wildlife and shelterbelt plantings, where it provides food and cover for birds. It may be pruned to a single stem and used as a small specimen tree in a smaller yard. Russet buffaloberry may be used for informal plantings, an understorey, and naturalization.

Above and left: silver buffaloberry *Below:* russet buffaloberry

Sara Williams

Sara Williams

Bill Remphrey

Ψ *Sorbaria sorbifolia* (Ural false spirea)

The genus name, *Sorbaria,* refers to its resemblance to *Sorbus* (mountain ash), as does the species name, *sorbifolia,* which means with leaves like *Sorbus.* Native to Asia, the false spirea is a fully hardy shrub with a very fine texture. The arching stems carry pinnately compound leaves, each with 13 to 23 leaflets. Large, soft panicles of creamy white flowers which somewhat resemble spirea are produced in late July and are highly attractive to bees. It is 1 to 2 m (4–6 ft) high, upright and spreading, tends to sucker, and can soon form a thicket.

Culture: False spirea will tolerate neglect, a wide range of

Brian Baldwin

Brian Baldwin

soils, drought, and full sun or full shade. It is susceptible to spider mites.

Use: Because of its tendency to sucker, it is little used in formal plantings or smaller urban lots. It is better placed in a more wild or naturalized setting, or to stabilize a slope or bank.

Brian Baldwin

Brian Baldwin

Right: fall color

Brian Baldwin

Spiraea trilobata (three-lobed spirea)

The genus name is derived from the Greek word *speiraira*, meaning a plant used for garlands, which in turn comes from *speira*, meaning spiral or twisted. *Trilobata* means three-lobed, alluding to the leaves. Native to Asia and up to 1 m (4 ft) in height, three-lobed spirea has arching branches covered with a profusion of single, white flowers in late May. One of the best white spireas, with a neat appearance and foliage retained to its base, it should be planted more often.

Culture: Plant in full sun on a range of well-drained soils.

Use: Spireas may be used as foundation plantings, in a mixed border, or a shrub border.

ψ *Symphoricarpos occidentalis* (western snowberry, buckbrush, wolfberry)

The genus name, *Symphoricarpos,* means fruit borne together and refers to the dense clusters of waxy, greenish-white berries. The fruit, believed by some to be poisonous, is retained through winter but changes color to a purplish light brown. The species name, *occidentalis,* means of the west and is similar to the common name.

A member of the honeysuckle family, snowberry is a native shrub, 0.5 to 1 m (1–4 ft) in height, which forms dense clumps or thickets and suckers readily. The inconspicuous, pink-and-white flowers are borne in late June and early July. The small, oval leaves are grey-green and opposite. Stems are hollow. *Symphoricarpos alba* is similar but has larger, bright white berries and will perform better in shade.

Culture: Grow in full sun to partial shade on well-drained soil.

Use: Snowberry can be massed as a ground cover, used as an understorey below trees, and for naturalization. It provides food and cover for birds and is a hummingbird nectar plant. It suckers too profusely for small or formal landscape use.

Department of Horticulture Science, University of Saskatchewan

Ψ *Syringa* spp. (lilac)

The genus name, *Syringa,* is from the Greek *syrinx*, a pipe, and refers to the hollow stems. One the most frequently planted shrubs on the prairies during the early part of this century, lilacs are vigorous shrubs, usually of 2 to 3.5 m (6–12 ft) in height. They are grown primarily for their large, fragrant panicles of white, pink, lilac, blue, or purple flowers, which may be single or double. Except for the Japanese tree lilac, their landscape value is not outstanding when not in flower.

The following species and their hybrids are recommended. They are listed in order of bloom, beginning with the earliest.

• The common lilac (*Syringa vulgaris*), originally from southeastern Europe, is a large, dense, and vigorous shrub, upright and spreading, with a very strong suckering habit. Its fragrant flowers are freely produced. A tough shrub for difficult situations, it is a parent to the French hybrids developed mostly by the Lemoine Nursery in France. Among these hybrids are: 'Congo' (single, magenta flowers in large, dense panicles), 'Charles Joly' (large, double, magenta panicles, which are heavily scented), 'Edith Cavell' (double, white, and an abundant bloomer), 'General Pershing' (double, deep purple), 'Madame Lemoine' (narrow panicles of double white flowers), 'Mrs. Ellen Willmott' (double, white), 'Ludwig Spaeth' (single, deep red-purple, abundant blooms), 'President Lincoln' (heavy clusters of single, Wedgwood blue panicles).

• Hyacinth-flowered lilacs (*Syringa* x *hyacinthiflora*) are 3 m (10 ft), upright, and spreading. They are hybrids between *S. vulgaris* and *S. oblata* var. *dilitata* developed mostly by Dr. Skinner of Dropmore, Manitoba. Their flowers are large, showy, and fragrant. They vary in the degree to which they sucker, but it is generally less than that of the common lilac. Among these cultivars are: 'Assessippi' (single, purple),

'Sister Justina'

Brian Baldwin

Top and bottom (detail): Japanese tree lilac

'Miss Canada'

'Minnehaha' (single, purple), 'Sister Justina' (pure white, fragrant, double, little or no suckering), 'Swathmore' (double, purple), and 'Pocahontas' (single, reddish-purple).

• Japanese tree lilac *(Syringa reticulata)* is the tallest of the lilacs, up to 8 m (27 ft). It blooms in late June or early July, with large, cream-colored flowers in loose, triangular-shaped panicles. An attractive tree, it may be pruned to a single trunk. It should be planted more often. 'Ivory Silk' is an improved selection.

• Late lilac *(Syringa villosa)* is 3 m (9 ft) in height and has pale pink to rosy lilac flowers, usually small and sparsely produced. The species name, *villosa,* means covered with hairs and refers to the leaves, which are large, coarse, and dull. It is non-suckering. Native to northern China, villosa lilacs form part of shelterbelts throughout the prairies.

• The Meyer lilac (*S. meyeri*) is a compact, dwarf plant of 2 m (6 ft) with small, glossy leaves. Almost ball-shaped, it produces an abundance of attractive, fragrant, small, pink to purple flowers in small clusters in late June. It is nonsuckering. The fine, twiggy growth makes a dense hedge. Introduced from northern China in 1908, it should be more widely used.

• 'Miss Kim' (*Syringa patula* 'Miss Kim') is a compact, 1 to 2.5 m (4–8 ft) shrub, native to Korea and northern China, with dark green foliage to its base. The foliage sometimes turns reddish purple in fall. It produces small but abundant clusters of fragrant, pale lavender flowers. It is ideal for a shrub border, a mixed border, and foundation plantings.

• The Preston lilacs *(Syringa* x *prestoniae),* hybrids of *S. villosa* and *S. reflexa,* were developed for the most part by Isabella Preston at the Central Experimental Farm in Ottawa in the early 1900s. They are fragrant, late blooming, and tend to be non-suckering. Sturdy, dense, and upright, they are 3 m (9 ft) in height, with a coarse texture and the large villosa leaves. Among this group of hybrids are: 'Coral' (compact, with clear, true pink flowers), 'Isabella' (large, dense, pyramidal flower clusters of pink), 'James MacFarlane' (single, clear deep pink in dense flower clusters), 'Jessica' (open flower clusters, deep purple), 'Minuet' (dense, dwarf compact plant with light purple flowers), 'Miss Canada' (dwarf, somewhat slower-growing plant; clear bright rose flowers borne freely in narrow upright spikes), 'Redwine' (compact plant, deep red buds, and deep pink flowers), 'Royalty' (compact plant with coarse foliage, fragrant, single, purple flowers), 'Hiawatha' (dense, deep rose), and 'Donald Wyman' (dense, red-purple, single flowers with attractive, small, dark green leaves, developed by Dr. Skinner of Dropmore, Manitoba).

Culture: Lilacs will grow in a wide range of soils in full sun.

They do not tolerate flooding or poor drainage. Most take two to three years to become established. Until they reach maturity they may not achieve their true color and form. Seeds add winter interest and are eaten by birds, and their removal has no effect on subsequent bloom.

Use: Use larger lilacs for screening, shelterbelts, and in informal shrub borders in larger yards. Japanese tree lilacs make excellent small shade trees. As a formal, sheared hedge, lilacs have little to offer — the very process of shearing substantially reduces their flowering capacity for the next season. Smaller lilacs are useful in a mixed border. Lilacs are nectar sources for bees and butterflies. Stems brought indoors in February may be forced for winter bloom.

Viburnum lantana (wayfaring tree)

The genus name is perhaps from the word *vieo* (to tie), describing the flexibility of the branches. It is believed to be the original *Viburnum* mentioned by Virgil. The herbalist Gerard called it the wayfaring tree because it brought joy to travellers. It was once planted by cow sheds to ward off witchcraft. Native to Europe and western Asia, this is either a large spreading shrub or a small tree, depending on whether it is left with multiple stems or pruned to a single trunk. It will reach 3 to 4.5 m (9–15 ft) in height. The grey-green leaves are rather dull and wrinkled with little fall color. White flowers are followed by fruit that turns from green to red to purple-black.

Culture: Plant in sun or partial shade on a range of soils. It has a neater appearance in full sun.

Use: The wayfaring tree may be used as a small specimen tree or in a mixed tree-shrub border. It is ideal for a smaller lot or as a grouping in a larger landscape.

ψ *Viburnum lentago* (nannyberry)

The species name, *lentago,* means flexible or supple and is from the Latin word *lentas.* This reference is presumably to the stems. Native to Manitoba, nannyberry is a small tree of 6 to 9 m (20–30 ft.), with shiny, oval, fine-toothed leaves that turn a glorious red-purple in fall. The creamy white flowers are produced in round clusters in May and June and are followed by berries that turn from green to yellow to red to blue. Often all colors are present at once in a single cluster. It is extremely attractive, has excellent landscape value, and is sadly underused.

Sara Williams

Culture: Plant in full sun or partial shade on a range of soils as long as they are well drained. Best mulched, since it may sucker if the roots are disturbed or damaged by tilling.

Use: Ideal as a specimen tree in a small landscape or grouped in a larger landscape. It can be multi-trunked or pruned to a single trunk. Use in a mixed border or informal tree-shrub border. The fruit is consumed by birds.

ψ *Achillea millefolium* (common yarrow)

The Greek hero Achilles is said to have used *Achillea* to heal his soldiers' wounds. The species name, *millefolium*, means a thousand leaves, and refers to the fine foliage. Native to Europe and naturalized over much of North America, yarrow has been in cultivation for many centuries. 'Cerise Queen' has aromatic, fern-like, dark green foliage and flat heads of rosy-pink flowers on 45 to 60 cm (18–24 in.) stems in late summer. 'Summer Pastels,' an AAS winner, is the same height and pink, rose, apricot, cream, red, beige, purple, or white. 'Moonshine' has grey-green foliage and lemon yellow flowers.

Culture: Grow in full sun on well-drained soils. They spread readily by rhizomes, and will need control (with a sharp spade!) within a border. Divide every three to four years.

Use: This long-flowering plant can be used massed, as a tall ground cover, in the perennial border, and in fresh and dried arrangements. It is a butterfly nectar plant.

Achillea ptarmica (sneezewort)

The roots and leaves of sneezewort were once used as a cheap replacement for snuff (*ptarmica* is the Greek word for sneezing). Native to Europe and Asia and naturalized in North America, sneezewort is covered with hundreds of tiny, double, pure white flowers in July and August on 45 to 60 cm (18–24 in.) stems. The foliage is fern-like and somewhat pungent. Improved cultivars are 'The Pearl' and 'Perry's White.'

Culture: Plant in full sun on poorer, well-drained soils. In richer soils it is invasive. Divide every three to four years.

Use: Used in both fresh and dried flower arrangements, sneezewort is useful in informal borders and for naturalizing.

'The Pearl'

ψ *Achillea tomentosa* (dwarf woolly yarrow)

Tomentosa means hairy or woolly. The "woolly" in both the botanical and common names refers to the foliage, which is aromatic, finely cut, and a soft woolly grey. The flowers are yellow and produced in flat clusters just above the foliage in June. The leaves form a mat.

Culture: Plant in full sun in well-drained soil on a hot, dry site.

Use: Woolly yarrow is excellent as a ground cover, for interplanting among paving stones toward the edges of a walk or patio, or in a rock garden. It is easily mowed for a neater appearance or rejuvenation in midsummer after flowering.

Hugh Knowles

Hugh Knowles

Aegopodium podagraria var. *variegatum* (goutweed, bishop's goutweed)

The species name is from the Latin *podagricus* and means used in treating gout or arthritis, presumably an occupational hazard of bishops of the time, perhaps for reasons of diet and lack of exercise. It is deep-rooted and persistent, and although it wilts during periods of heat and drought, it recoups immediately with the onset of cooler temperatures and moisture. Native to Europe, it has attractive, compound leaves with variegated white margins. Small, unattractive white flowers are produced in umbels above the dense foliage, which is 30 to 38 cm (12–15 in.) in height. On drier sites it may be shorter.

Culture: Goutweed will grow anywhere, but is best planted in poor soil in full sun or partial shade. It is extremely aggressive and will overpower less vigorous neighbors. Remove any shoots that revert to green. Mow if it appears untidy.

Use: Goutweed is excellent as a ground cover where it can be contained (between a driveway and a sidewalk or under a deck), where nothing else will grow, as an understorey below large trees, or to hold a slope. It will certainly brighten a shady corner. Do not use in a border or rock garden.

Sara Williams

Ψ *Alcea rosea* (hollyhock)

Alcea is the Greek word for mallow, which is in the same family as hollyhock. The word *rosea* means pink. Native to China, hollyhocks are tall (up to 2 m/6 ft), old-fashioned flowers available in a wide range of colors—white, pink, purple, red, and yellow. Single-flowered forms are hardier than double forms. They were introduced to Europe in the 1500s and were erroneously believed to be from the holy land (thus the common name). The annual, biennial, and perennial types are very similar. The perennials are short-lived and perpetuate themselves through reseeding. The singles are hardier than the doubles. *Alcea rugosa* is native to dry hills from Iran into Russia. It has pale yellow flowers on 2.5 m (8 ft) stalks. It has not been widely tested on the prairies but is worthy of trial. *Alcea ficifolia* has fig-like leaves, yellow flowers, and is longer lived than most hollyhocks. Native to Siberia, it too is worthy of trial.

Culture: Grow full sun in deep, well-drained soil. Leaf rust is sometimes a problem, as are spider mite infestations.

Use: Plant in the border, in large masses, as single specimens, and in the cottage garden. They are a nectar source for birds, bees, and butterflies.

Anemone sylvestris (wind flower, snowdrop anemone)

Native to Europe, snowdrop anemones produce single, pure white, nodding flowers in early spring, and may flower again in the fall. The plants are up to 40 cm (15 in.) in height, with attractive foliage.

Culture: Windflowers will grow in sun or shade in a wide range of soils.

Use: They self-seed too readily to be part of a formal border and are best left to naturalize in an area where they can reseed without becoming invasive: under a birch, apple, or plum tree, or in a wild or shade garden.

Sara Williams

Ψ *Antennaria rosea* (pussytoes, antennaria)

Antennaria is from the Greek word for antennae. The male flowers, produced on separate plants, have fine, short hairs with swollen tips similar to antennae. Pussytoes forms a low, woolly, grey-green mat of 5 to 8 cm (2–3 in.), with pink flowers in June. It is native to the prairies, where both pink and white flowered forms are found. *Antennaria aprica* is a white species more commonly found in the wild.

Culture: Plant in well-drained soil in full sun. They spread by stolons and need dividing and replanting every few years.

Use: Often used in dry bouquets, pussytoes are planted in rock gardens and among paving stones along an informal path.

Sara Williams

Ψ *Anthemis tinctoria* (golden marguerite, chamomile)

The species name, *tinctoria,* refers to its use as a dye source. Native to Europe and Asia, golden marguerite produces masses of yellow daisies 2.5 cm (1 in.) in diameter in June and July. 'Moonlight' has pale yellow flowers, 'Mrs. E.C. Buxton' lemon yellow, and 'Kelwayi' golden yellow. The foliage is aromatic, dark green, finely divided, and 60 cm (2 ft) in height. The species *A. sancti-johannis* has orange flowers. Although not widely grown on the prairies, it is worthy of trial.

Culture: Well adapted to poor soil and full sun. Do not fertilize. Cut back after flowering and divide every three to four years.

Use: Ideal as a cut flower and for naturalizing in areas beyond the reach of a garden hose—a dry bank or a back lane. It self-seeds too generously for a formal border, and seedlings may be inferior to cultivars.

Sara Williams

Sara Williams

Sara Williams

ψ *Arabis* spp. (arabis, rockcress)

A member of the mustard family, rockcress is a trailing, mat-forming plant only 15 to 20 cm (6–8 in.) in height, native to southeastern Europe, Turkey, and Iran. In May, it is covered with masses of tiny white or pink flowers, which practically conceal the soft grey-green evergreen foliage. *Arabis caucasica* (syn. *A. albida*), or wall rockcress, is available in both white and pink forms. 'Snowcap' is a single, white-flowered cultivar of 30 cm (12 in.) or less. Variegated forms are useful for their foliage but are less floriferous and usually less vigorous. *A. caucasica* 'Variegata' has green–and–creamy white leaves but is prone to sport reversion (reverting back to green). If this happens, the green parts should be removed. 'Snow Ball' is a dwarf, compact, white cultivar. 'Plena' is fully double, sterile, longer blooming, and produces no seedlings.

Culture: Plant in full sun to partial shade in a well-drained soil. For a tidier look, shear after flowering.

Use: Arabis is ideal for the rock garden, slopes, edging, the front of a perennial border, as a ground cover, or at the edge of paving stones to soften the appearance of a walk. Plant it where you will enjoy the fragrance. It is a butterfly larvae plant.

Sara Williams

Above: 'Silver Queen'
Left: 'Silver King'

B. J. Godwin

ψ *Artemisia ludoviciana* (artemisia, sage)

Artemisias are grown primarily for their aromatic, grey foliage, which has a sage-like smell. The flowers are generally inconspicuous. The genus was named after the Greek goddess of chastity, Artemis. The species name, *ludoviciana*, means of Louisiana, one of the areas to which it is native. 'Silver King' has attractive but undivided grey foliage, 60 to 90 cm (2–3 ft) in height, and a bushy, upright form. 'Silver Queen' is 75 cm (30 in.) in height with slightly wider, pointed leaves with a deeply cut, jagged margin. It is invasive and is best used for naturalizing. 'Valerie Finnis' is a more recent introduction with broad leaves and a compact form.

Culture: Native to western North America, they will tolerate poor, sandy soils, drought, and full sun. They spread by stolons.

Use: Naturalize in areas where other plants simply will not grow. In a border they are too invasive unless physically contained. The foliage is useful in dried arrangements.

Artemisia schmidtiana ('Silver Mound' artemisia)

'Silver Mound' forms a compact, mound-like plant, 30 cm (12 in.) in height, with a spread of 45 cm (18 in.). It seldom stirs from where it was originally planted. The foliage is a soft, finely cut, silver-grey with typical sage-like fragrance.

Culture: It does well in sandy, well-drained soils in full sun, and is quite drought tolerant. When grown in shade or under more fertile conditions it tends to lose its compact form. It may be sheared in midsummer for a neater appearance.

Use: 'Silver Mound' is excellent in the rock garden, used as an edging plant, and toward the front of the perennial border.

ψ *Artemisia stellerana* ('Silver Brocade' artemisia)

Native to northeast Asia, the species is naturalized over parts of North America. It was named for the German naturalist Georg Wilhelm Stellar (1709-1746), who brought it from Siberia. 'Silver Brocade' was introduced by the University of British Columbia Botanic Garden. It is a low, compact selection with deeply lobed leaves that remains prostrate until flowering. It thrives in the heat, and almost gleams at dusk.

Culture: Plant in full sun in well-drained soils. To prevent self-seeding, shear plants after flowering, before seeds set.

Use: It is extremely useful for edging, as a ground cover, naturalizing, holding slopes, and in pots or hanging baskets.

'Silver Brocade'

ψ *Aurinia saxatilis* (basket-of-gold, perennial alyssum)

Originally named *Alyssum saxatile* by Linnaeus in 1752, alyssum is native to Europe and Asia Minor. *Aurinia* is Latin for golden and refers to the flowers. *Saxatilis* means growing among rocks and alludes to its native habitat.

A low, mound-like plant of 25 to 30 cm (10–12 in.), its grey-green leaves are covered with masses of golden yellow flowers for several weeks in May and June. 'Compactum' is a dwarf form of 20 cm (8 in.). 'Citrinum' has lemon yellow flowers and is 30 to 38 cm (12–15 in.) in height. *Alyssum montanum* (mountain alyssum) has sulfur yellow flowers.

Culture: Plant in full sun in well-drained soil. Shear after flowering for a neater appearance. Do not overfertilize.

Use: Alyssum is ideal for the perennial border, rock garden, as a ground cover, or among paving stones or patio bricks.

Louis Lenz

Baptisia australis (false indigo, wild blue indigo)

An extract from the flowers was once used as substitute for the blue dye indigo, hence the common and genus names. *Baptisia* comes from the Greek word meaning to dye. *Australis* means south, and presumably refers to its native habitat in the southeastern United States.

A legume, false indigo has blue, pea-like flowers which bloom in May and June and somewhat resemble lupines. The inflated seed pods that follow are black, curled, and decorative. It is about 1 m (3–4 ft) in height, with an arching, upright form. The blue-green leaves are compound and remain attractive until hard frost. It is long-lived, with thick, strong roots.

Culture: Plant in full sun on well-drained soil. It does not tolerate root disturbance once established.

Use: Use in the perennial or mixed border, as a specimen plant, and in a wild garden. Both the flowers and seed pods are used in arrangements. It is a butterfly nectar plant.

Sara Williams

ᴪ *Bergenia cordifolia* (bergenia, giant rockfoil)

Named after Karl August von Bergen (1704-1768), a Frankfort botany professor, bergenia was introduced into Europe from Siberia in the 17th century. *Cordifolia* means heart-shaped and describes the leaves. The 30 cm (12 in.) spikes of pink to purple flowers are produced in May. The large, handsome, leathery, evergreen leaves (which turn a reddish bronze in autumn) resemble cabbage leaves. Depending on growing conditions, the flowers are produced either above or within the foliage. The root is thick and deep. Cultivars with white to rose-red flowers are available. Redder cultivars may be less hardy. *Bergenia crassifolia,* native from Siberia to northwest China, is similar to *B. cordifolia* but with slightly smaller, spoon-shaped leaves and flowers that are held higher above the foliage. The word *crassifolia* means thick-leaved.

Culture: Extremely adaptable, bergenia is equally at home in full sun or shade, and dry or moist soil.

Use: It is used in the perennial border, rock garden, as an edging plant, an underplanting below trees, a ground cover, a waterside planting, and in arrangements.

ψ *Bromus inermis* 'Skinner's Golden'
('Skinner's Golden' bromegrass)

The species was introduced from Europe. It is widely planted as a forage crop, and has escaped from cultivation in much of North America. 'Skinner's Golden' was selected near Dropmore, Manitoba, and is bright yellow with green variegation. It is 60 cm (24 in.) in height, with a graceful, arching form.

Culture: For the best color, grow in full sun in ordinary soil. Remove any sections that revert to green. It is a cool-season grass that performs best in early summer and fall. Mow if it becomes ragged during the heat of midsummer,.

Use: Mass plant as a transition area between the manicured area of a rural yard and surrounding bush, or use it to hold a bank or slope, or as a ground cover. If placed in the border, it must be contained, as it spreads rapidly by rhizomes.

Campanula carpatica (Carpathian bellflower)

Campanula is Latin for small bell and describes the bell-like flowers. The species name, *carpatica*, indicates its origin, the Carpathian Mountains. The blue, upfacing flowers, 2.5 to 5 cm (1–2 in.) in diameter, bloom for a long period in midsummer. They are held above a neat mound of foliage of 30 cm (12 in.). More compact cultivars are 'Blue Clips' and a white form, 'White Clips.'

Culture: Full sun or partial shade on well-drained soil.

Use: Carpathian bellflowers are ideal for the front of the border, the rock garden, and edging.

Campanula cochleariifolia (creeping bellflower)

A diminutive perennial from the mountains of Europe, creeping bellflower is a lot tougher than it looks. The bright green foliage, only 8 to 10 cm (3–4 in.) in height, is almost hidden by a myriad of tiny, outfacing, blue, bell-like flowers in June and July. *C. cochleariifolia* 'Alba' is a white form. 'Miranda' is taller, with larger, silver-blue, outfacing flowers. They spread by creeping rhizomes, soon forming a solid mat.

Culture: Grow in sun or partial shade in well-drained soil.

Use: This is an excellent plant for edging, the rock garden, a ground cover, among brick or paving stone walkways, cascading over walls, in crevices, and on garden steps.

Sara Williams

Centaurea macrocephala (globe centaurea)

The genus is named for the mythical Greek centaurs, creatures with the lower body of a horse and upper torso of a man. They were said to have used this plant medicinally. Native to the Caucasus Mountains, globe centaurea are easily identified by the overlapping bracts below the petals. *Macrocephala* means a large head, a reference to the large, yellow, thistle-like flowers borne in late summer. Up to 1 m (4 ft) in height, they are rather coarse, with long, wavy, green leaves.

Culture: Grow in full sun or partial shade in well-drained soil. They will need division every three or four years.

Use: Place at the back of a perennial or mixed border, use as specimen plants, or mass in large groups. They are used in both fresh and dried arrangements.

Sara Williams

Centaurea montana (perennial cornflower)

The species name, *montana*, refers to its habitat, the mountains of southeast Europe. The globular, thistle-like, blue flowers (2.5–5 cm/1–2 in. diameter), are held on 60 cm (24 in.) stems above grey-green foliage. They bloom profusely in June, with less intensive flowering later. 'Alba' is a white form thought to be less showy. 'Rosea' is a pale pink form.

Culture: Grow in full sun or partial shade in most soils.

Use: Because they self-sow, perennial cornflowers are best in an informal border or for naturalizing. They are used as cut flowers and are a butterfly and bee nectar source.

Sara Williams

Ψ *Cerastium tomentosum* (snow-in-summer)

The genus name, *Cerastium,* is from the Greek word for horn, a reference to the shape of the seed capsule. *Tomentosum* means hairy and describes the silver-grey leaves. The common name is derived from the masses of tiny white flowers produced in June. A member of the carnation family, it was introduced from Italy and Sicily. Each flower has five petals that are so deeply divided there appear to be ten. A mat-forming plant (20 cm/8 in. in height), it can be somewhat invasive. *Cerastium biebersteinii*, native to the mountains of Asia Minor, is more compact, with larger flowers.

Culture: Plant this tough perennial in full sun in poor, well-drained soils. Shear after flowering for a neater appearance.

Use: Excellent as a ground cover, on slopes, or trailing over walls. It has overwintered in large containers in sheltered areas. In a rock garden or perennial border, it may be too aggressive.

ꙮ *Coryphantha vivipara* (pincushion cactus)

Vivipara means bearing live young and refers to its offshoots. This native cactus is shaped like a pincushion and produces pink to violet-purple flowers with conspicuous yellow stamens in July. The fleshy stems are covered with spirally arranged bumps, each with a cluster of short, sharp spines. The edible fruit is a fleshy brown berry. Plants can form dense colonies 30 cm (12 in.) or more across.

Culture: Under normal border conditions, cacti will soon rot. Remember their origin and situate them in full sun on very well-drained, sandy soils.

Use: Cacti are useful in hotter, drier areas of a rock garden that are inaccessible to small children and pets.

Brendan Casement

ꙮ *Dianthus deltoides* (maiden pinks)

Deltoides is from the Greek word *delta* (triangular), a reference to the shape of the petals. An old-fashioned plant native from Scotland to Asia, maiden pinks form large mats, 8 to 15 cm (3–6 in.) in height, covered in tiny, deep pink flowers for six weeks in midsummer. The green foliage makes an attractive ground cover. 'Albus' is a white cultivar. 'Brilliant' is dark red.

Culture: Plant in full sun on well-drained soils. Shear after flowering for a neater appearance. They are short-lived but may self-sow. Taking cuttings will ensure their continuity.

Use: Maiden pinks are excellent in a rock garden, as an edging or ground cover, and among paving stones.

Sara Williams

Dianthus plumarius (grass pinks, cottage pinks)

The species from which most pinks originate are native to central and eastern Europe. Many cultivars are crosses between species, and their hardiness varies. The grassy, blue-green or grey foliage ranges in height from 15 to 60 cm (6–24 in.) and is attractive throughout the growing season. The fragrant flowers are produced from May to July and vary from white to pink to red, usually with fringed petals.

Culture: Grow in full sun in well-drained soil. Shear after flowering for a neater appearance. Divide every few years. The evergreen foliage benefits from snow cover.

Use: Use as cut flowers, in the rockery or perennial border, as a fragrant edging, and among paving stones.

Sara Williams

Louis Lenz

Dictamnus albus (gasplant)

Named after Mt. Dicte in Crete, gasplant is native from southern Europe to northern China. *Albus* means white, a reference to the flowers. The common name is a reference to the volatile oils that give the plant a pungent, lemon-like fragrance and may cause skin inflammation or blistering in sensitive individuals. Plant parts are poisonous if ingested. Long-lived and attractive, gasplant deserves greater use. The pinnately compound leaves are dark green and glossy. Racemes of white or pink flowers are produced on 90 cm (3 ft) stems in June. *D. albus* 'Purpureus' has dark purple flowers.

Culture: Gasplants do well in a loamy soil in full sun, and are drought tolerant after two or three seasons. Transplants will show reduced vigor for a few years.

Use: Use as specimen plants and in a perennial or mixed border.

Sara Williams

Ψ *Echinops ritro* (globe thistle)

A thistle is not an easy plant to market on the prairies, even if it is singularly attractive. *Echinops* comes from the Greek word for hedgehog and aptly describes its spiny nature. Native to Europe and Asia, it is 1 m (3–4 ft) in height, with large, globular, steel blue flowers in late summer. Improved cultivars are 'Veitche's Blue' and 'Taplow Blue.'

Culture: The globe thistle is at home in poor soils and full sun. It has sometimes been observed to die after flowering.

Use: A large plant, it is well suited to the back of a border, naturalizing, a specimen plant, and as a dried flower. It attracts bees and moths, and is a butterfly nectar plant.

Sara Williams

Ψ *Elymus arenarius* (blue lyme grass)

Native to European seacoasts, blue lyme grass is grown for both its foliage and flower heads. The genus name, *Elymus*, is from the Greek word for millet, while the species name, *arenarius*, means growing in sandy places, a reference to its native habitat. About 60 cm (2 ft) tall, with broad arching, blue-grey blades, it forms very loose, irregular clumps.

Culture: Grow in full sun. Given favorable conditions, it spreads rapidly and is invasive. A warm-season grass, it is not slowed by midsummer heat.

Use: Excellent for holding slopes, massed, or as a ground cover. Place it in the perennial border only if it can be physically contained. The flower heads are used for drying.

Erigeron speciosus 'Pink Jewel' ('Pink Jewel' Oregon fleabane)

A member of the composite family, the species is native to North America (including the prairies). The common name stems from the use of the dried flowers as flea repellant. Upright, well-branched plants of 50 to 75 cm (20–30 in.) produce small pink daisies with yellow centers. 'Pink Jewel' is 75 cm (30 in.) with flowers in various shades of pink.

Culture: Plant in full sun in well-drained soil.

Use: This is a long-lived perennial for either the rock garden or border and makes an excellent cut flower. It is a nectar source for butterflies.

'Pink Jewel'

Eryngium spp. (sea holly)

Sea holly resembles a metallic, blue-grey coneflower with a silvery, ruff-like bract at its base. The foliage is glossy, deeply cut, and very spiny. They bloom in July, holding their flowers until frost. The amethyst sea holly *(E. amethystinum)*, native to Europe, has silver-blue leaves and blue flowers on 45 cm (18 in.), amethyst-colored, branching stems. The alpine sea holly *(E. alpinum)*, from the Alps, is 60 to 90 cm (2–3 ft), with larger blue flowers and heart-shaped leaves. It tolerates clay soils and shade. The most common species is the flat-leaved sea holly *(E. planum)*. Native to Europe and Asia, it is 1 m (3 ft) in height, long-lived, with heart-shaped leaves.

Culture: Tolerant of poor and saline soils, sea hollies prefer full sun and well-drained soils. Our cooler evening temperatures enhance their flower and stem color.

Use: Perennial borders and fresh and dried arrangements.

Erysimum asperum (Siberian wallflower)

A member of the mustard family, Siberian wallflower is a biennial, perpetuating itself through self-seeding. In spite of its common name, it is native to the Mediterranean region. The bright orange flowers, each with four petals and four sepals, are produced in late spring in loose terminal clusters. Plants reach about 30 to 38 cm (12–15 in.) in height. Improved cultivars are 'Golden Bedder' and 'Lemon Queen.'

Culture: Full sun or partial shade in ordinary soil. Do not mulch, as it will prevent self-seeding.

Use: Because of its biennial nature, it is best left to naturalize where it can self-seed. Use in a wild garden below trees in filtered light.

Cushion spurge *(Euphorbia polychroma)*

Sara Williams

ψ *Euphorbia cyparissias* (cypress spurge)

The genus is named after Euphorbus, physician to a West African king. The species and common names refer to the needle-like foliage resembling that of a cypress tree. Native to Europe, cypress spurge is an attractive ground cover of 30 cm (12 in.), with finely divided, light green foliage and yellow bracts in late May and early June. The true flowers are very small and inconspicuous. If broken, the plant exudes a milky sap that may irritate the skin. It spreads by rhizomes.

Euphorbia polychroma (E. epithymoides), called cushion spurge because of its clump-like growth habit, adds color to the early spring garden with its bright greenish yellow bracts. It is 30 to 45 cm (12–18 in.) in height. It is not reliably hardy and should be grown in more protected locations. Its foliage turns red in the fall.

Culture: Plant in full sun on well-drained soils.

Use: Cypress spurge is excellent as a ground cover, for naturalizing where nothing else will grow, or holding a slope or bank. It is extremely aggressive in a rock garden or border.

Sara Williams

ψ *Festuca ovina* var. *glauca* (blue fescue, sheep fescue)

Festuca is the Latin word for a grass stalk, and *ovina* means of sheep—the species is used for pasture. The word *glauca* means blue and describes the bluish, waxy coloring of the leaves. An ornamental grass native to Europe and Asia, it has naturalized through much of North America. It is 15 to 30 cm (6–12 in.) in height, with thin, wiry blades that form tight, evergreen clumps and are very well-behaved within a border. 'Skinner's' has attractive golden seed heads which compliment the blue foliage. 'Elijah Blue' holds its color year-round.

Culture: Plant in full sun or partial shade on well-drained soils. A cool-season grass, it puts on vigorous growth in spring and fall. Divide older clumps every few years.

Use: Its neat form lends itself to more formal use, as edging, an accent plant in the rock garden, groupings in the perennial border, or a hummocky ground cover.

ψ *Gaillardia aristata* (gaillardia, blanket flower)

The genus name honors the French patron of botany, Gaillard de Marentonea. *Aristata* means bearded or with an awn, and describes the seed. Gaillardia is native to the North American prairies, and the common name suggests colors found in blankets of Indigenous peoples of the American Southwest: from yellow to orange, bronze, maroon, red, and burgundy. The flowers bloom from July until hard frost. Plants vary from 30 to 90 cm (1–3 ft) and have grey-green foliage.

Most hybrids are listed as annuals *(G. grandiflora)* but are usually crosses between annual and perennial types. With inherited characteristics of both, they tend to be relatively short-lived but have a long flowering season. 'Burgundy' is wine-red and 90 cm (3 ft). The 'Monarch' strain is a color mix. 'Goblin' is a more compact, mound-like cultivar of only 30 to 45 cm (12–18 in.), well suited to the perennial border or rock garden. 'Golden Goblin' is similar but yellow.

'Goblin'

Culture: Blanket flowers are adapted to full sun and well-drained soils, surviving with little care. Leave beds un-mulched so plantings can perpetuate themselves through self-seeding. Cutting back flowering stems prior to hard frost encourages new basal buds. They are slow to resume growth in spring, so be patient and refrain from digging them out.

Use: Use in the border or rock garden, as a cut flower, and for naturalizing. They are a butterfly and bee nectar source.

Ψ *Geranium macrorrhizum* (bigfoot geranium)

Geranium is from the Greek word for crane, describing the seed capsules, which resemble a crane's bill. The word *macrorrhizum* means big root and, like the common name, refers to the thick, fleshy rhizomes, which soon form dense, weedproof mats. Native to the Alps and Carpathian Mountains, they are 30 to 45 cm (12–18 in.) in height, with aromatic, lobed leaves once used by the pharmaceutical industry as a source of oil of geranium. The flowers are magenta. 'Ingwersen's Variety' has pink, darker veined flowers, 5 cm (2 in.) in diameter. 'Album' has white flowers with pink to red calyxes.

Culture: Plant in full sun to partial shade on well-drained soil. Divide every three to four years.

Use: Use in the perennial or mixed border, massed, as a ground cover, or under trees. They will tolerate dry shade.

Gypsophila repens (creeping babysbreath)

Gypso means gypsum and *philia* lover of, alluding to their preference for basic or alkaline soil. *Repens* means creeping and describes its growth habit. A native of central and south-

Creeping babysbreath

ern Europe, it is found in the Alps and Pyrenees. It forms a mound about 15 cm (6 in.) in height, with a spread of 90 cm (3 ft), and is covered in tiny white flowers in midsummer. 'Rosea' has pink flowers. All have deep tap roots and should not be moved once established.

Gypsophila paniculata (babysbreath) is a tall perennial of 90 cm (3 ft), whose narrow, grey-green leaves provide a fine, feathery texture. The deep tap root, coupled with its ability to self-seed, has allowed it to escape from cultivation and naturalize in ditches and pasture land. In Manitoba, the species has been declared a noxious weed; similar legislation may be drafted elsewhere. *Gypsophila paniculata* var. *flore pleno* is a mostly double form available from seed. 'Bristol Fairy' is a sterile double form of only 60 cm (2 ft) that is propagated vegetatively. 'Rosyveil' is mound-like, 45 cm (18 in.) in height, with semi-double to fully double pinkish to white flowers.

Culture: Plant in full sun on well-drained soils.

Use: Use creeping babysbreath in the rock garden or perennial border. Use standard babysbreath in the perennial border and in fresh and dried arrangements.

Hemerocallis spp. (daylily)

Hemerocallis is derived from the Greek phrase meaning beautiful for a day, a reference to its short-lived flowers (although a mature plant may have several hundred buds and be covered in bloom for two to three weeks). They are not true lilies, which belong to the genus *Lilium*.

A grassy-leafed perennial varying in height from 0.5 to 1 m (1.5–4 ft), daylilies are long-lived and require little maintenance. They are available in a wide range of forms and colors. Hundreds of cultivars are available, from the palest yellows to orange, peach, bronze, red, purple, and pink. Different cultivars bloom during different periods of the growing season from spring to late summer. A selection of early-, mid-, and late-season cultivars ensures bloom for most of the summer.

The species from which many of the garden cultivars were derived are the lemon daylily (*H. lilioasphodelus, formerly H. flava*) and tawny daylily (*H. fulva*), first introduced into Europe in the 1500s. Both are rugged and drought tolerant. The lemon daylily is native to Siberia and northern China, and is 1 m (3 ft) in height, with fragrant, lemon yellow, funnel-shaped flowers in May and June. It is one of the first daylilies to bloom. It spreads slowly. The tawny daylily is brownish orange with darker interior markings. Native from southern Europe through to China and Japan, it has naturalized in milder parts of North America through the spread of

Above, right: tawny daylily

rhizomes. It is 1 m (3–4 ft) in height, and blooms in July and August. *H. fulva* var. *kwanso* is a double form.

Modern cultivars are not as aggressive as the species and remain in tighter clumps. 'Stella D' Oro' and 'Happy Returns' have repeat bloom, giving them more extended flowering periods.

Culture: Daylilies grow in full sun or full shade (where they will flower less) in a wide range of soils. They bloom better with even moisture or when mulched, but are drought tolerant once established. They are long-lived and pest and disease free. They are easily transplanted.

Use: Daylilies are excellent massed, in the perennial or mixed border, naturalized, used as ground covers, or as waterside plantings. A few cultivars open late in the afternoon and remain open through the night. These are well placed in the night garden, especially if they are light in color or have fragrance. The roots have a crisp, nut-like flavor and may be eaten raw. The flower buds and young leaves are also edible. The flowers are a nectar source for hummingbirds, bees, and butterflies.

Above: 'Karen Lynn' *Right:* an older cultivar, possibly 'Hyperion'

Heuchera spp. (coral bells, alumroot)

The genus was named after Johann Heinrich von Heucher (1677–1747), a German professor of botany. The common name, alumroot, refers to the tannins found in the root. Like daylilies, coral bells are long-lived, long-blooming, and require little maintenance. A myriad of tiny pink bells are held on wiry stalks above rosettes of dark green, scalloped leaves, which turn bronze in winter.

Dr. Henry Marshall of the Agricultural Research Station at Morden, Manitoba, crossed the tender, bright red *H. sanguinea*, which is native to the southwestern United States, and our native *H. richardsonii*, a tough plant with nondescript greenish flowers. The resulting 'Brandon Pink' is a deep coral pink, while 'Northern Fire' is dark scarlet red. They are 50 to 60 cm (20–24 in.) in height and bloom in June and July.

The newer, purple-leafed cultivars are grown mostly for their foliage, and are not as hardy, vigorous, or drought tolerant as the Morden hybrids.

Culture: Plant in full sun on well-drained soils. Divide every three to four years.

Use: Coral bells are excellent as a ground cover, in the perennial border or rock garden, as edging, or as cut flowers.

'Brandon Pink'

Above: 'Eye Bright'; *below:* dwarf iris

Ψ *Iris* spp. (bearded iris)

The genus was aptly named for Iris, Greek goddess of the rainbow, whose steps on earth were said to have left these flowers in all colors of the rainbow. Mostly native to the Mediterranean, iris have been in gardens for centuries. There are hundreds of cultivars.

The flowers of bearded iris and *I. germanica* hybrids consist of six petals, three upright "standards," and three down-facing "falls." The fuzzy growth on the falls is called the "beard." The grassy foliage is sword-like and upright, providing interesting form and texture even when the plants are not in bloom. Iris bloom for two to three weeks in early June in a wide range of colors, from white through to yellow, pink, peach, blue, purple, and maroon. Heights range from 15 to 115 cm (6–45 in.). Generally speaking, taller bearded iris (those over 100 cm/3 ft) are less hardy.

Iris spuria, native to Iran and Turkey, are 60 cm (24 in.) in height, with yellow or blue flowers, and are heat and saline tolerant. *Iris pseudocorus,* the yellow flag iris, whose habitat is usually in or near water, is surprisingly adaptable to dry conditions. A native of Europe and Siberia, it is useful for its foliage alone: the tall (1 m/3 ft), sword-like, blue-green clumps resemble cattails. The flowers yield a yellow dye, and the seed capsules were once used as a coffee substitute.

Culture: Bearded iris require full sun and good drainage. Under shaded conditions they will not bloom, and they soon rot in soggy soils. Mulch around the base of iris prior to their first winter to even out temperature fluctuations and provide a measure of insulation. Divide every four years in July.

Use: Iris are excellent in the perennial border, the rock garden, massed, or for edging. The seed capsules are used in dried arrangements. They provide nectar for hummingbirds.

Leontopodium alpinum (edelweiss)

Leontopodium is from the Greek phrase for a lion's foot, which the flower head is supposed to resemble. *Alpinum* refers to its native habitat, the Swiss Alps. The common name, edelweiss, is the German phrase for noble white, a reference to the star-like bracts. The true flowers are yellow and inconspicuous. The whiteness of the bracts is affected by growing conditions and genetic variations. Its performance on the prairies is sometimes disappointing. The leaves are woolly and attractive.

Culture: Grow in full sun (or partial shade where summers are hot) on well-drained, sandy soil.

Use: Use in the rock garden, perennial border, for edging paths, and in dried arrangements.

Limonium spp. (sea lavender, statice)

The genus name, *Limonium,* is from the Greek word *leimon,* a meadow, the plant's native habitat. An airy plant with tiny flowers on finely branched stems, sea lavender is similar to babysbreath but more attractive. It is long-lived and deep rooted.

Common or wide-leaf sea lavender *(L. latifolium)* is native to the coastal salt marshes of Europe and Asia. It has billowy sprays of tiny, lavender blue flowers on 60 cm (2 ft) stems in July and August. 'Violetta' has deep violet flowers; 'Blue Cloud' has larger flowers; and 'Elegance' has deep blue flowers.

Tartarian or German sea lavender (formerly *L. tataricum,* now *Goniolimon tartaricum)* blooms in July and August and is a bit shorter, producing triangular, flat-topped sprays of silver-grey flowers. It has somewhat stiffer flower stalks. *L. tataricum* var. *angustifolium* (formerly *L. dumosum)* has silver-lavender flowers, while *L. tataricum* var. *nanum* has fluffy pink flowers and is only 24 cm (9 in.) high.

Culture: Plant in full sun in a loamy but well-drained soil. They perform better with even moisture, but are drought tolerant once established. Mulching is beneficial.

Use: Excellent as border plants, they have long been used in both fresh and dried arrangements.

Sara Williams

Ψ *Linum perenne* (perennial flax)

Linum is the Latin name for flax; *perenne* means perennial. The common name is derived from the Dutch *flas* and the German *flacks,* meaning to flay, part of the processing of flax. Native to Europe, flax has been grown since ancient times as a source of linen, rope, and linseed oil. Plants are about 60 cm (2 ft) in height, with tiny, narrow leaves, and 2.5 cm (1 in.) blue flowers. The overall appearance of the upright, arching clumps is light and airy. Individual flowers last only a day, but plants bloom over a four- to six-week period. Flowers close on cloudy, dull days. 'Alba' is a white cultivar.

Culture: Plant in full sun on well-drained soil. The plants have a woody base and resent disturbance once established. Although short-lived (three or four years), they do reseed.

Use: Flax are good subjects for the perennial border, massing, the cottage garden, or naturalizing in drier areas.

Sara Williams

Sara Williams

Malva spp. (malva hollyhock, musk mallow)

The genus name, *Malva*, is derived from the Greek *malakos*, meaning to soften. An extract from the sap was once used to soften and soothe the skin. *Malva moschata*, the musk mallow, is native to Europe, with very showy, satiny, rose-colored flowers on somewhat sprawling plants, 60 to 90 cm (2–3 ft) in height. *Moschata* means musky and describes the aromatic, deeply cut leaves. 'Alba' is a white-flowered cultivar. Although short-lived, plants are long-blooming and self-seed reliably. *Malva alcea* is 1 m (3–4 ft) in height and produces rose or white flowers for six to eight weeks. It too is short-lived. 'Fastigiata' has darker flowers on more upright plants. *Malva sylvestris* 'Primley Blue' is a dwarf cultivar with white flowers. 'Zabrina' has pink or white flowers with purple veins and is 1 m (3 ft) in height. Both cultivars flower from July to frost and are short-lived but will self-sow.

Culture: Full sun or partial shade on well-drained soils.

Use: These plants are well suited to borders, cottage gardens, naturalizing, or concealing unsightly objects. Use as cut flowers. They are a nectar plant for butterflies.

Ψ *Nepeta* x *ucranica* 'Dropmore' ('Dropmore' catmint)

Nepeta is the Latin word for mint. *Ucranica* means of the Ukraine, the origin of one of its parent plants. Catmint is characterized by square stems and opposite leaves. 'Dropmore' is a cross of *N. mussinii* and *N. ucranica* introduced by Dr. Frank Skinner of Dropmore, Manitoba, in 1932. It is very compact, 30 to 38 cm (12–15 in.) in height, with scalloped, grey-green leaves and light purple flowers. Because it is sterile, it blooms almost the entire summer and does not reseed, nor is it invasive.

Nepeta 'Six Hills Giant' is 1 m (3 ft) with dark blue flowers above grey foliage. It has not been widely tested but is worthy of trial. *Nepeta sibirica* 'Blue Beauty' (introduced as 'Souvenir d'Andre Chaudron' by Skinners Nursery in 1948) is about 0.5 m (2 ft) tall and more aggressive.

Culture: Plant in full sun or partial shade on well-drained soil.

Use: *Nepeta* 'Dropmore' is excellent as a border plant, as a companion to roses (for which it is used extensively in Great Britain), for edging, massing, as a cut flower, and a nectar source for bees. More aggressive catmints are best used for massing, naturalizing, in a cottage garden, or for stabilizing a slope. If you don't like cats, give one to your neighbor.

Above:
'Dropmore' catmint
Left: 'Souvenir d'Andre Chaudron'

Louis Lenz

Sara Williams

Oenothera missouriensis (Missouri evening primrose, Ozark sundrops)

The evening primrose should not be confused with the true primrose *(Primula)*—these two unrelated plants share only a common name. Missouri evening primrose produces delicate, tissue paper–like, pale yellow flowers that persist for many days and are borne from midsummer onward. The stems are about 45 cm (18 in.) in height, often trailing before turning upright as a flower stem. It has deep, woody roots. *Oenothera tetragona* 'Illumination' is more upright with larger flowers and is better suited to a border.

Culture: Plant in full sun on well-drained soil.

Use: Use for naturalizing and the cottage garden. The decorative, winged seed pods are used in dried arrangements. The seeds are eaten by several species of birds.

ψ *Opuntia polyacantha* (plains prickly pear cactus)

The fruit of this native cactus is a straw-colored, edible berry, but one would have to be pretty desperate to brave the spines in order to harvest it! The species name, *polyacantha*, means many spined. The stems are succulent and pear-shaped. The leaves have been modified to clusters of grey spines evenly distributed over the stems. The plant is 13 cm (5 in.) in height, and produces waxy, lemon yellow flowers, 5 to 7.5 cm (2–3 in.) in diameter, in June and July.

Culture: Plant in full sun on very well-drained, sandy soils.

Use: Cacti are useful in the hottest, driest areas of a rock garden that are inaccessible to small children and pets.

ψ *Paeonia* spp. (peony)

The peony was named to honor the mythical Greek physician to the gods, Paion. Most cultivars are hybrids of the Chinese peony, *P. lactiflora*, native to Siberia and northern China. Peonies have graced prairie gardens almost as long as European settlement. Noted for their longevity and low maintenance, they have attractive flowers and handsome, glossy green foliage. Flowers are white, pink, red, or purple, with single to fully double forms. Plants range from 60 to 90 cm (2–3 ft). Many are fragrant.

The tree peony (*Paeonia suffruticosa*) is not reliably hardy on the prairies. The fern-leaf peony (*P. tenuifolia*) is hardy but requires even moisture.

'John Harvard'

Brian Porter

Culture: Plant in deep, well-drained soil. Older cultivars with large, double flowers and relatively weak stems may need support in the form of a wire hoop. Plant buds on divisions or newly acquired peonies no lower than 5 cm (2 in.) below the soil surface; deep planting inhibits and delays flowering. It is better to plant too shallowly and mulch with dried leaves for the first winter than to plant too deeply. Allow three to four years for the plant to display its mature flower and leaf forms—juvenile foliage may not be as deeply divided as older divisions of the same cultivar, nor will the doubleness of flowers be stabilized.

Use: Peonies are valuable in the perennial and mixed border, either singly or massed, and as cut flowers.

Edgar Toop

Papaver nudicaule (Iceland poppy)

Papaver is from the Greek word for milk and refers to the milky sap. *Nudicaule* means a bare or nude stalk—there are no leaves present on the wiry flower stems. Iceland poppies are circumpolar, native to Arctic and subarctic regions of Europe, Asia, and North America. Biennial in habit, they produce dainty, tissue paper–like flowers throughout the summer in vibrant shades of orange, yellow, white, cream, and salmon pink. The flowers are up to 7.5 cm (3 in.) in diameter and held 30 to 45 cm (12–18 in.) above the basal rosette of finely divided foliage.

Culture: Plant in full sun on well-drained soils. Do not mulch. Plants are short-lived but self-seed.

Use: Iceland poppies are valuable in the border and rock garden because of their extended period of bloom. The decorative seed capsule is used in dried arrangements.

Sara Williams

Papaver orientale (Oriental poppy)

The common name, poppy, is from the Anglo-Saxon word for sleep, a reference to the narcotic properties of a different species. Oriental poppies are native to the Caucasus, Iran, and Turkey, and both the species and common names allude to the Orient. The species is 60 to 75 cm (2–2.5 ft), with bright scarlet flowers in May and June with a prominent purple-black blotch at the base of each petal. Many cultivars exist—pink, salmon, white, orange, red, and purple—both single and double. The satiny flowers are large, up to 12 to 15 cm (5–6 in.) in diameter. The leaves are hairy, deeply lobed, and sharply toothed. Roots are deep, fleshy, and brittle.

Culture: Plant in full sun and well-drained soil. They go dormant in August, forming new rosettes of basal leaves by September, when they can be divided. They are often planted in narrow diagonal drifts surrounded by later-blooming plants to hide their dying foliage after they finish blooming.

Use: While in bloom Oriental poppies make an enormous visual impact in the perennial border and as a cut flower. The decorative seed pods are used in dried arrangements.

Phalaris arundinacea var. *picta* (ribbon grass)

Native to Europe and North America, ribbon grass is 60 to 120 cm (2–4 ft) in height, with variegated green-and-white leaves forming loose, upright clumps.

Culture: It will tolerate a variety of soils in full sun to partial shade. Under favorable conditions, it spreads quickly by rhizomes. It is a cool-season grass, and its growth is curtailed during the heat of midsummer. Mowing at that time improves its appearance and stimulates growth in early fall.

Use: It is excellent massed, naturalized, or as a ground cover, but is too aggressive for the perennial border.

Sara Williams

Phlox spp. (Arctic phlox, moss phlox, creeping phlox)

Phlox is Greek for flame and describes the bright pink flowers. Garden cultivars are usually hybrids of two or more species. *Phlox borealis* (Arctic phlox) is native to Alaska and Canada. *Borealis* means northern. It forms a low mound about 10 cm (4 in.) high of narrow, needle-like, evergreen foliage. The small pink, white, lilac, or lavender flowers bloom in May. The stems are woody. *Phlox subulata* (moss or creeping phlox) is native to the eastern United States. *Subulata* means awl-shaped and refers to the leaves. It is similar to *P. borealis,* but not as hardy, vigorous, or long-lived.

Most of the species were introduced to England from North America by plant explorer John Bartram in 1745. Ironically, within two centuries the hybrids developed there had made their way back to North America through the nursery trades.

Culture: Plant in full sun or part shade with good drainage. In exposed sites, winter desiccation often occurs. Shear after flowering to promote vigorous growth. Divide every three years.

Use: Phlox are excellent in a rock garden, as ground covers, edging a path, among paving stones, a perennial border, trailing over low walls, and nestled in garden steps.

Sara Williams

Polygonum bistorta 'Superbum' (knotweed, fleece flower)

Polygonum means many jointed knees, referring to the stems. *Bistorta* means twisted and describes the roots. Knotweed is 45 to 75 cm (18–30 in.), with spikes of pink flowers that resemble bottle brushes held well above the foliage. The distinctive basal leaves are 10 to 15 cm (4–6 in.) long, with wavy margins and a white midrib. The roots are very thick. The cultivar 'Superbum,' meaning superior, has larger flowers than the species. *Polygonum affine* 'Dimity,' called the Himalayan fleece flower, forms a low mat with pink or white flowers.

Culture: Grow in sun or shade on well-drained soil.

Use: Knotweed is excellent in the perennial border, massed, used as a ground cover in the shade, and as a cut flower.

Orangespot cinquefoil

Ψ *Potentilla* spp. (potentilla, cinquefoil)

Potentilla comes from the word *potens*, powerful, and refers to its reputed medicinal and magical properties. Gardeners are usually more familiar with the woody, shrubby cinquefoil than the herbaceous forms. All have five-petalled, buttercup-like flowers. The orangespot cinquefoil *(P. crantzii,* syn. *P. alpestre),* native to Europe and Asia, has bright yellow flowers in June and July and a height of 30 to 38 cm (12–15 in.). Silverweed *(P. anserina)* is native to the prairies, only 15 cm (6 in.) high, with 2.5 cm (1 in.) yellow flowers above a thick mat of silver-green foliage in May and June.

Culture: They do well in full sun on well-drained soils.

Use: Ideal as ground covers on hot, dry slopes, potentillas also fit into a rock garden.

Salvia x 'Superba' (salvia 'Superba')

Salvus is Latin for safe or healthy, a reference to the plant's ancient medicinal uses. A member of the mint family, it has square stems and opposite leaves, and dense racemes of tubular, two-lipped flowers. 'Superba,' introduced at the turn of the century, is long-flowering and trouble-free. It is probably a hybrid of *S. nemorosa* and other species native to Turkey, Iran, and Afghanistan. Cultivars include 'Blue Queen,' 36 to 60 cm (18–24 in), with rich violet flowers; 'East Friesland,' a deep purple of 36 cm (18 in.); and 'Rose Queen,' a rosy violet.

Culture: Grow in full sun in ordinary, well-drained soil.

Use: Excellent in the border, massed, as specimen plants, and for cut flowers.

Saponaria ocymoides (rock soapwort)

The genus name is from the Latin *sapo*, meaning soap. The bruised leaves will produce a lather. *Ocymoides* means resembling basil, alluding to the tiny leaves. A member of the pink or carnation family, the star-shaped flowers range from pink to white, blooming in June and July. Only 10 to 20 cm (4–8 in.) in height, it is a vigorous trailing plant, native to the European Alps.

Culture: Plant in full sun in well-drained soil. Shear after flowering for a neater appearance.

Use: Good for trailing over low walls, on slopes, and in the rock garden.

Sara Williams

Ψ *Sedum* spp. (stonecrop)

The genus name is from the Latin word *sedo*, to sit, and alludes to the way in which these plants sit on walls and rocks. A large group of low (15–30 cm/6–12 in.), succulent perennials, sedums are valued as much for their foliage as for their flowers. Many cultivars exist, some of which are very similar, and there is some confusion about nomenclature. With some truth, my son used to comment, "You sedum one, you sedum all," yet their charm remains.

　　Among the cultivars recommended for the prairies are:
• 'Autumn Joy,' a hybrid of *S. telephinum* and *S. spectabile*, 60 cm (2 ft) high, with pink flowers in late August or early fall • evergreen stonecrop *(S. hybridum),* with glossy green leaves and yellow flowers in early summer • Ewer's stonecrop *(S. ewersii),* with blue grey foliage and pink flowers in July • goldust stonecrop *(S. acre),* only 8 cm (3 in.) tall, with masses of tiny leaves and tiny yellow flowers in late spring • *S. kamtschaticum,* with yellow flowers, 15 to 20 cm (6–8 in.) in height • *S. kamtschaticum* 'Middendorffianum,' which forms a clump of dark green leaves with yellow flowers • *S. kamtschaticum* 'Variegatum,' with attractive, green-and-white variegated leaves • *S. reflexum,* with blue-green, needle-like leaves and yellow flowers in midsummer • *S. spurium,* with pink flowers and a low spreading habit, has a number of attractive cultivars: 'Bronze Carpet,' with bronze foliage, 'Roseum,' and 'Tricolor,' with variegated leaves • showy stonecrop *(S. spectabile),* with pink flowers in late summer • 'Vera Jameson,' 22 to 30 cm (9–12 in.), with red-purple leaves and pink flowers in late summer.

Culture: Plant in full sun on well-drained soils.

Use: Sedums are excellent as ground covers in hot, dry areas, in the rock garden, as edging, or as plantings among path or patio paving stones. Butterflies are attracted by their nectar.

Sara Williams

Above: S. telephinum atropurpurea ***Right:*** 'Autumn Joy' ***Below:*** *S. reflexum* 'Jenny Stone'

Sara Williams

Sara Williams

ψ *Sempervivum* spp. (hens and chicks, house leek)

The genus name, *Sempervivum,* means always alive and refers to the plant's longevity and the belief that its presence on a rooftop would ward off fire and lightning. It often grows on roofs in Great Britain, hence the common name, house leek. It bears a close resemblance to a miniature artichoke (the hen) surrounded by even more diminutive artichokes (the chicks). It is monocarpic—the "hen" dies after flowering—but the "chicks" live on. Grown primarily for its succulent evergreen foliage, which is seldom over a few centimeters (2 in.) high, in midsummer it produces a weird, umbrella-shaped flower stalk with small, daisy-like flowers in white, cream, or pink.

Culture: Plant in a hot, sunny location on poorer, well-drained soils.

Use: They are excellent in the rock garden, for edging, among paving stones, or as a ground cover in hot, dry locations.

Sara Williams

ψ *Silene vulgaris* var. *maritima* (sea campion)

Sea campion is a member of the pink family, native to the seacoasts of western Europe. From June to October, it is covered with masses of tiny white flowers with distinctly notched petals. The calyx are often inflated. The leaves are a silver-green, and the trailing stems give the 15 cm (6 in.) plant a soft, mound-like appearance. Plants are short-lived but self-seed.

Culture: Plant in full sun in a well-drained location.

Use: Excellent as a ground cover, in a cottage garden, or for naturalizing in a hot, dry location. Seedlings would soon overrun a rock garden.

B. J. Godwin

ψ *Solidago* hybrids (goldenrod)

The genus name is from the Latin *solido,* meaning to make whole or strengthen, a reference to its medicinal use. Native to North America, where the species is a pernicious weed, they were long blamed for causing hayfever. Outstanding hybrids developed in Europe, including 'Golden Fleece,' 'Cloth of Gold,' and 'Crown of Rays,' are now finding their way into North American gardens. Many lack the invasive tendencies of the species but remain terrifically drought tolerant.

Culture: Plant in full sun and well-drained soil. Powdery mildew may be a problem.

Use: Use in the perennial border, cottage garden, as a cut flower, massed, and naturalized. A bee and butterfly nectar plant.

ψ *Sphaeralcea coccinea* (prairie mallow)

Sphaer is from the Greek word for globe and refers to the spherical-shaped fruit; *alcea* is a reference to its relationship with the genus *Alcea*, or hollyhock. *Coccinea* means scarlet and describes the flowers, which vary from a deep salmon to orange-red. They are held above attractive, silver-green foliage from May to June. These prostrate plants form a mat only 15 to 20 cm (6–8 in.) in height. Native to the prairies, mallow has deep, woody roots and is often found along road allowances in some of the least inviting, gravely soils.

Culture: Plant in full sun on well-drained soils.

Use: This is a good plant for the rock garden, the perennial border, among paving stones, or for edging.

Sara Williams

Stachys byzantina (lambs ears)

Stachys is from the Greek word for spike and describes the flower. *Byzantina* means of Byzanthium, or Istanbul. It is native to the Caucasus, Turkey, and Iran. A member of the mint family, lambs ears has square stems and opposite leaves. The whorls of pink to purplish flowers are held on 10 to 15 cm (4–6 in.) spikes from midsummer to frost. It is grown mainly for the silver-grey, woolly foliage, which indeed resemble lambs' ears. Plants are 30 to 45 cm (12–18 in.) in height and spread slowly. 'Silver Carpet' is a dwarf cultivar which seldom flowers and makes an excellent ground cover.

Culture: Plant in full sun in well-drained soil.

Use: *Stachys* is excellent in the border, rock garden, or cottage garden, for edging, or massing. It is a bee nectar source. In England it is much used as a companion plant with roses.

Sara Williams

Stachys grandiflora (big betony)

This species differs from the previous one in that it is grown primary for its flowers rather than its foliage. The species name, *grandiflora,* means large-flowered. Whorls of purple flowers are held above mounds of bright green but somewhat wrinkled, heart-shaped leaves with scalloped edges.

Culture: Plant in full sun or partial shade in well-drained soil.

Use: Use in the border, rock garden, or cottage garden, for edging, or massing. It is also valuable as a cut flower.

Sara Williams

ψ *Symphytum officinale* (comfrey)

Symphytum is from the Greek phrase meaning to grow together, an allusion to its healing properties. *Officinale* refers to its use as a pharmaceutical. Comfrey is from the Middle English *cumfirie*, meaning to cause coagulation of wounds. Native to Europe, comfrey has escaped from cultivation in many parts of North America. Pink or blue flowers are produced on 1 m (3 ft) plants from June to August. The root system is deep and penetrating. 'Argenteum' is a very attractive variegated cultivar. *Symphyum* x *rubrum* has dark red flowers on 50 cm (20 in.) plants and is said to be less aggressive. Both need further testing for hardiness on the prairies.

Culture: Comfrey will grow practically anywhere and do well.

Use: Use as a hedge, massed, for naturalizing, and as a ground cover. It is too aggressive for the perennial border.

Above: comfrey
Left: 'Argenteum'

Sara Williams

J. G. N. Davidson

ψ *Tanacetum vulgare* (common tansy)

Tanacetum is from the Greek *athanasia*, a medicine to prolong life; *vulgare* means common. Common tansy was rubbed on corpses in the Middle Ages to preserve them. It was also used as a flea and lice repellent. It is believed to be toxic. Native from Europe to Siberia, it is 1 m (3 ft) in height, with dark green, aromatic, ferny foliage. The flat, button-like, yellow flowers bloom from July until frost. The species is quite invasive. 'Crispum' has parsley-like leaves and is shorter.

Culture: Plant in well-drained soil in full sun.

Use: The species is too invasive for a border but is used for naturalizing, massed, or on slopes. 'Crispum' can be used in a border or a cottage or herb garden.

Brian Porter

Thermopsis caroliniana (false lupine, thermopsis)

Thermopsis is from the Greek and means lupine-like. The species name, *caroliniana*, is a reference to the Carolinas, an area to which it is native. Yellow, lupine-like flowers bloom in spring and are followed by flat seed pods. Plants are 1 m (3–4 ft) high, with attractive, blue-green, compound leaves. Like other legumes, thermopsis is adapted to poor soils and has the ability to fix nitrogen from the atmosphere.

Culture: Plant in full sun in ordinary soil. It spreads slowly and resents root disturbance.

Use: Use in the border, for naturalizing, and as a cut flower.

Gail Rankin

♆ *Thymus* spp. (thyme)

Thymus is the ancient Greek name for this plant. Thymes are miniature members of the mint family, with square stems, opposite leaves, and flowers on short spikes. Among the more drought-tolerant thymes is mother-of-thyme *(Thymus serpyllum),* which forms a tight mat of dark green foliage, 15 cm (6 in.) in height, and is covered in a mass of tiny purple flowers in midsummer. It spreads by creeping rootstock. 'Album' has white flowers. Woolly thyme *(T. pseudolanuginosus)* is even lower, forming a mat of grey foliage with pink flowers.

Culture: Plant in full sun on well-drained soils. The leaves are evergreen, so wind protection and snow cover are helpful.

Use: Ideal in the rock garden, planted among paving stones, as a ground cover, or for edging a path. Some species are used as culinary herbs. It is a nectar source for bees and butterflies.

Above: thyme as a ground cover
Right: white-flowered mother-of-thyme

♆ *Verbascum nigrum* (verbascum, dark mullein)

Verbascum is an ancient name for this group of plants. *Nigrum* means black or dark, perhaps describing the purple anthers. The common name, mullein, is from the Latin *mollis* and means soft, a description of the leaves. Mulleins are native to Europe, but many species are widely naturalized in eastern North America. Biennial in nature, verbascum perpetuates itself through reseeding. Plants are 90 cm (3 ft) in height, with tall spikes of yellow flowers in midsummer. The large basal leaves are heart-shaped, and arise from thick, fleshy roots.

Culture: Plant in full sun in light, sandy soil.

Use: Excellent for large borders, a cottage garden, naturalizing, and cut flowers.

♆ *Veronica* spp. (veronica, speedwell)

The genus name, *Veronica,* is associated with St. Veronica for reasons lost to antiquity. Speedwells form a large group of perennials, only a few of which are drought tolerant. Comb speedwell *(Veronica pectinata)* forms a prostrate grey mat of 5 cm (2 in.), with tiny, white-centered, blue or rose flowers in June or July. Both the common and species name describe the

Comb speedwell

leaf shape, which resembles a comb used to card wool, a reference that is probably lost on most gardeners today. The woolly speedwell (*V. spicata* var. *incana,* formerly *V. incana*) also has grey leaves but is taller and clump forming. Its spikes of violet blue flowers are 30 to 45 cm (12–18 in.) in height and bloom in July. 'Rosea' is a pink cultivar.

Culture: Speedwells prefer full sun and well-drained soils. Woolly speedwell can be rejuvenated after flowering by shearing.

Use: They are valued for their soft grey foliage and are useful as dense ground covers, among paving or patio stones, as edging, or in rock gardens. They are a bee nectar source.

Viola canadensis (Canada violet)

Viola is thought to be derived from the Latin word *via,* which means road or way. The implication is that these are flowers found along the way. The genus name *canadensis* means of Canada, to which they are native. The fragrant, white flowers, 25 to 38 cm (10–15 in.) in height, are produced above heart-shaped leaves. The plants spread by rhizomes and can be quite invasive.

Culture: Plant in shade and well-drained soil.

Use: Excellent as a ground cover in dry shade, or for naturalizing. In a shady border they are too aggressive.

ψ *Viola tricolor* (johnny-jump-up)

Native to Europe, johnny-jump-ups are biennial in nature. They have escaped from cultivation and become naturalized in much of North America. The species name, *tricolor,* means of three colors and describes these small blue, yellow, and white blossoms. Only 10 to 15 cm (4–6 in.) in height, they flower through most of the summer. They have been used in the breeding of many of the modern pansies.

Culture: Johnny-jump-ups will grow in sun or shade in any sort of soil.

Use: Useful for naturalizing or the wild garden. They self-seed too readily for a perennial border or rock garden.

Ψ *Yucca glauca* (yucca, small soapweed)

Yucca is the Caribbean name for a plant that early botanists thought it resembled. The species name, *glauca*, means glaucous—grey-blue or covered with a powdery bloom. The common name alludes to the early use of the roots in soap. A member of the lily family, yucca is grown primarily for its evergreen foliage: narrow, stiff, grey-green leaves with shedding white margins and tipped with very sharp spines. The creamy white flowers are bell-shaped, pendulous, and produced on 60 to 90 cm (2–3 ft) stalks in July. It has deep roots and is native to the Dakotas, Montana, and southern Alberta.

Culture: A desert plant, yucca does best on well-drained soils in full sun, but will only flower in response to adequate moisture. It will not tolerate heavy, wet soils. The flowers are fertilized by the pronuba moth, which deposits her eggs where the seed pod will develop, assuring her larvae of a reliable food source upon hatching. The larvae consume some of the flat, black seeds, but generally leave enough to per-petuate the plant.

Use: Because of its unusual form and texture, yucca is an exceptional accent plant in the rock garden, or as a ground cover for hot, dry locations. Cattle browse buds and flowers if given the opportunity.

Sara Williams

Gail Rankin

Brian Porter

Celastrus scandens (American bittersweet)

Native to North America, bittersweet is seldom seen in prairie gardens, which is unfortunate. The genus name is derived from the Greek *kelastros*, meaning late season, a reference to the prolonged retention of the fruit. *Scandens* means climbing. The flowers are small and white. The orange fruit split to reveal scarlet seeds, giving it unusual fall and winter landscape value. The oval, pointed leaves are bright yellow in the fall. A plant may produce male, female, or perfect flowers. To ensure fruit, plant several in close proximity.

Culture: Plant in full sun in a wide range of well-drained soils.

Use: Bittersweet is used to cover fences and pergolas, as a ground cover, and to hold slopes. The fruiting stems are attractive as winter bouquets and in dried arrangements, and the fruit is eaten by birds.

Brian Baldwin

Brian Baldwin

Top and bottom (detail): golden clematis

Clematis spp. (clematis)

Clematis is the Greek word for a climbing plant. Native to the northern temperate regions of the world, the small-flowered species of clematis and their hybrids are hardier and more drought tolerant than the larger-flowered types. The leaf stalks of these perennial vines act as tendrils, wrapping around whatever support is available, and the vines may reach 4 m (12 ft) or more.

Clematis ligusticifolia (western virgin's bower) is 4 m (12 ft) in height. Native to the prairies, it bears small white flowers, 2 cm (1 in.) in diameter, in late summer. It has pinnately compound leaves. It is dioecious. If plants of both sexes are grown in proximity, it can set copious quantities of seed.

Ψ *Clematis tangutica* (golden clematis) is native to northwest China and has nodding, soft yellow, bell-shaped flowers in midsummer followed by silvery, feather-like seed heads. It is 3 m (9 ft) or more in height and very vigorous.

Clematis macropetala (big petal clematis) has been used to produce many attractive hybrids. The species name, *macropetala*, means with large petals. Since clematis have no true petals this is a reference to the large, petal-like stamens. Introduced from China in 1910 by Reginald Farrar, the big petal clematis has great profusions of small, nodding, lavender blue flowers in May and June. It is 2.5 to 3.5 m (8–12 ft) high.

Among the hybrids are: • 'Bluebird,' with flat, outward-facing, deep blue flowers, 6 cm (2.5 in.) in diameter, blooming for up to eight weeks on new wood • *Clematis* x 'Blue Boy' (*C. macropetala* and *C. viticella*), a prolific bloomer of 2 m (6 ft), with 6 cm (2.5 in.), outward-facing, blue flowers produced over a long period in midsummer on new wood • Ψ *Clematis* x 'Rosy O'Grady' *(C. macropetala* and *C. alpina),* with large, dark pink flowers with long pointed sepals that bloom on old wood in May and June and on new wood in August • 'Maidwell Hall,' which has dark blue flowers with a purple tinge • 'Markham' (also listed as *C. markhamii* and 'Markham's Pink'), which has semi-double, pink, nodding flowers with white stamens • Ψ 'Prairie Travelers' Joy,' a very drought-tolerant selection, with star-like, white flowers produced over a long season • 'Snowbird,' which is pure white and late flowering • 'White Swan,' a profusely blooming, double, snow white hybrid with 12.5 cm (5 in.), nodding flowers on both old and new wood on a 2.5 m (8 ft) vine.

Clematis alpina is another species that has been used in the development of some excellent hybrids. From the mountains of southern Europe, the species is 2 to 2.5 m (6–8 ft) in height, with satiny, nodding, blue flowers blooming in May and June. Its hybrids may not be as drought tolerant as those of *C. macropetala* and will benefit from mulching and several deep waterings per season: • 'Francis Rivis,' a deep blue • 'Pamela Jackman,' a rich, mid-blue • 'Ruby,' with nodding, rosy-red blooms with white petaloid stamens • 'Willy,' a pale pink.

Culture: Plant clematis in full sun or partial shade in a deep, loamy soil to which peat moss has been added. Keep evenly moist through the first few growing seasons. Mulching is beneficial. Once established, they are surprisingly drought resistant. They will need a support on which to climb.

Use: Use clematis to cover an arbor or trellis, break up a large expanse of fence or wall, screen unsightly objects, or provide shade. They are also useful as a ground cover or to hold a slope.

Western virgin's bower

'Rosy O'Grady,' a pink introduction developed by Frank Skinner

Echinocystis lobata (wild cucumber)

Native to North America, including the Canadian prairies, wild cucumber is an annual vine capable of climbing up to 6 m (20 ft) in a long, warm growing season. The genus name comes from the Greek words *echinos*, hedgehog, and *krystis*, bladder, a reference to the 5 cm (2 in.), spiny, oval seed pods. The small, greenish-white flowers are inconspicuous and borne in midsummer. The lobed leaves are 7.5 to 13 cm (3–5 in.) across.

Culture: Wild cucumber thrives in hot weather. Plant in a warm location in full sun to partial shade. The tendrils will need some support to cling to.

Use: Often used to cover unsightly objects, it will also do well over a fence or trellis.

Brian Baldwin

Brian Baldwin

☙ *Humulus lupulus* (hops)

The genus name, *Humulus,* is from the same root as the word *humus,* meaning soil. Hops hug the soil and act as a ground cover when they have no support on which to climb. The species name, *lupulus,* means wolf, and comes from an older name, willow wolf, referring to its habit of climbing through willows. Native to the Qu'Appelle Valley, hops are a fast-growing, vigorous climber. They are herbaceous in habit, dying down to the snow line each winter, but are capable of quickly climbing 6 m (20 ft) or more in a single season. They climb by twining shoots and will form a dense cover.

The small, greenish-white flowers are produced in panicles in the leaf axils in June. The female flower matures to form a papery cone, known commonly as a hop, which imparts the characteristic bitter taste to beer. Male and female flowers are borne on separate plants. A plant of each sex is required to ensure fruit production.

Culture: Hops thrive on neglect. Plant in a sunny location on well-drained soil. If grown in the shade, flower and fruit production are reduced. Once established, it is heat and drought tolerant. It will need support.

Use: An excellent vine for screening or as a ground cover, hops have the added bonus of being a raw ingredient for beer. The perfect plant for the brewer turned gardener!

Sara Williams

Ipomoea tricolor (morning glory)

Native to Mexico, morning glories were used by the ancient Aztecs both as medicine and hallucinogens. They were introduced to Europe in the 1600s. Related to the sweet potato, they are fast-growing annual vines of 2.5–3.5 m (8–12 ft), with large, heart-shaped leaves. The species name, *tricolor,* is a reference to the flowers, which are trumpet-like, 8 to 12 cm (3–5 in.) in diameter, single or double, in white, blue, purple, red, or pink, with a white throat. Older cultivars close at midday, but many newer cultivars remain open until dusk. All plant parts are said to be poisonous.

Culture: Morning glories prefer full sun and poorer soils. Richer soils and too much water or fertilizer results in lush growth and few flowers. The vines are surprisingly heavy and need sturdy support around which to twine, whether fencing, lattice, or trellis.

Use: Use to screen unsightly objects, break up expanses of fence, as a ground cover, and in boxes and hanging baskets.

Lonicera x brownii 'Dropmore Scarlet Trumpet' ('Dropmore Scarlet Trumpet' honeysuckle)

'Dropmore Scarlet Trumpet' is a woody vine introduced by Dr. Frank Skinner of Dropmore, Manitoba, in 1950. A hybrid of *Lonicera sempervirens* and a *L. hirsuta* collected in northern Minnesota, the flowers are sterile. They begin blooming in June and continue less profusely until frost. It is 3 m (9 ft) in height, with clusters of bright orange, trumpet-shaped flowers.

Culture: Plant in full sun or partial shade in a loamy soil, well amended with organic matter. In shadier locations, flowering will be reduced. Mulching is recommended. Keep evenly moist during establishment. Netting or trellis is needed to support the twining stems.

Use: It is excellent on a lattice or trellis.

Ψ *Parthenocissus quinquefolia* (Virginia creeper)

The genus name is from the Greek *parthenos* (virgin) and *kissos* (ivy), which is also a rough translation of the common name. The species name, *quinquefolia*, means five leaves and describes the palmately compound leaves. Virginia creeper is known for its brilliant scarlet fall color. It is an extremely vigorous woody vine, climbing to 15 m (50 ft) or more. The flowers are inconspicuous. The fruit is a small, blue berry that resembles a grape. It climbs by tendrils, which will need a support of wire or netting.

    Parthenocissus quinquefolia var. *engelmannii* (Engelman's ivy) differs from the species in that it is less susceptible to powdery mildew, and it has holdfasts or "adhesive pads" at the ends of each tendril, allowing it to climb without additional support. It may damage painted surfaces.

Culture: Plant in full sun or partial shade in a variety of soils. Powdery mildew and leaf hoppers are sometimes a problem.

Use: It will cover a large expanse of wall very quickly, and can also be used as a ground cover or over a large arbor.

Right: fall color

Tropaeolum majus (nasturtium)

Its nomenclature is somewhat warlike. The genus name is from the Latin *trapaeum*, meaning a trophy. The flowers are said to resemble helmets, and the leaves, shields. The common name is from the Latin *nasus*, nose, and *tortum*, twist, which would describe one's face after tasting the leaves and

National Garden Bureau

flowers, which contain mustard oil and have a tangy, peppery flavor. These annual vines are native to the highlands of Mexico and Chile. In cultivation for over three centuries, they are most recently being marketed for use in salads.

The flowers are funnel-shaped, single or double, in yellow, orange, pink, and red. Some are fragrant. The vines are 0.5 to 3.5 m (1–12 ft) in height. The leaves are round, with veins radiating from their centers.

Culture: Plant in full sun in well-drained soil. Nasturtiums climb and cling with twisting leaf stalks on string, wire, trellis, or fence. Excess fertilizer or rich soil reduces flowering. Flea beetles are sometimes a problem.

Use: Taller selections are used for screening and over trellises, dwarf types in beds, hanging baskets, and boxes. Both are useful as ground covers.

Brian Baldwin

Brian Baldwin

ψ *Vitis riparia* (riverbank grape, Manitoba grape)

The genus name, *Vitis*, is the Latin word for grapes. Both the species and common names allude to their presence on river banks using nearby trees as support. Native to the prairies, Manitoba grape is a vigorous, woody climber reaching up to 5.5 m (18 ft). Grown primarily for its foliage, it does produce small, blue fruit suitable for jams and jellies. Plants are dioecious, so male and female plants must be nearby to ensure fruit production. It climbs using tendrils, which need support.

The hybrids 'Beta' and 'Valiant' produce superior fruit but require a more sheltered location and even moisture. These cultivars are not dioecious, so only one plant is required.

Culture: Plant in sun or partial shade in a loamy soil to which organic matter has been added. Mulch is beneficial. Even moisture is needed during the first few years. Once established, the species is drought-resistant. Leafhoppers and powdery mildew are sometimes problems.

Use: Riverbank grape is excellent for covering a large expanse of wall, as a "garden ceiling" for a large arbor, or as a ground cover.

Allium spp. (ornamental onion, allium)

Allium is from the Latin word for garlic. Attractive, drought-tolerant, long-lived, and trouble-free, alliums are among the most under used hardy bulbs available to prairie gardeners. Related to lilies, there are over 600 species worldwide.

Most of the alliums grown in prairie gardens are from Asia. Colors include white, pink, yellow, red, purple, and blue. Heights range from 25 to 90 cm (10–36 in.). • *Allium aflatunense* (aflatun onion) is drumstick in shape, with lilac-purple or light violet flowers, 6 to 10 cm (2.5–4 in.) in diameter, in May and June. It is 45 to 75 cm (17–30 in.) in height, with strap-shaped leaves. • *Allium caeruleum*, formerly *A. azureum* (blue globe or Azure onion), has deep blue, globular flowers (described by the species name, which means dark blue), 3 to 4 cm (1–1.5 in.) in diameter, on 30 to 60 cm (12–24 in.) stems in June. • *Allium flavum* (the Latin word for yellow) has graceful, lemon-yellow florets which form the umbel and are tier-like in effect, with the center ones erect and the outer ones falling. It is 40 cm (16 in.) high, blooming in late summer. • *Allium karataviense*, named after a mountain range in Kazakhstan, is only 25 cm (10 in.), but has one of the largest flower heads of the hardy onions. The spherical, pale pink or purple flower heads, which bloom in early spring, are 7 to 10 cm (3–4 in.) in diameter and composed of star-shaped florets. The broad basal leaves are grey-purple. • *Allium moly* (golden garlic) has star-like, buttercup yellow flowers in early spring on 30 cm (12 in.) stems above wide, grey-green basal leaves. • *Allium oreophilum*, formerly *A. ostrowskianum* (ostrowsky onion), has carmine pink flowers on 15 to 20 cm (6–8 in.) stems in midsummer above graceful, curled leaves. *Oreophilum* means mountain-loving; it is native to the Caucasus Mountains and Turkey into Iran and Afghanistan. 'Zwanenburg' is a deeper pink. • *Allium* x 'Purple Sensation' has bright purple flowers, 10 cm (4 in.) in diameter, which bloom in early summer on 90 cm (36 in.) stems. • *Allium schoenoprasum* (chives) forms dense clumps, 30 to 45 cm (12–18 in.) high, with pink flowers 2 to 5 cm (1–2 in.) in diameter. The species name is from the Greek *schoinos* (a rush) and *prasum* (leek) and describes the rush-like, edible leaves. 'Forescate' has deeper pink flowers. • *Allium senescens* has small, mauve-lilac flowers on 45 to 60 cm (18–24 in.) stems above glossy leaves in late summer. • *Allium sphaerocephalon*, native to Europe, Asia, and North Africa, has drumstick-shaped flowers the color of red wine; they bloom in midsummer on 60 cm (24 in.) stems. The species name is from the Greek word for round head.

Culture: Plant in full sun on well-drained soil.

Use: Use in fresh or dried arrangements, the perennial or mixed border, and the rock garden.

Above:
Allium flavum
Right:
Allium karataviense

Sara Williams

Sara Williams

Sara Williams

Above:
Allium x 'Purple Sensation'
Right:
Allium oreophilum

International Flower Bulb Center

Siberian fritillary

Sara Williams

ψ *Fritillaria* spp. (fritillary)

Native to central Asia, the Siberian fritillary *(F. pallidiflora)* is the most hardy and widely grown fritillary on the prairies. The genus name is from the Latin *fritillus,* a dicebox, a reference to the checkered flowers of some species. The word *pallidiflora* means pale flower. Up to 30 cm (12 in.) in height, it soon forms large clumps of nodding, soft yellow, bell-like flowers, blooming in early spring. It is a terrific plant, and under used. *F. michailowski,* native to Turkey and equally hardy, is only 15 cm (6 in.) in height, with nodding, purple-bronze bells edged in yellow in spring. *F. persica* and *F. meleagris* are only marginally hardy. The widely marketed *F. imperialis* is *not* hardy on the prairies.

Culture: Plant in sun or shade in any well-drained soil.

Use: They soon naturalize in a mixed or perennial border, appearing in unexpected but always welcome places.

'Red Carpet'

Allan Daku

'Happy Thoughts'

Allan Daku

Lilium spp. (lily)

Most of the lilies grown in prairie gardens are hybrids of Asiatic species. Their ancestors originated in Asia in a very similar climate. They vary in height from 25 to 150 cm (10–60 in.) and come in a generous range of colors, blooming variously from June to late August.

The following lilies are tried and true: • **White:** 'Sterling Star' (1.2 m/4 ft), 'Blizzard,' also called 'Apollo' (0.9 m/3 ft), 'Snow Bird' (1 m/3.25 ft), 'Happy Thoughts' (1 m/3.25 ft) • **Yellow:** 'Connecticut King' (75 cm/30 in.), 'Yellow Joy' (1.1 m/3.5 ft), 'Kenora' (1.2 m/4 ft), 'Dreamland' (1 m/3.25 ft), 'Spacious Living' (1.2 m/4 ft), 'Amulet' (1 m/3.25 ft), 'Yellow Blaze' (1.2 m/4 ft), 'Destiny' (1 m/3.25 ft) • **Peach:** 'Tiger Babies' (1.5 m/5 ft), 'Peach Pixie' (40 cm/16 in.) • **Orange:** *L. lancifolium* (or *L. tigrinum),* the tiger lily (0.9 m/3 ft), 'Bingo' (60 cm/24 in.), 'Honey Bear' (40 cm/16 in.), 'Avignon' (0.9 m/3 ft), 'Pirate' (0.9 m/3 ft), 'Jolanda' (1.5 m/5 ft), 'Kismet' (1.2 m/4 ft), 'Earlibird' (75 cm/30 in.), 'Maxwill' (1.2 m/4 ft) • **Pink:** 'Carol Jean' (45 cm/18 in.), 'Malta' (0.9 m/3 ft), 'Tristar' (0.9 m/3 ft), 'Embarrassment' (1.3 m/4.25 ft), 'Appleblossom' (1 m/3.25 ft) • **Red:** 'Rhodes' (0.9 m/3 ft), 'Red Torch' (50 cm/20 in.), 'Wanda' (1 m/3.25 ft), 'Bold Knight' (1.2 m/4 ft), 'Red Carpet' (40 cm/16 in.), 'Red Velvet' (1.2 m/4 ft).

Culture: Grow in full sun in deep, well-drained soil in which organic matter has been incorporated. Fertilize with bonemeal, 5–10–0, or 5–10–10 in early spring just prior to the stems emerging. Botrytis is sometimes a problem.

Use: Lilies are excellent in the perennial border, in a mixed border, and as cut flowers.

Scilla sibirica (squill)

The genus name is from the Greek *skilla*, meaning sea-squill, an old-fashioned house plant to which *Scilla* are related. The species name, *sibirica*, indicates its origin. Sometimes called bluebells, Siberian squills are 15 cm (6 in.) in height and one of the earliest harbingers of spring, blooming in May. 'Spring Beauty' is darker, taller, and more robust. 'Taurica' is a more intense blue. A white form, 'Alba,' is also available. Given moderately favorable conditions, they soon colonize through reseeding.

Culture: Plant in full sun in well-drained soil.

Use: These small bulbs are excellent in the rock garden.

Brian Baldwin

Tulipa (tulip)

Tulipa is from the Turkish *tulbend*, a turban. Native to the Near East, they were cultivated and hybridized in Turkish gardens for centuries prior to their introduction to Europe in the 1500s.

Tulips come in a wide range of colors, shapes, and heights. Cultivars vary in hardiness and durability depending on microclimate and the particular winter. Most perform well the first spring after planting and then gradually decline. Tulips classified as single early and Darwin are generally the most reliable and long-lasting. Single early tulips bloom early, and are 25 to 40 cm (10–16 in.) in height. Darwins have long, slender stems and large, globe-like flowers, and are the most reliable, blooming later and avoiding late spring frosts.

Of the shorter species tulips, the following are considered both hardy and reliable. All of these are from Asia and will form colonies through self-seeding and bulb offsets. • Ψ *Tulipa tarda*, from central Asia, is 10 to 15 cm (4–6 in.) in height, with yellow, white-tipped blooms. No garden should be without it! *Tarda* means late, perhaps because it blooms later than other bulbs in its native habitat. • *Tulipa kolpakowskiana*, also from central Asia, is 15 cm (6 in.) in height with a curved flower stem and orange-yellow petals which may be purple on the outside. • Ψ *Tulipa urumiensis*, native to Lake Urumia in Iran, is 12 cm (5 in.) in height and has yellow petals which may be olive or red on the outside. • The multi-flowered *Tulipa turkestanica*, from Turkestan, has pointed, white petals with an orange-yellow center and is 20 cm (8 in.) in height.

Culture: Tulips need full sun and good drainage. Plant bulbs in the fall. Darwins should be planted 15 to 20 cm (6–8 in.) deep, and shorter species more shallowly. Divide every three years.

Use: Tulips add spring color to a perennial or mixed border and are often used in annual beds. The species are shorter and well adapted to rock garden plantings.

Above: Darwin tulips
Right: Tulipa tarda
Below: Tulipa urumiensis

Sara Williams

Brian Baldwin

Sara Williams

Bulbs

Sara Williams

Ageratum houstonianum (ageratum, flossflower)

Ageratum, from a Greek phrase for not growing old, refers to the long-lasting color of the cut flowers. The species name honors William Houston (1695–1733), a Scottish physician who collected plants in Central America. Low in stature (13–30 cm/5–12 in.) and long in bloom, ageratum is covered in fluffy clouds of tiny blue, pink, or white flowers from early summer until frost. The plant is mound-like in form, with heart-shaped leaves. Among the recommended cultivars are 'Dwarf Blue Bedder,' 15 cm (6 in.); 'Blue Mink,' 25 to 30 cm (10–12 in.) in height, with larger, powder blue flowers; 'Bavaria,' a bicolor of white and powder blue of 36 cm (14 in.); 'Summer Snow,' only 13 cm (5 in.) and white; 'Blue Horizon,' one of the taller ageratums at 75 cm (30 in.), with large flower clusters; 'Adriatic,' an early blue of 20 cm (8 in.); 'Madison,' 20 cm (8 in.), free-flowering, and mid-blue.

Culture: Plant in full sun to light shade, in organic but well-drained soil. Although drought tolerant, they will have better bloom with more even moisture. Pinch for a more compact plant. Native to Mexico and Central America, ageratum are very frost tender.

Use: Dwarf ageratums are ideal for edging, containers, and as winter house plants. Taller types are used in drifts in borders and as cut flowers. They are butterfly nectar plants, and the seeds are eaten by finches and juncos.

Sara Williams

Ψ *Amaranthus caudatus* (love-lies-bleeding, tassel flower)

The Greek word *amarantos* means unfading and alludes to the long-lasting flowers. The species name, *caudatus,* means with a tail, a description of the long, drooping flowers. Native to India, and a close relative of redroot pigweed, the flowers are blood-red, rope-like panicles hanging from plants 60 to 120 cm (24–48 in.) in height, which, of course, give the plant its rather melodramatic common name. The cultivar 'Green Thumb' is 40 to 60 cm (15–24 in.), with green panicles.

Culture: Plant in full sun on poorer, well-drained soils. They are very drought- and heat-tolerant. Excessive moisture or poor drainage may cause root rot. Transplant with as little disturbance to the root ball as possible.

Use: Love-lies-bleeding is well-placed in an annual or mixed border. It is also used in fresh and dried arrangements. As a focal point, it often invites comments.

ѱ *Ammobium alatum* (winged everlasting)

The genus name is derived from the Greek *ammos* (sand) and *bio* (to live), meaning a plant that lives in sand, a reference to its native habitat in Australia, where it is a perennial. *Alatum* describes the winged stems. Small yellow daisies are produced on branched stems of 45 to 90 cm (18–36 in.) with grey, felty leaves. 'Grandiflora' has white flowers with yellow centers, 5 cm (2 in.) in diameter.

Culture: Plant in sandy to loam soils in full sun.

Use: Winged everlastings are generally grown as everlasting flowers. The white flowers are especially valued because they do not fade with age. Cut stems just before the flowers open and hang them upside-down.

B. J. Godwin

Anagallis monelli var. *linifolia* (flaxleaf pimpernel)

Anagallis, which means delightful, was the Greek common name for this plant. *Linifolia* means narrow leaved. Native to the Mediterranean, where it is a perennial, flaxleaf pimpernel produces clusters of tiny blue, purple, or red flowers on plants 15 to 45 cm (6–18 in.) in height. Blue petals with reddish undersides are common. 'Phillipsii' is 30 cm (12 in.) in height, with deep gentian blue flowers. 'Gentian Blue' is a compact plant of only 15 to 23 cm (6–9 in.) with a profusion of blue flowers.

Culture: Plant in full sun on well-drained soil.

Use: Place toward the front of an annual or mixed border, in a rock garden, as edging, or in containers or hanging baskets.

Brian Porter

ѱ *Arctotis stoechadifolia* (blue-eyed African daisy)

The genus name is derived from the Greek words *arktos* (bear) and *otos* (ear); the seed is supposed to resemble a bear's ear. Native to South Africa, these daisy-like flowers are 7.5 cm (3 in.) in diameter, with blue centers rimmed in gold. The petals range from white through cream, yellow, pink, mauve, wine, and red, with lavender undersides. The finely cut foliage is grey, and plants are from 30 to 60 cm (12–24 in.) in height. A tender perennial, it is treated as an annual.

Culture: Plant in sandy soil and full sun. They perform well where nights are cool.

Use: Use in annual and mixed beds.

Steven Still

Mexican poppy

Gail Rankin

ψ *Argemone grandiflora* and *Argemone mexicana* (prickly and Mexican poppies)

The genus name is from the Greek word *argema,* meaning cataract, which this plant was once used to treat. The word *grandiflora* means large-flowered. Native to the deserts of Mexico, both plants are considered poisonous. The prickly poppy has silky, white flowers up to 10 cm (4 in.) in diameter, prickly leaves, and a height of 1 m (3 ft). The Mexican poppy has yellow to orange flowers, 5 to 6 cm (2–2.5 in.) in diameter, and is 0.5 to 1 m (2–3 ft) tall. Its leaves have minute spines on the edges, and some forms have white-spotted foliage. 'Yellow Luster' is 40 to 50 cm (15–20 in.) high with pale orange to lemon flowers and foliage veined in silver.

Culture: Grow in light, sandy soil in full sun.

Use: They are well suited to an annual or mixed border.

Calendula officinalis (calendula, pot marigold)

Calendula is from a Latin phrase meaning throughout the months, a reference to its long blooming period. The word *officinalis* means of the pharmacopoeia and refers to its past medicinal use for ulcers, cuts, bruises, and warts. Native to the Mediterranean and southern Europe, calendulas have long been a favorite in rural prairie gardens. They bear large, daisy-like flowers in shades of orange, apricot, yellow, and cream. The flowers close at night. Plants are upright, 30 to 45 cm (12–18 in.) in height, with a spread of 30 to 60 cm (1–2 ft). All plant parts are strongly aromatic when crushed. 'Pacific Beauty Mixed' is 45 cm (18 in.) in height, with long-stemmed, double flowers in shades from cream to red. 'Mandarin' is a newer orange hybrid. 'Bon Bon' is an early, free-flowering, dwarf hybrid of 30 cm (12 in.). 'Prince' is long-stemmed and 60 to 75 cm (24–30 in.).

Culture: Plant in full sun or light shade in poorer soils with good drainage. Calendulas are heat- and drought-tolerant. Deadhead for continuous bloom. Aster yellows, a viral disease, is sometimes a problem.

Use: Use in annual borders, cottage gardens, for mass bedding, and in containers. The flowers have long been used as a dye (not so long ago to color butter) and both flowers and leaves are used in salads and stews. It is a butterfly nectar plant.

Catharanthus roseus (vinca, Madagascar periwinkle)

Native from Madagascar to India, vinca is becoming more widely used by prairie gardeners. *Catharanthus* is from a Greek phrase meaning a pure flower. *Roseus* means rose-colored. The single, pink-centered flowers are available in white, pink, rose, lavender, and purple. The pointed leaves are a glossy dark-green. Plants are up to 30 cm (12 in.) in height, with a spread of twice that. All plant parts are poisonous.

'Polka Dot,' an All-America Selections winner, is an extremely dwarf plant that has white flowers with cherry-red centers. 'Vinca Parasol,' another AAS winner, is bigger, with larger flowers and overlapping petals. 'Little Linda' is very floriferous, with deep rose-pink flowers. 'Pretty in Rose,' also an AAS winner, has velvety, rose-purple flowers. 'Apricot Delight' is a unique color on compact, early-blooming plants.

Culture: Plant in full sun or partial shade in sandy loam soils.

Use: Use in beds, baskets, and containers, and as ground covers.

All-America Selections

Celosia cristata (cockscomb)

Celosia is from the Greek word *kelos,* meaning burned, and describes the brilliant flower color. Both the common and species names allude to the crested form of the flowers, which resemble the comb of a rooster. Native to tropical Asia, the velvety flowers have also been described as resembling coral or the human brain. Colors range from pink, red, orange, and salmon through to gold and white. Flowers are long-lasting (up to two months!). Plants vary from 15 to 60 cm (6–24 in.) in height, with green or bronze foliage. 'Jewel Box' is dwarf and used for edging. 'Toreador' is an All-America Selections winner of 45 to 50 cm (18–20 in.) with huge combs. 'Fireglow' and 'Pink Castle' are AAS winners of the same height, with velvety, cardinal-red flowers. Cultivars such as 'Flamingo Feather' and 'Pink Feather' are useful in dried arrangements.

Culture: Although cockscomb prefer a fertile soil high in organic matter with even moisture, they are somewhat drought-tolerant once established. Mulching is beneficial. Plant in full sun or partial shade. These frost-tender tropical plants need an exceptionally long, hot summer to perform well.

Use: Cockscomb are well-suited to the front, middle, or back of a border. Dwarf types are used for edging. All are excellent in fresh or dried arrangements.

All-America Selections

Right: 'Pink Castle'

All-America Selections

Sara Williams

ψ *Centaurea cineraria* (dusty miller)

Native to Italy, the genus *Centaurea* was named after the mythical Greek centaurs, who were said to have used these plants to heal wounds. *Cineraria* means ashen grey, the color of the deeply lobed, felt-like leaves, which look a bit like a "dusty" miller covered in flour. Varying in height from 15 to 45 cm (6–18 in.), with a spread of about 20 cm (8 in.), these plants are grown mainly for their foliage. The purple flowers are small and inconspicuous. 'Silver Feather' has fine, delicate foliage, is compact, and 30 cm (12 in.) in height.

Culture: These heat- and drought-tolerant plants do well in full sun in well-drained soil such as sandy loam.

Use: Excellent for edging, bedding, and containers. The soft grey serves as a foil for the flamboyant colors of brighter annuals.

Sara Williams

ψ *Centaurea cyanus* (bachelor's button, cornflower)

An old-fashioned annual that has graced our gardens for centuries, cornflowers are native from Europe into western Asia. *Cyanus*, a Greek word for blue, refers to the flower color. Cornflowers were a common weed in wheat—which the British call corn—fields, hence the common name. The flowers are in shades of blue, purple, wine, deep rose, pink, and white, and up to 5 cm (2 in.) in diameter. The narrow leaves are grey-green. Plants vary in height from 30 to 90 cm (12–36 in.), with a spread of about 30 cm (12 in.).

Among the cultivars are 'Blue Diadem,' 60 cm (24 in.), with deep blue, double flowers; 'Frosty Mixed,' 16 cm (30 in.), a bicolor with white or pink contrasting petal tips; and 'Polka Dot,' a dwarf mixture of only 38 cm (15 in.). The Florence series, with 3 cm (1 in.) pink, white, and blue flowers, is well-suited to containers.

Culture: Cornflowers thrive in poorer, well-drained soils in full sun or partial shade. Deadhead for prolonged bloom.

Use: Use in the annual border, cottage garden, for naturalizing in a back lane or wildflower garden, and for cut flowers.

ψ *Chrysanthemum parthenium* (feverfew, matricaria)

A perennial usually treated as an annual on the prairies, this old-fashioned plant is native to Europe and Asia. The genus name is from the Greek *chrysos* (gold) and *anthos* (flower).

Used to relieve fevers in ancient times, feverfew ranges in height from 15 to 60 cm (6–24 in.) and is covered in masses of small, white, double flowers, each with a button-like yellow center. The leaves are scented. 'Butterball' is 15 to 25 cm (6–10 in.), with large, golden-yellow flowers with white edging. 'Snowball' has pure white flowers on dwarf (20 cm/8 in.), compact, bushy plants. 'White Stars' is mound-shaped, only 15 cm (6 in.), with star-shaped, white flowers. 'White Wonder' is 30 cm (12 in.), with double flowers on compact plants.

Culture: Feverfew tolerates poor soil, in full sun or partial shade.

Use: Good for naturalizing in a wildflower garden or back lane, it is also used as edging, in an annual or mixed border, for a cottage garden, in pots and containers, and as a cut flower.

Clarkia unguiculata (clarkia, garland flower)

Clarkia was named after Captain William Clark (1770–1838), co-leader of the Lewis and Clark expedition, which explored the area from Louisiana to the Pacific Ocean. The species name, *unguiculata*, means narrow-clawed and describes the base of the petals. Native to California, clarkia is an upright plant of 0.5 to 0.75 m (2–2.5 ft). The long racemes of single or double flowers, each with four clawed petals, are in white, pink, red, and purple, and about 8 cm (2.5 in.) in diameter.

Culture: They grow best in full sun or partial shade on a dry, sandy loam. Pinch growing points when young to encourage bushiness. They do well under crowded conditions and with cool prairie nights. Do not fertilize with nitrogen. They suffer during hot weather and may be better planted in partial shade.

Use: Excellent in the border, as mass plantings, and cut flowers.

Ψ *Cleome hasslerana* (cleome, spider flower)

Cleome is presumably from the Greek word *kleos,* meaning glory, alluding to the beauty of the flowers. The common name is derived from the long, protruding stamens, which resemble the legs of a spider. Native to Brazil and Argentina, this stately (up to 2 m/6 ft), old-fashioned annual has a soft, airy appearance, with fragrant flowers in shades of white, pink, rose, and purple, followed by decorative seed pods. The leaves are attractive, strongly scented, and palmately compound, with sharp, back-curving spines. 'Helen Campbell' is 90 cm (36 in.) in height, with glistening, pure white flowers. The Queen series are similar in height in pink, rose, and purple.

Steven Still

Culture: Cleomes prefer well-drained soil in full sun to partial shade.

Use: Mass toward the rear of a border or the center of an island bed, or use as a summer hedge, an accent plant, to screen unsightly objects, and as cut flowers. Cleome is a nectar source for bees and hummingbirds, and the seed is eaten by finches and juncos.

Sara Williams

Ψ *Coreopsis tinctoria* (calliopsis, tickseed, coreopsis)

The Greek word *koris* means bug; *opsis* means like. As the common name tickseed suggests, the seeds resemble bugs. *Tinctoria* means used for dyeing, an early use of the flower heads. Native to the central and western United States, these somewhat sprawling plants range in height from 20 to 90 cm (8–36 in.). The long-stemmed, single, daisy-like flowers are in bright shades of yellow, orange, brown, pink, purple, and red, with some bicolor or banded cultivars. The flowers are 2.5 to 5 cm (1–2 in.) in diameter, with notched or toothed petals. Generally available in catalogues as dwarf mixed or tall mixed types, 'Tiger Flower Improved' is a dwarf, compact bicolor of 20 to 23 cm (8–9 in.), and 'Early Sunrise' is an AAS winner, with early, semi-double flowers, 5 cm (2 in.) in diameter.

Culture: Coreopsis need full sun and good drainage and tolerate poor soil.

Use: Use taller types on sunny banks, in waste spaces, for massing, as cut flowers, or naturalized in a wildflower garden or back lane, and shorter types in beds and borders, as well as for edging.

Sara Williams

Cosmos bipinnatus (cosmos)

Kosmos is the Greek word for beautiful and orderly. *Bipinnatus* refers to the attractive, finely divided foliage. Native to Mexico, this tall (1–2 m/4–6 ft), old-fashioned annual produces single, daisy-like flowers, 8 to 10 cm (3–4 in.) in diameter, with yellow centers and pink, red, violet, lavender, or white petals. Cultivars include: 'Versailles Tetra,' with deep slate pink flowers; 'Purity,' with white flowers; 'Candy Stripe,' 75 cm (30 in.), with white petals edged with crimson; 'Sonata,' with single flowers in white, red, pink, and rose; 'Sunny Red,' a *C. sulphureus* hybrid and AAS winner, only 30 cm (12 in.) in height, with single, bright red flowers; the

Ladybird series, also *C. sulphureus* hybrids, with semi-double flowers in yellow, orange, and red.

Culture: Plant in full sun on poor, well-drained soils. Taller types may require staking. Do not fertilize.

Use: Plant taller cultivars in a border, cottage garden, or waste spaces. Use dwarf cultivars for edging and bedding. Use as cut flowers. Cosmos is a bee and butterfly nectar plant.

Ψ *Cynoglossum amabile* (Chinese forget-me-not, hound's tongue)

The genus name comes from the Greek words *kyon,* meaning dog, and *glossa,* meaning tongue. Like "hound's tongue," it refers to the texture and shape of the leaves. *Amabile* means lovely. A biennial, it produces a profusion of small, blue flowers the first year from seed. Native to eastern Asia, it is 45 to 60 cm (18–24 in.) in height, with blue, pink, and white flowers. 'Firmament' has deep indigo blue flowers on dwarf plants. 'Snow Bird' is white. 'Avalanche' has white flowers on dwarf, compact plants of 40 to 45 cm (16–18 in.). 'Blue Showers' is slightly higher, 60 to 75 cm (24–30 in.), with grey-green foliage. 'Mystery Rose' is 38 to 45 cm (15–18 in.), with white flowers with a hint of pink.

Louis Lenz

Culture: Grow in full sun or partial shade, in hot, dry locations.

Use: Use in mixed or annual borders, a cottage garden, or for naturalizing. It makes a dainty and fragrant cut flower.

Ψ *Datura* spp. (trumpet flower, angel's trumpet)

Native to southwest China, *Datura metel* (trumpet flower) grows to 1.5 m (5 ft), and has large leaves and fragrant, trumpet-shaped, mostly white, single or double flowers which open in the late afternoon or evening. *Datura* is from the common name used in India. *Metel* is the common name used in China. All plant parts are poisonous. 'Huberana' has blue, yellow, or red flowers. 'Alba' is white, 'Caerulea' blue, and 'Ivory King' creamy yellow. 'Belle Blanche' is pure white, 80 cm (32 in.) in height, and suitable for large pots. 'Double Golden Queen' is 1 to 1.5 m (3–5 ft).

Datura inoxia (angel's trumpet) is native to Mexico and the United States. *Inoxia* means without spines. It reaches 90 cm (3 ft), with single or double flowers in white, pink, and lavender.

Sara Williams

Culture: Grow in rich but well-drained soil in full sun.

Use: Datura can be used as specimen plants, in annual or mixed borders, in large containers, or as an annual hedge.

Steven Still

Dianthus chinensis (China pink, dianthus)

From the Greek *dios* (divine) and *anthos* (of flowers), the genus name aptly describes this flower's beauty and fragrance. The species name, *chinensis*, reflects its Asian origin. Dianthus are dwarf, compact, mounded plants only 30 cm (12 in.) in height, with grey-blue, grassy foliage. Because many of the annual cultivars are hybrids of annual and perennial types, they may live three or four years, especially when snow cover is adequate. The fragrant flowers are 2.5 cm (1 in.) in diameter, with fringed petals in shades of white, red, pink, lilac, and purple, with many bicolors.

Cultivars include: 'Fire Carpet,' with 5 cm (2 in.) flowers in vermilion-scarlet; the Princess series, only 20 cm (8 in.) in height, which are ideal for edging and containers; 'Black and White Minstrels,' with blackish crimson petals with white tips; 'Snowfire,' a 20 cm (8 in.) bicolor with fringed, white petals and cherry red centers; 'Bravo,' a scarlet AAS winner found growing wild in Japan; the Parfait series, with 5 cm (2 in.) flowers that bloom early, continuously, and prolifically and may persist for years; and the Ideal series, also an AAS winner.

Culture: Dianthus are tolerant of poor soil. Plant in full sun to light shade.

Use: Use as cut flowers, in borders, and as mass plantings. The shorter cultivars are ideal for edging, container planting, and in the rock garden. They are a hummingbird nectar plant.

Sara Williams

ψ *Dimorphotheca sinuata* (African daisy, cape marigold, star-of-the-veldt)

The genus name, *Dimorphotheca*, comes from the Greek words *di* (twice), *morphe* (shape), and *theka* (fruit or receptacle), a reference to the two types of seeds produced by the ray and disc flowers. The species name, *sinuata*, means with a wavy edge and describes the leaf margin. Native to South Africa, African daisies have shimmering, daisy-like flowers with white, cream, yellow, orange, or salmon petals with darker centers. They close at night or when it is cloudy. The plants are 30 to 75 cm (12–30 in.) in height. 'Tetra Pole Star' is 38 to 45 cm (15–18 in.) in height and spread, with 8 cm (3 in.) flowers with white petals and violet centers. 'Star Shine' is a compact, mound-like plant with 5 to 8 cm (2–3 in.) flowers of pink, rose, or white with a yellow eye.

Culture: Grow in full sun in hot, dry, well-drained soil.

Use: They are excellent in containers, massed in the border, or in rock gardens.

ψ *Dorotheanthus bellidiformis* (livingstone daisy)

Dr. Martin Schwantes named the genus after his mother, Dorothea. *Bellidiformis* is a reference to its similarity to *Bellis perennis*, the English daisy. The common name suggests its resemblance to small stones. Succulent, frost-tender plants from South Africa, they have daisy-like flowers, 2.5 to 5 cm (1-2 in.) in diameter, with dark centers and crimson, white, pink, purple, yellow, buff, apricot, or orange petals. Low and spreading, they are 20 to 30 cm (8–12 in.) in height. 'Magic Carpet Mixed' is available in mixed colors with flowers 8 cm (3 in.) in diameter. 'Lunette' and 'Yellow Ice' are yellow.

Culture: Plant in full sun on sandy, well-drained soils.

Use: Ideal in hot, dry areas of a rock garden, as edging, and container plants.

ψ *Dyssodia tenuiloba* (Dahlberg daisy, golden fleece)

The genus name, *Dyssodia*, comes from the Greek phrase meaning evil-smelling and refers to the attractive but odoriferous foliage. The species, *tenuiloba*, means narrow lobed, and also describes the finely divided leaves. Native to Texas and Mexico, the Dahlberg daisy is a spreading, bushy plant of 20 to 30 cm (8–12 in.) in height, with pungent, fern-like leaves, and a profusion of small yellow daisies.

Culture: Dahlberg daisies thrive in light, well-drained soil, in full sun and heat but where nights are cooler.

Use: Use for edging, annual or mixed borders, the rock garden, or as a cut flower.

ψ *Emilia javanica* (tassel flower)

The Emile honored by the genus name remains unknown. It is native not only to Java (from which the species name is derived) but to the tropics of both hemispheres. The common name is very apt, as the bright orange-red flowers look very much like the tassels with which formal drapery is held. The flowers are held on wiry stems, 45 to 60 cm (18–24 in.) in height, above the grey-green leaves. *Emilia javanica* var. *lutea* has yellow flowers.

Culture: They grow best in full sun on dry soil.

Use: Tassel flowers do well in an annual or mixed border or as cut flowers.

Steven Still

ψ *Eschscholzia californica* (California poppy)

The genus was named for Johann F. von Eschscholtz (1793–1831), a German naturalist who collected plants in California, South America, and the Pacific Islands. Native to the dry hills of California, they are 20 to 38 cm (8–15 in.) in height, with finely dissected, grey-green leaves. The satiny, single or double flowers are 5 to 8 cm (2–3 in.) in diameter, in white, lemon, gold, orange, salmon, pink, purple, and violet. Cultivars include 'Cherry Ripe,' a bright cerise; the compact 'Dalli,' scarlet; 'Milky Way,' with a butter-and-eggs appearance; and 'Thai Silk Mixed,' with fluted petals.

Culture: Plant in full sun to light shade on well-drained soil.

Use: Use in wildflower or cottage gardens and for naturalizing.

Sara Williams

ψ *Euphorbia marginata* (snow-on-the-mountain)

Euphorbus was a physician in ancient Mauritania. The word *marginata* refers to the white margins on the upper leaves. Native to the United States, snow-on-the-mountain is 60 cm (24 in.) in height, with grey-green leaves and bracts with distinctive white margins. The true flowers are inconspicuous. 'Summer Icicle' is a dwarf cultivar.

Culture: It tolerates heat and poor soil. Plant in full sun to light shade in well-drained soil.

Use: Use as a foil for brighter colors, as an accent plant in formal and cottage gardens, and for foliage in arrangements.

Brian Baldwin

Brian Baldwin

ψ *Gaillardia pulchella* var. *picta* (annual gaillardia, blanket flower)

The genus was named to honor a French patron of botany, M. Gaillard de Charentonneau. *Pulchella* means pretty. *Picta* means painted or brightly marked. Native to North America, blanket flowers produce single or double, daisy-like flowers about 5 cm (2 in.) in diameter in an autumnal array of colors: yellow, orange, red, brown, and bicolors, with purple centers. 'Double Mixed' is 60 cm (24 in.), with 8 cm (3 in.), double flowers in cream, gold, and crimson, as well as bicolors. 'Red Plume' is an AAS winner with double burgundy or brick red blooms on dwarf, compact plants. 'Double Lorenziana Mixed' has bell-shaped, double, crimson flowers with yellow tips.

Culture: Plant in full sun on a range of well-drained soils.

Use: Excellent in beds, borders, cottage gardens, containers, for naturalizing on dry banks or back lanes, and as cut flowers.

Gazania ringens (gazania)

The genus name honors Theodore of Gaza (1398–1478), who translated the botanical works of Theophrastus from Greek to Latin. *Ringens* means rigid and may refer to the stout bracts below the flowers. Native to South Africa, gazania has satiny, single flowers, 5 to 8 cm (2–3 in.) in diameter, in glowing shades of yellow, orange, bronze, pink, and white. They close at night and on cloudy days. The thick, dark green leaves have white undersides and are formed in basal rosettes. The Daybreak series are in shades of yellow through bronze.

Culture: Grow in well-drained soil in full sun. Water during extended hot periods. They are wind tolerant.

Use: Useful in borders, massed, in the rock garden, as edging, in containers, and brought indoors as a winter houseplant.

'Mini-Star'

Ψ *Gomphrena globosa* (globe amaranth)

Globosa describes the shape of the flowers. Native to India, globe amaranth range in height from 15 to 75 cm (6–30 in.), with almost iridescent, clover-like flowers in white, yellow, orange, pink, rose, and purple. Cultivars include: 'Dwarf Buddy,' 15 to 20 cm (6–8 in.) in height, with royal-purple flowers; 'Strawberry Fayre,' 60 cm (24 in.), in a strong red that is retained when dried; *G. haageana* 'Orange,' with apricot-orange flowers; 'Gnome,' 20 to 30 cm (8–12 in.), with pink, rose, purple, and white flowers; and 'Strawberry Field,' 38 cm (15 in.), with exceptionally large, red blossoms.

Culture: Plant in full sun in well-drained soil.

Use: Excellent in borders, rock gardens, cottage gardens, containers, as edging, and in fresh and dried arrangements. It retains its color for a long time.

Ψ *Gypsophila elegans* (annual babysbreath)

The genus name, from the Greek *gypsos* (gypsum) and *philos* (lover of), indicates its preference for alkaline soils. *Elegans* means elegant. The common name alludes to its sweet fragrance. Native to Europe and Asia, this old-fashioned annual is 45 to 60 cm (18–24 in.) in height, with masses of tiny flowers above small, narrow leaves. White-flowered cultivars include 'Covent Garden,' 'Giant White,' and 'Snow Fountain.' 'Rosea' has rose-pink flowers. 'Red Cloud' is shorter, with carmine to pink flowers. 'Garden Bride' is pink and only 30 cm (12 in.) high.

Culture: Plant in full sun on well-drained soil. Successive plantings ensure continuous bloom.

Use: Ideal in fresh and dried arrangements, they are also useful in the border, a cottage garden, and in containers.

'Italian White'

Sara Williams

ψ *Helianthus annuus* (sunflower)

Helios is the Greek word for sun, *anthos* for flower. The large, yellow flowers resemble the sun, and turn to follow it through the day. The edible seeds have long been used by Native peoples of North America. The common sunflower, ranging from 2 to 3 m (6–10 ft) or more in height, has huge yellow flowers. Newer cultivars are shorter, often branched, and in colors from white through yellow, orange, bronze, mahogany, purple, and red, including bicolors and single and double forms. 'Mammoth Russian' is 2 m (6.5 ft) in height, with 25 cm (10 in.), single, yellow flowers. 'Valentine' is 1 m (4 ft) and excellent as a cut flower. 'Color Fashion Mixed' is 2.5 m (8 ft), with single flowers of yellow, bronze, red, and purple. 'Italian White' is 1 m (4 ft), branching, with cream petals and black centers. 'Sunspot' is 45 to 60 cm (18-24 in.), with yellow flowers 20 to 25 cm (8–10 in.) in diameter.

Culture: Plant in full sun to partial shade and in poor soil.

Use: Useful as accent plants, summer hedges or screens, in mixed or annual beds, and in fresh or dried arrangements.

ψ *Helichrysum bracteatum* (strawflower, immortelle)

The Greek words *helios* (sun) and *chryso* (golden) refer to the flower. The species name, *bracteatum*, describes the stiff bracts around the flowers. Native to Australia and 30 to 60 cm (12–24 in.) in height, strawflowers are classic, old-fashioned everlastings—long-stemmed, daisy-like, up to 8 cm (3 in.) in diameter, in shimmering shades of white, yellow, orange, salmon, red, pink, and purple. The papery, petal-like bracts are dry and sharp to the touch. Cultivars include 'Bright Bikini Mixed,' dwarf plants of 38 cm (15 in.); 'Hot Bikini,' in mixed colors described as a "river of molten lava"; and 'Monstrosum,' with larger flowers on more compact plants.

Culture: Plant in full sun on well-drained soil. Deadhead.

Use: Long a favorite in fresh and dried arrangements, they are also useful as border plants. If used for drying, cut before they are fully open, as further maturation will occur during drying.

ॐ *Helipterum* spp. (acrolinium)

The genus name is from the Greek *helios* (sun), referring to its sun-loving nature, and *pterum* (wing), describing the papery bracts, or petals. There is much confusion over the names of the three species now classified under this genus. They are often listed under their former names, and they all resemble strawflowers. All are native to Australia. *Helipterum humboldtiana* (Humboldt's sunray) is 45 cm (18 in.) in height, with narrow, silver leaves and tiny clusters of yellow flowers. *H. manglesii* (Mangle's sunray, Swan River daisy) is 30 to 45 cm (12–18 in.), and has slightly larger, solitary flowers in white to bright pink with yellow centers. *H. roseum* (rose sunray, acrolinium) is up to 60 cm (24 in.), with semidouble to double, solitary flowers ranging from white through rose and red with darker centers. It is not as heat resistant as the others.

Culture: Plant in dry soil in full sun.

Use: Excellent as fresh or dried flowers and in a rock garden.

'Bonnie Red'

Louis Lenz

ॐ *Kochia scoparia* var. *trichophylla* (burning bush, summer cypress)

The genus name honors Wilhelm Daniel Josef Koch (1771–1849), a German botanist. The species name, *scoparia*, is Latin for broom-like or floor sweeper. "Summer cypress" alludes to the resemblance of its narrow leaves to those of a cypress tree. "Burning bush" describes its scarlet fall color. Grown primarily for its dense, bushy, light green foliage, it is oval shaped, 0.5 to 1.0 m (2–3 ft) in height, with a spread of about 0.5 m (2 ft). Native to southern Europe and Asia, burning bush has become widely naturalized. The species has been classified as a noxious weed in Manitoba. 'Acapulco Silver,' an AAS winner, has silver-tipped foliage that gives it a frosted appearance.

Sara Williams

Culture: For best fall color, plant in full sun on well-drained soil. It appears very tolerant of wind and urban air pollution. Plants from seed may not be uniform in height or form, a drawback in a formal design, although it is easily sheared.

Use: Somewhat formal in appearance, it is used as an accent plant, in large pots or planters, in the border, or as a temporary summer hedge.

ॐ *Limonium sinuatum* (statice, notch-leaf sea lavender)

Limonium, from the Greek *leimon* (a meadow), alludes to its native habitat near salt flats along the coast of Europe from

Steven Still

the Mediterranean to Asia Minor. *Sinuatum* means wavy margin and describes the leaves. Although the species is yellow, cultivars of sea lavender produce masses of winged or crescent-shaped, papery flowers in white, yellow, pink, blue, or purple, usually with white centers. Plants are about 75 cm (30 in.) in height, with a spread of 60 cm (24 in.). The leaves are basal, and the stems winged. 'Petite Bouquet' is 30 cm (12 in.), in mixed or single colors; it is ideal for containers. 'Sunset' is 75 cm (30 in.) in orange, apricot, peach, and rose.

Culture: Heat- and salt-tolerant, sea lavender does well in full sun in a fertile but well-drained sandy or loamy soil.

Use: Attractive massed in the border, they are excellent as dried or fresh cut flowers and are a butterfly nectar plant.

Sara Williams

ψ *Mesembryanthemum crystallinum* (iceplant)

Much confusion surrounds the nomenclature of these South African plants. The genus name, *Mesembryanthemum*, is from the Greek phrase for midday; the flowers open only on sunny days. The species name, *crystallinum*, means crystalline and refers to the ice-like specks on the foliage. Grown as much for its foliage as its blooms, iceplant has succulent leaves and a prostrate form. The shimmering, daisy-like flowers are yellow, pink, or white.

Culture: Grow in full sun in light, well-drained soils. Despite the common name, it flourishes in heat and will not stand frost.

Use: Excellent for hot, windy areas, they are used in containers, as edging, and in the rock garden.

Louis Lenz

ψ *Nolana paradoxa* (Chilean bellflower)

Nolana means little bell in Latin and describes the flowers. The species name, *paradoxa*, means unusual. Native to Chile and Peru, these are prostrate plants of about 15 cm (6 in.) with fleshy leaves. The dark blue flowers are tubular and 5 cm (2 in.) in diameter, with ruffled petals and a yellow or white throat.

Culture: Plant in full sun to partial shade, in dry, well-drained soil. Due to their long tap root, they may not transplant well.

Use: Use in the rock garden, tumbling over a wall, covering a bare bank, or as edging. They are outstanding in containers.

✴ *Papaver rhoeas* (corn poppy, Flanders poppy, Shirley poppy)

Papaver, the Latin name for poppy, is derived from the word *pap*, meaning milk, a reference to the milky sap. The species name, *rhoeas*, is from the Greek *rhodo*, meaning rose-colored, alluding to their use as a red dye in ancient times. Up to 1 m (3 ft) in height, these are the common field poppy of Europe. The silky flowers are single or double, in pink, red, white, salmon, and apricot, and about 5 to 7 cm (2–3 in.) in diameter. Shirley poppy, in white, pink, or red, has a white blotch at the base of each petal.

Culture: Plant in full sun in well-drained soil. Deadhead for longer flowering.

Use: Use for naturalizing, massing, and the cottage garden. The decorative seed pods are used in arrangements.

✴ *Pelargonium* x spp. (geranium)

The Greek word *pelargos* means stork, alluding to the seed's resemblance to a stork's bill. The species name, *hortorum*, means of the garden. Native to South Africa, geraniums were first introduced to England in the 1690s, and are now among the top three annuals planted in North America. In East Africa, where they are a perennial, they are commonly used as a 2 m (6 ft) hedge. Colors include white, pink, rose, red, orange, salmon, and some bicolors. Cultivars are 30 to 60 cm (12–24 in.) in height, with a spread of 30 cm (12 in.). The rounded, scented leaves are often attractively "zoned" with darker or lighter bands of color. Newer cultivars tend to hold their petals better in the wind. The Sprinter series are compact, 45 cm (18 in.) in height, and bloom profusely. The Ringo series has zonal leaves; they flower earlier than the Sprinters. 'Stardust' has quilted petals. 'Freckles,' a dwarf cultivar of only 30 cm (12 in.) and an All-America Selections winner, has rose spots on each pink petal. For continuous bloom, indoors and out, 'Schoene Helena,' a salmon pink, is hard to beat. 'Multibloom' is floriferous and early. The ivy-leaved geranium is ideal in pots and containers.

Ivy-leaved geranium

Culture: Plant in full sun in a fertile, loamy soil to which organic matter has been added. Geraniums need both good fertility and good drainage. Overwatering may result in stem rot and oedema, which causes brown, corky thickenings on the leaves. Spent flowers should be removed.

Use: Geraniums are used for bedding, containers, hanging baskets, and as houseplants over winter. They are a hummingbird nectar plant.

Louis Lenz

Perilla frutescens 'Crispa' (perilla)

Perilla is the Hindu name for this plant. The word *frutescens* means shrubby, perhaps a reference to its form in its native habitat in India, China, and Japan. A member of the mint family, perilla is grown for its remarkable, reddish-purple, metallic, wrinkled, cinnamon-scented foliage. It is about 60 cm (24 in.) in height and resembles coleus, to which it is related. The flowers are insignificant.

Culture: Grow in full sun to very light shade in average, well-drained soil.

Use: Use in the border, large containers, and as a houseplant.

Sara Williams

Ψ *Petunia* x *hybrida* (petunia)

One of the most popular annuals in North America, petunias are dependable, long-blooming, and fragrant, but perhaps overused. *Petun* is an aboriginal Brazilian name for tobacco, to which petunias are related. Petunias are native to Argentina and were introduced to Europe in the mid 1800s. There are hundreds of cultivars, in red, pink, purple, blue, white, and yellow, as well as bicolors, ruffled or striped, and single or double forms. Heights range from 15 to 38 cm (6–15 in.).

Culture: Grow in full sun to partial shade. They prefer fertile, well-drained soil, but will survive a wide range of conditions. Slugs and tobacco mosaic virus are sometimes problems.

Use: Petunias are used as edging, in hanging baskets and other containers, and massed for bedding and borders. They are a hummingbird nectar plant.

Brian Porter

Ψ *Phacelia campanularia* (California bluebell)

Phacelia is the Greek term for bundle or cluster and describes the flower. The species name, *campanularia*, refers to their similarity to bellflowers. Native to the southwest United States and Mexico (including California), these dainty desert plants of 20 to 25 cm (8–10 in.) have small, grey-green leaves and blue flowers. The leaves may cause an allergic skin reaction.

Culture: They perform well in full sun in a wide range of soils, with hot days and cool nights. They transplant poorly.

Use: Use massed, in the rock garden, or as a ground cover. They are attractive to bees.

ψ *Portulaca grandiflora* (portulaca, rose moss)

The genus *Portulaca* was named by Linnaeus, who observed that the lid of the seed capsule opened like a gate. *Portula is* Latin for little gate. *Grandiflora* means large-flowered. Portulaca is a dwarf, trailing, succulent plant of only 15 cm (6 in.), with a spread of 60 cm (24 in.). It produces masses of 5 cm (2 in.), satiny, single or double flowers, in white, cream, yellow, orange, red, and purple. The flowers close at night and on cloudy days. It has succulent stems and fleshy leaves, which often have a reddish tinge. Cultivars include: 'Swan Lake,' with large (10–15 cm/4–6 in.), double, white flowers; 'Cloud Beater Mixed,' which is double and doesn't close if its cloudy; and 'Sundial Mixed,' which flowers earlier and has more basal branching.

Culture: Grow in full sun on well-drained, sandy soils.

Use: Excellent for edging, beds, rock gardens, in containers, as a ground cover, or on dry banks.

ψ *Psylliostachys suworowii* (Russian statice)

Russian statice is closely related to *Limonium*. The genus name, *psylliostachys*, is from the Greek words *psyllion*, meaning a type of plantain, and *stachys*, a flower spike. The species was named after Ivan Petrowitch Suworow, medical inspector in Turkestan (to which it is native) in 1886. The spikes of tiny lavender, pink, or white flowers, each surrounded by a papery calyx, are on thin stems of 45 to 75 cm (18–30 in.).

Culture: Plant in well-drained, sandy loam in full sun. They soon develop a taproot, which makes transplanting difficult.

Use: Use in mixed borders and as a cut flower. Russian statice is a butterfly nectar plant.

ψ *Salvia farinacea* (mealycup sage, salvia)

Salvia is the Latin word meaning to heal and alludes to the plant's medicinal properties. *Farinacea* means mealy. Each flower is supported by a floury-looking calyx, or cup, hence the species and common names. Native to Texas and New Mexico, salvias are members of the mint family, with typical square stems and opposite leaves. Flowers are produced on long spikes, and plants reach 60 cm (24 in.). 'Silver White' is a fine white cultivar. 'Victoria' is a dwarf violet blue.

Culture: Plant in fertile, well-drained soil in full sun to light shade. Do not overwater. It may self-sow once established.

Use: Use in beds, borders, a cottage garden, massed, and in fresh and dried arrangements.

M.P.M. Nair

ψ *Salvia viridis* (clary sage)

Clary sage has the square stems and whorled flowers typical of the mint family. The species name, *viridis*, means green and describes the green bracts of some forms. Clary means "clear-eyed," alluding to its former use in healing eye afflictions. Native to the Mediterranean, clary sage is 50 to 60 cm (20–24 in.) tall. Showy bracts are in pastel shades of blue, pink, purple, and cream. The true flowers above the bracts are small and inconspicuous. 'Claryssa' is a dwarf plant of 45 cm (18 in.) that is used as an everlasting. 'White Swan' is 45 cm (18 in.) and white. 'Blue Bird' is 38 cm (15 in.) and deep blue.

Culture: Grow in full sun and well-drained soil.

Use: Good for naturalizing in a dry area, on a slope, in annual or mixed beds, in a cottage garden, or in arrangements.

Steven Still

ψ *Sanvitalia procumbens* (creeping zinnia)

The genus name honors Federico Sanvitali (1704-1761), an Italian professor. *Procumbens* means lying flat on the ground without rooting. Native to Mexico, creeping zinnia is a low, mound-shaped plant with a spread of about 60 cm (24 in.). The trailing stems produce an abundance of single or double, yellow or orange flowers with dark-purple centers that resemble zinnias. 'Gold Braid' is a double-flowered gold cultivar. 'Mandarin Orange,' an All-America Selections winner, has bright-orange, double flowers with black centers.

Culture: Plant in full sun on well-drained soils.

Use: Use in containers, hanging baskets, rock gardens, trailing over walls, as edging, or a ground cover in hot, dry areas.

'Silver Dust'

Sara Williams

ψ *Senecio cineraria* (dusty miller)

The genus name, *Senecio*, is from the Latin word for old man, an apt description of the fluffy white seed heads, which are not always seen in our short growing season. The species name, *cineraria*, is Latin for ashen grey, a reference to the leaf color, as is the common name. Native to southern Europe, dusty miller is grown for its deeply cut, silver foliage. The yellow flowers are insignificant. Plants range in height from 20 to 40 cm (8–15 in.). Dwarf cultivars include 'Cirrhus,' with spoon-shaped leaves, and 'Silver Dust.'

Culture: Grow in full sun in ordinary, well-drained soil.

Use: Plant in borders, containers, the cottage garden, and as edging. It is useful for separating stronger clashing colors.

ѱ *Tagetes* spp. (marigold)

This genus was named for Tages, a grandson of Jupiter, who is said to have sprung from the ploughed earth in the form of a boy. The common name, a shortened form of Mary's gold, is associated with the Virgin Mary. Among the most popular annuals in North America, marigolds vary from 15 to 60 cm (6–24 in.) in height, with flowers in yellow, orange, burnt copper, and creamy white. The finely cut foliage has a distinctive odor. They are very heat- and drought-tolerant, long-blooming, and prolific.

Although some types are called "French" (usually shorter with smaller flowers) or "African" (taller with larger flowers), the marigold is originally from Mexico, where it was cultivated by the Aztec Indians. It was introduced to Spain over 400 years ago and was popular in monastic gardens. Modern hybrids have varied parentage, having been developed from four different species.

Some marigold species repel nematodes (of which there are few in prairie soils). This has given it a mostly undeserved reputation as having insect-repellent properties.

Culture: Plant in full sun on well-drained soils. Avoid overfertilizing, especially with nitrogen, which will produce an abundance of leafy growth at the expense of flowers. All marigolds are susceptible to aster yellows.

Use: Dwarf cultivars are used as edging plants and in containers, while taller types are placed toward the back of the border. All are useful as cut flowers. The flower heads were once used to produce a yellow dye. The petals are edible and are employed as a saffron substitute. They are a butterfly, bee, and hummingbird nectar plant.

'Dainty Marietta'

Steven Still

All-America Selections

ѱ *Tithonia rotundifolia* (Mexican sunflower)

The genus name honors Tithonus of Greek mythology. Granted immortality but not eternal youth, he eventually shrivelled to the size of a grasshopper. How this relates to a flower native to Mexico is unclear. *Rotundifolia* describes the large, round, velvety foliage. Plants can reach 2 m (6 ft) in height. The 7.5 cm (3 in.) flowers resemble single dahlias. 'Goldfinger' is 75 cm (30 in.), with burnt orange, single blooms; 'Yellow Torch' is a brilliant yellow; 'Torch' is 1 m (4 ft), with single, orange-vermilion flowers.

Culture: They are adapted to heat, sun, and poor soil.

Use: In the border, as accents, annual screens, and cut flowers.

Steven Still

Gail Rankin

Ursinia anethoides (dill-leaf ursinia, jewel-of-the-veldt)

The genus was named to honor Johannes Ursinus, a 17th century German botanist. *Anethoides* means dill-like and describes the leaves. Like other South African annuals, it resembles gazania or dimorphotheca. The bright orange-yellow, daisy-like flowers have a dark purple ring in the center and are held on thin, wiry stems 30 to 45 cm (12–18 in.) above the finely cut, dill-like, aromatic leaves. They close at night and on cloudy days.

Culture: Plant in light, well-drained soil in full sun.

Use: Use in annual or mixed borders and in containers.

'Zulu Prince'

Brian Porter

Ψ *Venidium fastuosum* (cape daisy, monarch-of-the-veldt)

Venidium is Latin for veined and describes the ribbed seed pod. Both the species name, *fastuosum,* and the common name, monarch, mean proud, perhaps a reference to the plant's promience on the South African veldt, to which it is native. The large (10–13 cm/4–5 in.) flowers are brilliant orange with a dark purple-black center and close at night and on dull days. The silver foliage is deeply cut and has a fuzzy, cobweb-like texture which is more predominant in young plants. Cultivars are available in ivory, cream, pale yellow, and white.

Culture: Grow in well-drained, light soil in full sun.

Use: Use in annual or mixed borders and as a cut flower.

Gail Rankin

Ψ *Xeranthemum annuum* (immortelle)

The genus name comes from the Greek words *xeros* (dry) and *anthos* (flower) and refers to its use as a dried flower or everlasting. The common name is a similar allusion. Native from the Mediterranean to Iran, it has been in cultivation for centuries. The small daisies are single or double, in white, pink, purple, and rose, with petal-like bracts. The leaves are silver-grey. The plants are 0.5 to 1 m (2–3 ft) in height, with erect, branching stems. 'Snowlady' is white. The Lumina Double series has flowers in purple, red, rose, and white.

Culture: They grow best in sandy soil in full sun.

Use: Useful in the border or for fresh or dried arrangements.

ψ *Zinnia elegans* (zinnia)

Linnaeus named this genus for botanist Johann Gottfried Zinn (1727–1759). *Elegans* means elegant. Originally from Mexico, zinnia is one of our most popular annuals. The flowers, held on stiffly erect stems, are single or double, in forms ranging from cactus-flowered to pompom in every color but blue. Cultivars range in height from 15 to 100 cm (6–40 in.) and include: 'Persian Carpet,' a bicolor mix; 'Parasol Mixed,' compact plants of 25 to 30 cm (10–12 in.), with fully double flowers in a wide range of colors; 'Ruffles Mixed,' 70 cm (28 in.) in height, with fully double flowers in yellow, pink, scarlet, and cherry; 'Star White,' a compact white; 'Scarlet Splendor,' 55 cm (22 in.) high, with flowers 13 cm (5 in.) across.

Culture: Plant in full sun on well-drained soil.

Use: Use in beds, containers, as edging, and as cut flowers. They are a butterfly and hummingbird nectar source.

Steven Still

Wild white geranium (*Geranium richardsonii*)

Alumroot (*Heuchera richardsonii*)

Dotted blazingstar (*Liatris punctata*)

Three-flowered avens (*Geum triflorum*)

Potentilla silverweed (*Potentilla anserina*)

Blue: Smooth fleabane (*Erigeron glabellus*); *purple:* Western wild bergamot (*Monarda fistulosa*)

Smooth blue beardtongue (*Penstemon nitidus*)

Harebell (*Campanula rotundifolia*)

Smooth aster (*Aster laevis*)

ature can be imitated quite effectively and even used as a model for the urban landscape."

Robin Smith

Chapter 8

Native Plants

In the xeriscape

T he use of native plants—grasses, flowers, shrubs, and trees that grow naturally within a few hundred kilometers of your home—is becoming an increasingly popular approach to xeriscape design in both private and public landscapes. For many gardeners, native plants represent a return to nature and a restoration of a landscape that is becoming endangered.

We have become so accustomed to the presence of some native plants—bur oak, green ash, pincherry, chokecherry, horizontal juniper—in our landscapes that we may not think of them as indigenous at all, but like all native plants, they have evolved to thrive in this climate.

Like anything else, it is often better to start small. As your knowledge of and familiarity with naturalization increases, there's always room for expansion.

Designing with native plants

Native plants can be used along with introduced plants as part of a conventional landscape design. They may also be naturalized—introduced and allowed to spread through seed, suckers, or rhizomes—to create a self-sustaining ecological plant community.

Think about what you actually want to do. You may decide to include only native plants in your xeriscape, but to

Tall grass prairie demonstration project at The Forks in Winnipeg.

treat these as individual plant specimens rather than as an integrated plant community. Because we are familiar with the former approach and know what to "do" with it and how to maintain it, it may be an easier way to deal with native plants.

The alternative is to create a sustainable, evolving landscape using a particular "community" of native plants. Charles Thomsen has done this in his urban yard in Winnipeg, as did Robin Smith in Saskatoon (see pp. 196–97).

Self-sustaining plant communities, especially in the front yard, may be perceived by more manicured neighbors as somewhat "weedy." Naturalization is allowed to proceed and the homeowner gives up the control that would be exercised in a more formal landscape.

Before you begin, check provincial legislation to determine what is or is not a legal weed. *Kochia* (burning bush), *Gypsophila paniculata* (babysbreath), and *Lythrum salicaria* (purple loosestrife), although widely naturalized in North America, are actually European plant introductions and have been declared noxious weeds in some provinces. Also determine if naturalization can be carried out on municipally owned boulevards which are visually a portion of your front yard.

Establishing an aspen forest or a short grass prairie requires a great deal of knowledge. Which plants are involved? An aspen forest involves not only trees, but the shrubs, grasses, and annual and perennial flowers that make up the understorey. What type of soil are these plants suited to?

Some of the plants move around, a function of biennial self-sowing and birds. This evolving landscape may start out with a predominance of certain plants, but this will change as it evolves, matures, and comes of age over the years. Are you the kind of person who can tolerate an evolving landscape where the wiles of wind and birds contribute to change?

And remember, there's a fine line between naturalization and allowing dandelions, quack grass, and sow thistle to invade and become dominant.

Propagation

There is also the question of establishment. Will these plants be started from seed sown directly in place or will you start them indoors under lights or in a greenhouse? If the former, can you distinguish between a seedling of a blanket flower and that of a sow thistle? If your knowledge of native plants is limited, you may be better off purchasing plants from a nursery. There are now quite a few nurseries that specialize in or carry native plants (see p. 198).

It's not instant

Although seed packets of wildflowers have been widely marketed in recent years to give the impression that they will produce "instant meadows," this image is misleading. Natural plant communities take many centuries to evolve. It's simply not possible to duplicate that balance within a few growing seasons.

These seed packets usually include a mixture of annuals and perennials. Although they are labelled as "wild" or "native," one must ask, "Native to where?" While many of these collections contain seeds that are native to North America, some of the plants contained in the mixture may not be hardy on the Canadian prairies. Others may not be drought-tolerant.

As well, the germination requirements of the seeds within a packet may be quite different from one another. Some may require a pretreatment such as cold or scarification in order to break dormancy. Some may require light and others darkness.

If your intention is to sow these seeds directly where they are to be grown, it's also important that you are able to recognize them as seedlings. Can you distinguish between a seedling gaillardia and a seedling sow thistle? What does wild flax look like as a seedling? If you are unable to do this, chances are that the sow thistles will win out every time. The end result may well be a weed patch rather than a native flower meadow.

Native grasses as ornamentals

Many of the native grasses that once provided forage for bison have come into their own in the last decade as their ornamental value has gained greater recognition. For gardeners who are a part of a larger agricultural community, it means a shift in our mindset: overcoming the predominant view of these plants as weeds or forage and recognition of their beauty and use in the landscape.

The species that follow have a wide range of uses: massed in large curved beds as "transition zones" between the more manicured portion of a large acreage or farmyard and the outlying areas or bush; as specimen or accent plants, as ground covers, in a border, and on slopes or banks to control erosion.

Little bluestem (*Schizachyrium scorparium*) is a loose, clump-forming grass, 45 cm (18 in.) in height, with blue-green to purple foliage and racemes of hairy, silver seed heads. In fall, the foliage turns a warm bronze-red, making it ideal for the winter landscape. It grows in full sun and ordinary soil and is fairly drought tolerant once established. It may be used in mass plantings or small groupings in the perennial border. It spreads by rhizomes.

Fringed brome (*Bromus kalmii*) is 1 m (3 ft.) in height, with attractive and showy cascading seed heads. It is useful in the border or as a specimen plant.

Indian grass (*Sorghastrum avenaceum*) is 1 m (4 ft) in height, with reddish stalks and bronze seed heads. Use it in a mixed border or as a specimen or accent plant.

Sheep fescue (*Festuca ovina*) is a short (20 cm/8 in.), green or grey-green, tufted bunch grass that is excellent as a ground cover. The fact that very few weed seeds germinate among the clumps means the maintenance required is minimal.

Canada wild rye (*Elymus canadensis*) is a tall, showy bunch grass with pointed, waxy green leaves. The attractive seed head has very long, thread-like awns protruding from each seed. It is a cool-season grass that does well in partial shade and may reach 1 m (4 ft) in height. It will grow in all soils. It may be massed or used as an accent plant.

Collecting seed of wild plants: An ethic

Extracted from a pamphlet by the Native Plant Society of Saskatchewan

• identify plants before collecting seeds
• avoid rare or endangered species or fragile habitats such as sand dunes or wetlands
• collect from large local populations, both to maximize genetic diversity of your collection and to minimize effects on the natural population
• choose species native to an area within a 300 to 500 km (200–300 mi) radius of where the seed will be used
• select plants from your own ecological zone (aspen parkland, boreal forest, or mixed prairie)
• use caution when purchasing "wildflower mixtures," which may contain European species that are potentially invasive
• only use weed-free commercial seed
• if purchasing native plants, ensure they are nursery propagated rather than dug from the wild
• collect from sites that are least susceptible to damage, such as road allowances and ungrazed areas
• collect ripe seeds, not entire plants
• leave at least 50 percent of seed in place for natural regeneration: native seed production is generally low and infrequent
• it is illegal to collect seed in national, provincial, and regional parks and protected natural areas
• obtain necessary permits to collect in forest reserves and community pastures
• obtain permission from landowners.

Native plants for the xeriscape

by Mack Miller

Concerns about water conservation and environmental pollution have led to an increased interest in the use of drought-tolerant native plants which thrive without irrigation.

Many species found within a small natural area can be used in residential landscaping. My favored approach is to naturalize as much as possible. It has a somewhat "wild" look and the advantage of very low maintenance once established. An alternative is to develop a border containing only native species.

If you wish to grow your own plants, collect only a few seeds. Do not dig up plants from the wild. Transplanting is seldom successful, and their removal is in conflict with the conservation ethic.

Unless you are familiar with the appearance of seedlings, begin plants in beds or containers or indoors under lights. Exceptions to this are large areas where grasses are to be planted and for species (especially legumes) that do poorly in the confines of a pot or transplant poorly.

Key

Height: L = low, to 30 cm (12 in.); M = medium, 30–60 cm (12–24 in.); T = tall, over 60 cm (24 in.)

Propagation: S = seed; D = division; C = cuttings

Seed treatment: w/s = warm stratification; c/s = cold stratification; sc = scarification

Light: Sh = shade tolerant

Plants native to moderately dry or very dry sites
Perennials (listed in order of bloom):

Anemone patens (prairie crocus)   L, S (seed outdoors immediately after collection)
Geum triflorum (three-flowered avens)   L, S (c/s)
Penstemon nitidus (smooth blue beardstongue)   L, S (c/s)
Thermopsis rhombifolia (golden bean)   L, S (c/s, sc)
Astragalus crassicarpus (ground plum)   L, S (c/s, sc)
Antennaria aprica (low everlasting)   L, S (c/s)
Eriogonum flavum (yellow umbrellaplant)   L, S (c/s)
Gaura coccinea (scarlet gaura)   L, S (c/s, sc) or D
Malvastrum coccineum (scarlet mallow)   L, S (c/s, sc) or D
Mamillaria vivipara (pincushion cactus)   L, C (stem sections)
Opuntia polyacantha (plains prickly pear cactus)   L, C (stem sections)
Opuntia fragilis (brittle prickly pear cactus)   L, C (stem sections)
Gaillardia aristata (blanket flower)   M, S (c/s)
Linum lewisii (wild blue flax)   M, S (c/s)
Allium textile (prairie onion)   M, S (c/s)
Campanula rotundifolia (harebell)   M, S (c/s)
Erigeron caespitosus (tufted fleabane)   L, S (c/s)
Chrysopsis villosa (hairy golden aster)   L, S (c/s)
Ratibida columnifera (prairie coneflower)   M, S (c/s)
Liatris punctata (dotted blazingstar)   L, S (c/s)
Aster laevis (smooth aster)   T, S (c/s)
Solidago rigida (stiff goldenrod)   M, S (c/s)
Gutierrezia diversifolia (broom weed)   L, S (c/s)

Grasses:

Boutelua gracilis (blue grama)   L to M, S
Koeleria cristata (June grass)   L to M, S
Stipa comata (speargrass)   M to T, S

Shrubs:

Symphoricarpos occidentalis (western snowberry)   S (w/s, c/s, sc) or D
Rosa arkansana (prairie rose)   S (w/s, c/s, sc) or D
Juniperus horizontalis (creeping juniper)   S (w/s, c/s, sc) or C

Mack Miller owns Miller's Native Plants in Saskatoon, Saskatchewan.

Plants native to areas of moderate moisture
Perennials:

Viola adunca (early blue violet)   L, S (c/s), Sh
Fragaria glauca (wild strawberry)   L, D, Sh
Penstemon gracilis (lilac flowered beardstongue)   L, S (c/s)
Anemone multifida (cut-leaved anemone)   M, S (c/s)
Anemone canadensis (Canada anemone)   M, S or D, Sh
Zizia aptera (heart-leaved alexander)   M, S (c/s)
Astragalus striatus (ascending purple milk vetch)   M, S (c/s)
Galium boreale (northern bedstraw)   M, S (c/s), Sh
Heuchera richardsonii (alumroot)   M, S
Psoralea esculenta (Indian breadroot)   M, S (c/s, sc), seed directly
Erigeron glabellus (smooth fleabane)   M, S (c/s), Sh
Oxytropis splendens (showy locoweed)   L, S (c/s)
Potentilla arguta (white cinquefoil)   M, S (c/s)
Potentilla pensylvanica (prairie cinquefoil)   M, S (c/s)
Agastache foeniculum (giant hyssop)   T, S (c/s), Sh
Rudbeckia serotina (black-eyed susan)   M, S (c/s)
Monarda fistulosa (bergamot)   M, S (c/s), Sh
Liatris ligulistylus (meadow blazingstar)   M, S (c/s)
Aster ciliolatus (Lindley's aster)   M, S (c/s), Sh

Grasses:

Agropyron dasystachyum (northern wheatgrass)   M to T, S or D (rhizomatous)
Agropyron smithii (western wheatgrass)   M, S or D (rhizomatous)
Agropyron subsecundum (awned wheatgrass)   M to T, S
Festuca hallii (plains rough fescue)   M, S or D (rhizomatous)

Shrubs:

Elaeagnus commutata (silverberry)   S (c/s)
Shepherdia argentea (silver buffaloberry)   S (c/s)
Amelanchier alnifolia (saskatoon berry)   S or D
Cornus stolonifera (red osier dogwood)   S (c/s), Sh
Corylus cornuta (beaked hazelnut)   S (c/s), Sh
Crataegus spp. (hawthorn)   S (w/s, c/s), sc
Shepherdia canadensis (Canada buffaloberry)   S (c/s)

Trees:

Fraxinus pensylvanica (green ash)   S
Populus tremuloides (trembling aspen)   S
Prunus pensylvanica (pincherry)   S (c/s)
Prunus virginiana (chokecherry)   S (c/s)
Quercus macrocarpa (bur oak)   S (c/s)

Edmonton: Naturalizing a public green space

by Eugene Y. Lin

Naturalization is the process that can be used to revert a formerly manicured landscape to a natural plant community, or preserve natural vegetation in an area to be developed. Declining funds for parks and strong public opinion on environmental protection are the major forces behind this trend. There is a high financial cost, which includes energy and chemical inputs, to maintaining manicured parks with few tree species and large expanses of mowed grass.

Naturalizing an open space has many benefits. It is low-cost in the long run, ecologically sound, conserves the original ecological resource, enhances wildlife habitat, is aesthetically pleasing, and provides both educational and recreational opportunities.

If not properly implemented, this concept leads to problems with public resistance, increased risk of fire and crime (due to increased cover), and wildlife. Implementation may also be limited by the availability of native plant material, and, until recently, the lack of technical information and experience regarding its use.

One option is planting beds and borders in layers made up of tall trees, shorter trees, tall shrubs, ground covers, and ornamental grasses. Using this concept, trees are never planted in straight lines but grouped into clumps and staggered. Within the clumps or groupings, species are arranged randomly but in homogenous clusters. Shrubs form an understorey below and adjacent to trees. Plantings are made at close spacings, averaging about one tree and three shrubs per 3 m by 3 m (1 yd x 1 yd) space.

Eugene Lin is a horticulturist, design consultant, and owner of Country Gardens Landscape Ltd. in Calgary. Design adapted from a design by Eugene Y. Linn so as to include only plants native to the prairies.

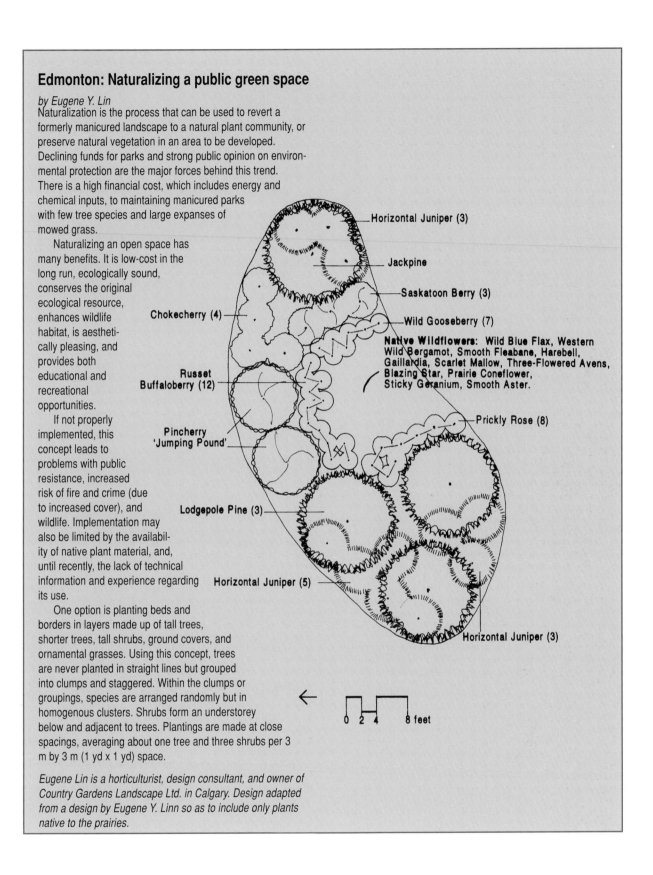

Horizontal Juniper (3)

Jackpine

Saskatoon Berry (3)

Wild Gooseberry (7)

Native Wildflowers: Wild Blue Flax, Western Wild Bergamot, Smooth Fleabane, Harebell, Gaillardia, Scarlet Mallow, Three-Flowered Avens, Blazing Star, Prairie Coneflower, Sticky Geranium, Smooth Aster.

Chokecherry (4)

Russet Buffaloberry (12)

Pincherry 'Jumping Pound'

Prickly Rose (8)

Lodgepole Pine (3)

Horizontal Juniper (5)

Horizontal Juniper (3)

0 2 4   8 feet

Native plant communities in the urban xeriscape

by Charles H. Thomsen

Those of us who have been advocating a greater appreciation and use of native plant material now have a strong ally in the concept of xeriscape. Managing naturally occurring water is crucial in creating a sustainable landscape. Rather than removing rainfall as quickly and efficiently as possible (as has been the engineering approach in the past) we must make every effort to "hold and percolate" it into the soil.

The typically flat prairie landscape can be easily shaped to create a warped surface that will trap runoff and encourage the development of a more diverse community of plants. We should be replacing irrigated lawns with alternative materials such as native grasses and wildflowers and drought-tolerant shrubs and ground covers.

Every time we clear bush to build houses, or pave over the landscape, we are in effect raising temperatures within our cities. The term "urban heat island" illustrates the phenomenon where mean temperatures are higher within the built-up area than in the surrounding rural landscape. Solar energy is reflected back into the atmosphere. In a recent study of Tucson and Phoenix, Arizona, where the total vegetation cover has been reduced by 9 percent during the past 40 years, there has been an increase in temperature of one or two degrees during the same period. Higher temperatures have caused increased evapotranspiration rates in what little vegetation remains. This water must be replaced through irrigation. Electrical demands have also increased due to nonstop air conditioning. One man-made problem exacerbates another.

In my own suburban home landscape in Winnipeg, we have tried to reintroduce native Manitoba plant species and their associated plant communities. This is in sharp contrast to the well clipped, overfertilized and overwatered landscapes that dominate most suburban communities. While the landscape we created is often referred to as "the weed patch," its minimal watering and low maintenance requirements are a direct application of xeriscape principles and the issue of sustainability.

Rather than an extensive Kentucky bluegrass lawn, our yard is filled with a great diversity of indigenous trees, shrubs, and ground covers. Planted areas are heavily mulched with wood chips and dead leaves collected from other parts of the city. This mulch reduces weed competition, retains soil moisture, and over time, through decay, adds valuable nutrients to the soil, as well as improving the soil's water retention capacity.

In addition, a stream channel and pond are fed by water from a basement sump pump as well as roof and yard runoff. Water from rain barrels and the pond is used to irrigate house plants and garden. Goldfish fill the pond and rain barrels to check algae growth and control mosquitoes.

A sustainable landscape is a regenerative landscape: a landscape in which species of plants support each other and the wastes of one become the inputs of another. This is

Sara Williams

Except for the boulevard, an aspen forest replaces a conventional lawn at the Thomsen residence in Winnipeg.

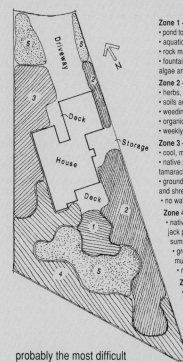

Zone 1 – Wetland/pond
- pond to collect surface runoff and sump water
- aquatic and bog plants
- rock mulch along edges of pond
- fountain to aerate water, and fish to control algae and mosquitos.

Zone 2 – Kitchen garden
- herbs, vegetables, fruit trees/shrubs
- soils aerated and compost added
- weeding as necessary
- organic mulch of grass clippings
- weekly watering or as needed.

Zone 3 – Boreal forest
- cool, moist, shaded
- native plants: birch, aspen, fir, spruce, tamarack, cherry, dogwood
- ground cover of perennials, wood chips, and shredded Christmas trees
- no watering.

Zone 4 – Upland forest
- native plants: oak, aspen, green ash, jack pine, buffaloberry, saskatoon, sumac, cherry
- ground cover of perennials, heavy mulch of leaves
- no watering.

Zone 5 – Grassland
- mixed prairie grasses
- biweekly mowing or as needed
- no watering.

Zone 6 – Service area
- firewood storage, potting table, equipment storage.

Zone 7 – Deck

probably the most difficult principle to follow. With our landscape design and horticultural traditions we have come to think of landscapes and their component parts as pictures or individual artifacts, not as living systems. To create truly sustainable landscapes, we must be cognizant not only of the requirements of individual species for survival, but more importantly, conditions necessary for the survival of the entire ecological community. Rather than removing fallen leaves each year, we should consider their value and functions as a natural fertilizer, an insulator of the soil, and a food source for other organisms.

By following these principles, we will be on the road to creating more sustainable landscapes, as well as introducing new and exciting design potentials for our homes and communities.

Charles Thomsen is head of the Department of Landscape Architecture, University of Manitoba.

What do your neighbors think?
An epistle on an alternative landscape

by Robin Smith

My father's garden, the garden of my youth, was a horticultural wonder—annuals, roses, manicured trees and shrubs, lawns with concrete edges around everything. Even the lily pond and wishing well were concrete (and both leaked more often than not!). It was a yard suitable for entry into local horticultural contests in Edmonton.

As years passed, my father's attention turned to golf, leaving me to tend the garden. Where could I have gone awry? The biologist side of my dad had also introduced us to nature. On walks in the woods attention was drawn to a fungus on an old stump, a wildflower tucked into the understorey or a bird in song. I began to appreciate how natural systems worked, and the soft edges appealed to me. Soon the concrete edge was being selectively removed, organic curves introduced, beds enlarged, and more perennials added.

Obtaining a degree in landscape architecture further instilled in me the notion that nature can be imitated quite effectively and even used as a model for the urban landscape—an idea strengthened by a sense that urban folk are out of touch with their environment as more and more of our natural areas are paved over.

When someone views my natural garden in Saskatoon, they either love it or think "there goes the neighborhood!" When we purchased our home some years ago, the landscape was fairly typical—a large expanse of front lawn, two large blue spruce on each side, and a foundation planting of tall cedars and junipers. A sidewalk bisected the lawn and terminated at a concrete porch, which seemed somewhat elevated because of the settling of the front yard. The back yard was more of the same.

The first year I mowed the less-than-perfect lawn, watered, and mowed again. The winter was spent planning for the demise of this same lawn. Off-street parking took out a nice chunk. When the driveway was cored out for a gravel base, I asked the contractor to leave the good topsoil in a large pile adjacent to the driveway. This was shaped into a raised bluff. That took care of 80 percent of the lawn area. The rest of the lawn proceeded to wither and die. Slowly the bluff area was planted with aspen, wild rose, buffaloberry, snowberry, chokecherry, and saskatoons.

Boulders were brought in and placed randomly around the bluff to simulate outcroppings, and mostly native, drought-tolerant ground covers were introduced. Those plants that required more than one season of regular watering were out of luck. Only the strong survive in my landscape. The narrow prairie zone along the sidewalk and a small swale-cum-pathway were seeded with wildflower mixes and sheep fescue, a clump-forming, nonaggressive grass. Native plants were nursed under grow lights in the basement through the depths of winter and added to the landscape each spring. Soon a wide variety of native plants were blooming: coneflower, gaillardia, goldenrod, asters, fleabanes, blue flax, and fescue grasses.

As with most landscapes, the composition of our prairie is dynamic, changing with the seasons. Some of the plants move around, a function of biennial self-sowing and birds.

The back yard has been treated a bit more formally, with the addition of an alpine rock garden, a vine-covered garden swing and arbor, a pond and waterfall, and a host of perennials. The area under the mature trees on the north edge of the lot has been allowed to naturalize and is now a varied assortment of understorey shrubs and herbaceous plants, contributed mainly by birds. Leaf litter is encouraged and stays where it falls. About one-fifth of the back yard remains a lawn for kids and pets to enjoy. A rabbit enclosure and compost pile complete the picture.

Nature has a free rein in my urban landscape. The yard is always full of birds and bees and butterflies. It may be many things but it is not boring. It is very much alive, a respite where one can find order in chaos and forget for a moment that one is in a city.

What do my neighbors think? Quite frankly, I haven't bothered to ask!

Robin Smith was landscape architect for the Meewasin Valley Authority in Saskatoon, Saskatchewan, from 1986 to 1994.

Fall color of naturalized native plants in the front yard of the Smith residence, Saskatoon.

Sara Williams

Suppliers of native seeds and plants

Note: *This list is not complete, nor is it intended as an endorsement of suppliers.*

Alberta

Alberta Nurseries & Seeds Ltd.
Box 20
Bowden AB T0M 0K0
Chris Berggren (403) 224–3545

ALCLA Native Plant Restoration, Inc.
3208 Bearspaw Drive NW
Calgary AB T2L 1T2
(403) 282–6516

Blooming Prairie
10351–76 Avenue
Edmonton AB T6E 1K9
Katie Benschop, P.Ag., (403) 431–1451

Bow Point Nursery Ltd.
(native plants of southern Alberta)
Box 16, Site 3, R.R. 12
Calgary AB T3E 6W3
Ken and Pam Wright (403) 242–8018

Calgary Zoological Society
P.O. Box 3036, Stn. B
Calgary AB T2M 4R8
(403) 232–9300, fax (403) 237–7582

Coaldale Nurseries
Box 1267
Coaldale AB T1M 1N1
(403) 345–4633

The Conservancy
51563 Range Road 212A
Sherwood Park AB T8G 1B1
(403) 434–7401 (phone & fax)

Devonian Botanic Garden
University of Alberta
Edmonton AB T6G 2E1
(403) 987–3054

Eagle Lake Nurseries Ltd.
Box 2340
Strathmore AB T1P 1K3
Anita Heuver (403) 934–3622

Eastern Slopes Rangeland Seeds Ltd.
Box 273
Cremona AB T0M 0R0
Clare Tannas (403) 637–2473
fax: (403) 637–2724

EnviroScapes
Box 38
Warner AB T0K 2L0
Vince Petherbridge (403) 733–2160

Foothills Nurseries (wholesale only)
2626–48 Street SE
Calgary AB T2B 1M4
Arnold Heuver (403) 272–3200

Greenview Nurseries
Box 12, Site 16, R.R. 7
Calgary AB T2P 4G7
Hans Bron (403) 936–5936

Hannas Seeds
5039–49 Street
Macombe AB T4L 1Y2
Patricia Hannas (403) 782–6671

Knutson & Shaw Growers
Box 295
Vulcan AB T0L 2B0
Ray Shaw, Bev Knutson-Shaw
(403) 485–6688

Laidlaw Nursery
(fruit-bearing bushes only)
Box 316
Tofield AB T0B 4J0
Ted and Eleanor Laidlaw (403) 662–2778

Parkland Nurseries Ltd.
R.R. 2
Red Deer AB T4N 5E2
Dwayne Beck (403) 346–5613

Prairie Seeds Inc.
Box 428, 1805–8 St.
Nisku AB T0C 2G0
Kerby Lowen/David Ingledew
(403) 955–7345

Rangeland Seeds (native grass seeds,
50 lb minimum order)
Box 928
Vulcan AB T0L 2B0
Warden Budd (403) 485–6448

Sunstar Nurseries
810–167 Ave NE
Mailing address: R.R. 6, Site 6, Box 17
Edmonton AB T5B 4K3
Harold Voogd (403) 472–6103

Manitoba

Living Prairie Museum
2785 Ness Avenue
Winnipeg MB R3J 1S4
(204) 832–0167

Prairie Habitats
P.O. Box 1
Argyle MB R0C 0B0
Carol and John Morgan (204) 467–9371

Prairie Originals
17 Schreyer Crescent
St. Andrews MB R1A 3A6
Shirley Froehlich (204) 338–7517

Saskatchewan

Blazingstar Wildflower Seed Co.
Box 143
St. Benedict SK S0K 3T0
(306) 289–2046 (phone and fax)

Millers' Native Plants
Hwy 16 East, 426 Keeley Way
Saskatoon SK S7J 4B2
Mack and Lee Miller (306) 374–4785

Prairiescape
2815 Pasqua Street
Regina SK S4S 2H4
(306) 586–6576/(306) 596–4150

Prairie Grown Garden Seeds
Box 118
Cochin SK S0M 0L0
Jim Ternier (306) 386–2737

Prairie Mountain Seeds
Box 273
Arcola SK S0C 0G0
(306) 455–2513

Paule Hjertaas
15 Olson Place
Regina SK S4S 2J6
(306) 584–2835

T & E Williamson Seeds Ltd.
Box 6
Pambrun SK S0N 1W0
Tom and Elaine Williamson
(306) 582–6009

hen you don't have a lot of water, deficit irrigation applies what little you have when it will do the most good.

Chapter 9

The Edible Xeriscape

By convention, we tend to separate food production areas from the rest of our landscape. This is evident even in the words we use. In England, the entire landscape—trees, shrubs, lawn, flower beds, fruit and vegetable patches—is referred to as "the garden." On the prairies, "the garden" is the area, almost always rectangular in shape, where we grow our beans, peas, and corn, almost always in straight lines.

Many edible plants are highly ornamental, and many prairie gardeners are now integrating these fruits (such as Nanking cherry, crabapple, and pincherry), herbs (purple sage, curled parsley), and vegetables (red leaf lettuce, New Zealand spinach, peppers, cherry tomatoes) into their mixed borders.

Vegetables

If you opt for a separate vegetable garden, employ appropriate xeriscape techniques: deep soil well amended with organic matter, drip irrigation, weed control, mulch, and

Purple sage, a colorful and drought-tolerant herb.

Sara Williams

grouping plants according to water needs. Cultivar selection and timing of irrigation are also important factors in water conservation.

Select cultivars that can be planted early in the growing season when temperatures are lower and more stored soil moisture is available. Those with a shorter "days to maturity" requirement will need water over a shorter period. Some cultivars may be more resistant to water stress. Sometimes "heritage" varieties fare better than newer hybrids.

Weed control is critical. Weeds compete with vegetables for water and decrease yields. They also harbor insects and disease.

Most vegetables need a minimum of six hours of sunlight a day. If they receive morning sun, some can tolerate dappled shade in the heat of the afternoon; partly shaded conditions will also conserve soil moisture. Cabbage, broccoli, lettuce, peas, spinach, and carrots are more tolerant of shade than cucumbers, melons, squash, tomatoes, green peppers, and corn. If trees provide shade they may also compete for soil moisture. Buildings do not.

In rural areas, shelterbelts are essential because they decrease wind velocity, slowing evaporation from both plants and soil. Using wide row planting (beds 30 to 45 cm/12–18 in. wide) makes better use of drip irrigation or soaker hoses.

Black plastic mulches hold heat and are ideal for warm-season vegetables such as tomatoes, peppers, corn, melon, squash, and eggplant. Use organic mulches for cool-season vegetables like potatoes, carrots, cabbage, broccoli, cauliflower, lettuce, beets, and spinach. Allow the soil to warm up in spring prior to applying organic mulches.

Most garden vegetables will need about 2.5 cm (1 in.) of water per week once the transplants are established. Allow the soil surface to dry between waterings.

Tomatoes and vine crops allowed to sprawl on the ground shade the soil surface, somewhat reducing evaporation. Because plants are lower, they are out of the direct path of drying winds.

Deficit irrigation

Deficit irrigation is the practice of replacing only a small portion of the water used by plants. When you don't have a lot of water, deficit irrigation applies what little you have when it will do the most good. While water stress can cause reductions in yield as well as quality in crops like lettuce and celery, it can improve tomato quality, enhancing flavour by increasing sugars and flavor constituents.

Timing is critical! Water stress can be very harmful at some stages of growth and not harmful at others. Avoid water stress at these critical times. The most critical time for watering most vegetables is from flowering to fruit formation.

Cole crops: cabbage, cauliflower, broccoli, and Brussels sprouts
These are cool-season crops with a 90 cm (2 ft) rooting zone. If directly seeded, irrigate just prior to seeding to increase the firmness of the seedbed and provide optimum soil moisture during germination and emergence. If you are using bedding plants, water immediately after transplanting to a depth of 15 to 30 cm (6-12 in.). During May and June, plants will need only 10 to 15 mm (0.5 in.) of water weekly. During July and August they will need 25 to 50 mm (1–2 in.) of water weekly. Do not subject to drought stress during head and sprout formation and expansion. Even moisture during this period should reduce splitting in cabbages and buttoning, browning, and bolting in cauliflower.

Vine crops: cucumber, melon, pumpkin, and squash
These vegetables are heat loving and deep rooted (90 cm/3 ft). Short-season cucumbers will need 300 mm (12 in.) of water over the growing season, while late-season pumpkins and squash require up to 500 mm (20 in.). They have large seeds which must absorb two to three times their weight in water before germinating. A single irrigation in mid-June is generally sufficient. Vine crops are most sensitive to drought stress during flower initiation and pollination, when lack of sufficient moisture may result in misshapen fruit or aborted flowers.

Moisture stress during fruit development results in smaller fruit of lower quality. Infrequent but deep irrigation (50–75 mm/2-3 in.) is recommended from fruit set to early August. This will ensure moisture through the root zone while discouraging disease development due to wet foliage. Cucumbers are sensitive to overhead irrigation and cold water.

Onions
Onions generally need 400 mm (16 in.) of water over the growing season. They have an effective rooting depth of less than 60 cm (2 ft), and single irrigations should be limited to less than 50 mm (2 in.). Irrigation is critical for rapid and even germination. Because onion seed is sown at a shallow depth, it is very vulnerable to surface drying even when subsurface moisture is high. Keep the top 3 cm (1.2 in.) of soil moist after seeding. This may necessitate daily irrigation during hot, windy weather. Once they have germinated, their water needs for the next six to eight weeks are quite low, 20 to 25 mm (0.75–1 in.) per week. During July this may be increased to 25 to 35 mm (1–1.4 in.) per week. August and early September are periods of rapid bulb enlargement. Water use is high and drought stress will significantly reduce yield.

Sweet corn
Sweet corn needs 350 to 500 mm (14–20 in.) of water over the growing season. Water use is particularly high during hot,

---

Group vegetables with similar water needs, and water accordingly

Vegetables requiring moderate irrigation (300–450 mm/12–17 in.):
beans
broccoli
Brussels sprouts
cabbage
cucumbers
early onions
turnips
watermelons

Vegetables requiring generous irrigation (450–600 mm/18–24 in.):
beets
carrots
sweet corn
eggplant
lettuce
muskmelons
onions (late)
parsnips
peppers
potatoes
summer squash
winter squash
tomatoes

windy weather. Late-season cultivars will need more water than early-season ones. Corn has a 60 cm (2 ft) root zone. If stored soil moisture at seeding time is sufficient for rapid germination, do not irrigate until plants are 20 to 25 cm (8–10 in.) high. Irrigation cools the soil, slows germination, and encourages disease. It's better to irrigate prior to seeding and seed once the soil surface is warm. Supersweet corn is especially sensitive to cold soil at seeding time. Moisture is most critical from tassel emergence to harvest. Moisture stress at tasselling and the week following usually results in poor cob formation. During hot, windy weather, corn will need 50 mm (2 in.) of water per week.

Potatoes

Potatoes are shallow rooted (80 cm/30 in.) and drought sensitive. Maintain soil moisture in the top 60 cm (24 in.) of the soil. Total water use over the growing season will be 450 to 600 mm (18–24 in.). The most critical stage at which adequate moisture is needed is from stolon initiation to tuber set. Stolon initiation begins at about the same time as flower bud formation. A water shortage early in the season reduces the number of tubers. A water shortage later limits tuber size. If water is limited, water once at flowering time and once three weeks later.

Root crops: carrot, parsnip, beet, and rutabaga

If the soil is dry, irrigate prior to seeding beets and rutabagas. Irrigation after seeding may result in cool soil, delayed emergence, and crusting, which impedes emergence. Carrots and parsnips benefit from frequent light irrigations during germination. Once established, these crops have a rooting zone of 60 to 90 cm (24–36 in.) and fairly low water needs until the roots begin to rapidly enlarge.

If the soil below the root is dry, the tips of carrots or parsnips will lose moisture to the soil and wither. Subsequent good moisture conditions may not overcome this deformity.

These root crops reach their maximum water use in September, especially if the weather is hot. Moisture shortages during the last third of their growth period will have the greatest effect on their yield and quality.

Herbs

Most herbs are native to the Mediterranean region and thrive under conditions of heat, full sun, and good drainage—perfect plants for the xeriscape!

Drought-tolerant herbs include: anise, borage, chamomile, chives, dill, fennel, sage, rosemary, lavender, thyme, and savory.

The unwatered orchard

Much of the fruit grown in the prairies is drought tolerant and will survive in a unirrigated orchard. Prior to planting, amend the soil with organic matter. Afterwards, mulch and weed as required.

Most fruit trees and small fruits capable of living through our winter are also quite drought tolerant. Drought-tolerant fruit can live, once established, without additional water for an almost unlimited number of years. They may, however, fail to produce fruit every year, and in dry years, the fruit may be of low quality.

The following practices will help ensure your plants' survival:
1) Cultivate (summerfallow) for the year previous to planting.
2) Water and weed newly planted trees for the first three to five years until their roots are established. Plant only the number of trees that you can water and care for in any one year.

Fruit cultivars suitable for the unwatered orchard tend to share certain characteristics. They are fully hardy (any fruit that suffers winter damage is likely to attempt extra growth to replace dieback and as a result will be less drought-tolerant). Plants that put on their growth early in the growing season tend to be more tolerant of dry summers, as are those that develop moderately and grow a small amount each year.

A well developed shelterbelt is essential for the unwatered orchard. It is also recommended that enough space be left between the fruit trees and the small fruit so that the roots and canopies of the fruit trees do not compete with the smaller bush fruit for light or moisture.

Tom Ward is with the Department of Horticulture Science, University of Saskatchewan.

Drought-tolerant fruit

Fruit is listed in order of drought-tolerance, with those that are the most drought-tolerant first, and those with lesser drought tolerance last.

Introduced fruit:
rhubarb *(Rheum rhabarbarum)*
golden currant *(Ribes aureum)*
sea buckthorn *(Hippophae rhamnoides)*
Missouri currant *(Ribes odoratum)*
apple *(Malus spp.)*
gooseberry *(Ribes spp.)*
Mongolian cherry *(Prunus fruticosa)*
plums *(Prunus spp.)*
- hybrids
- sand cherry x plum
red currants *(Ribes spp.)*
black currants *(Ribes spp.)*
Nanking cherry *(Prunus tomentosa)*

Native fruit:
chokecherry *(Prunus virginiana* var. *melanocarpa*
saskatoon berry *(Amelanchier alnifolia)*
pincherry *(Prunus pensylvanica)*
buffaloberry *(Shepherdia argentea)*
hawthorn *(Crataegus spp.)*
wild plum
- Canada plum *(Prunus nigra)*
- American plum *(Prunus americana)*
- sand cherry *(Prunus besseyi)*
blueberry *(Vaccinium myrtilloides)*
hazelnut *(Corylus cornuta)*
wild raspberry *(Rhubus spp.)*
wild strawberry *(Fragaria spp.)*
highbush cranberry *(Viburnum trilobum)*
lingonberry *(Vaccinium vitis-idaea)*

Part 3

Appendices

he greatest barriers are lack of public awareness, unrealistically low-priced water, and the negative image of xeriscape as an unattractive landscape of rocks, cacti, and plastic.

Implementing Change in Your Community

A public parking lot in Kamloops designed with drought-tolerant green ash and junipers to provide color, screening, and shade with minimal water use.

The landscapes of a community or country reflect its culture, the availability of water, and the value its people place on water. Changing the way people perceive their landscape is what xeriscape is all about.

Many Japanese gardens use little water. The classic gardens of the Moors of Spain and North Africa, influenced by the desert, used water sparingly in shallow canals, giving a visual and auditory impression of a lot more water than was actually present. In contrast, the North American landscape consists mainly of irrigated lawn, which requires enormous inputs of water. Our landscape reflects our comparatively low population and, until very recently, an abundant supply of water.

Water is a limited resource. We cannot make more of it. We must use the same water again and again. Our increasing population puts greater pressure on water resources. The environmental and monetary cost of supplying ourselves with clean water is increasing.

Pricing Water Realistically

Environment Canada estimates that by the year 2011, water use in Canadian municipalities could double if growth and consumption patterns continue. The average Canadian uses 390 L (100 U.S. gal.) of water a day, compared to 200 L

(50 U.S. gal.) in the British Isles and Sweden, and 150 L (40 U.S. gal.) in France and Germany. Drought-stricken areas of California are considering regulations that would limit water use to 200 L (50 U.S. gal.) of water per day.

The less we pay, the more we tend to use. The 1987 Federal Water Policy identified low water pricing as the main factor preventing expansion of present water treatment facilities. Canadian water rates vary enormously, from flat rates to metered billing. Even metered rates seldom reflect the true cost of water. The rate structures of many utilities actually reward waste by charging less per litre as more is used. Pricing water realistically encourages conservation. A 10 percent hike in water price has been shown to prompt a 3 to 7 percent decrease in consumption.

When water shortages occur, the alternative to conservation is expansion of existing facilities to meet the peak demand of summer landscape water use. This is an enormously expensive undertaking. Water must be piped, purified, and distributed, and sewage facilities expanded to equal capacity. As Sandra Postel, author of *Last Oasis*, commented, "managing demand rather than continually striving to meet it is a surer path to water security." Most water-conservation programs are implemented or strongly supported by the water-management agency within a community.

The largest single demand for residential water is landscape irrigation (estimated at 40 to 70 percent). Yet half of the water applied to our landscapes is either wasted or unneeded.

A large concrete public space is softened and made more inviting by allowing junipers to spill over a center planter.

The Xeriscape Movement

The xeriscape movement began in the western United States with the droughts of the late 1970s. Because it is not essential, landscape irrigation was the first use to be curtailed. A California community of 150,000 people lost nearly $30 million worth of landscape plants during the 1977–78 drought when irrigation was restricted.

In the "hydrological cycle," inappropriate landscapes put pressure on local water supplies, which are then forced to restrict water use. These restrictions are most detrimental to the very landscapes that caused the cycle. Unfortunately, once the immediate

'Morden Centennial' rose and thyme grace what would otherwise be a harsh expanse of asphalt in a public walkway.

shortage is over, people revert to their pre-drought irrigating practices.

In 1981, a task force consisting of the Denver Water Department, Colorado State University, and the Associated Landscape Contractors of Colorado met to determine what steps the landscape industry could take to reduce the effects of future droughts. They formed the National Xeriscape Council, Inc., a nonprofit organization interested in promoting xeriscape landscaping. By 1990, xeriscape programs had been established in many areas of the United States and Canada, often with the municipal water supply agency as a key participant.

Implementing Change

The greatest barriers to implementing a community xeriscape program are lack of public awareness of the issue, unrealistically low-priced water, and the negative image of xeriscape as an unattractive landscape of rocks, cacti, and plastic.

A positive attitude toward a water-conserving landscape is crucial if changes are to be made. The realization that water is a limited resource is a first step. Xeriscape is more effective in promoting this concept than is the imposition of bylaws restricting water use on our landscape.

A Saskatoon boulevard planting of drought-tolerant tawny daylily, a more water-conserving choice than a conventional turf planting.

Brian Baldwin

Communities can build awareness of xeriscape through mass media, brochures, public workshops, and demonstration gardens. Integrating all of these strategies is extremely effective. Why not xeriscape a public park, the grounds of a library, a town office, school, recreation centre, post office, tourist office, seniors home, or city hall? Ask for volunteers. Invite the local landscape industry to participate with donations of materials or labor. Use the hands-on xeriscape process as a public workshop. Install signage to explain what you've done and why. Encourage local media coverage. Distribute fact sheets and brochures explaining the xeriscape concept, why the project was initiated, and its benefits.

Many prairie communities, faced with a water shortage and impending restrictions, have just done that. Some of these programs are described below.

Xeriscape programs can broaden our vision. Good ideas catch on. People notice. Our landscape begins to change.

Regina

Located in the centre of the prairies and far from a major river system, the city of Regina decided in 1986 to adopt landscape water conservation as a cheaper alternative to major expansion of its water and sewer facilities. Its peak summer demand was three times that of the winter demand, and peak demand is what governs the size of facilities.

The concept of xeriscape was crucial to reducing peak

The Regina Xeriscape Demonstration Project

by Arnie Thiessen, Crosby Hanna & Associates

This project was conceived as a teaching tool to show Regina residents what xeriscape is all about and to help individuals visualize its application in their own yards. In partnership with SaskTel, the project was developed on a community switching station located in a residential area. The building, on a corner lot, was designed to blend into the neighborhood with a similar character to area houses.

Our approach was to provide a visually interesting landscape able to accommodate visitors and to incorporate a variety of materials and plant species. A winding bed around the building was flanked with two focal planting beds at the edge of the public walk. The beds were separated by a band of turf that encourages visitors to circulate through the site. Signage provides information.

Subsoil was cultivated to facilitate drainage through the ubiquitous Regina clay, and topsoil added. Existing grades were sloped from the building toward the street, but adjusted to make rainwater available to plants. Rainwater from the driveway was diverted to an adjacent shrub bed. Shallow catchment areas, mulched to make them less visible, were used to retain runoff water for plant use. Low berms were built into the shrub beds to provide visual interest and to reduce runoff from the lawn area into the gutter.

In order to give visitors a sense of the wide range of suitable plant material, over 40 species were used in the design: deciduous and evergreen trees and shrubs, perennials, and five species of grass. Plants were selected and arranged to provide a range of color and texture throughout the growing season. Silver- and grey-foliage plants unify the site through color repetition. Color contrast was provided by flowering shrubs and perennials. With the exception of one tree, all plants were placed within beds to ease lawn maintenance.

The front area encourages visitors to wander around the mixed borders. Two alternative grasses were used in the side yard. The sheep fescue in the semicircular bed is a very low maintenance turf often used as a ground cover. Adjacent to the bus stop are cool-season grasses, which become dormant during the heat of summer. For people who like to spend their summers at the lake, a backyard that doesn't need mowing or watering in the middle of summer could be a real plus.

A wood chip mulch was applied to a depth of 15 cm (6 in.) in shrub beds, and coarse peat moss to a depth of 10 cm (4 in.) in perennial

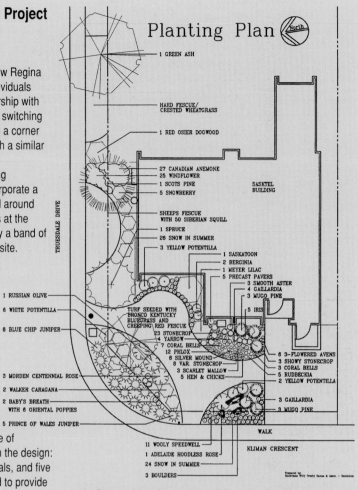

Planting Plan

1 GREEN ASH
HARD FESCUE/ CRESTED WHEATGRASS
1 RED OSIER DOGWOOD
27 CANADIAN ANEMONE
25 WINDFLOWER
1 SCOTS PINE
5 SNOWBERRY
SASKTEL BUILDING
SHEEPS FESCUE WITH 50 SIBERIAN SQUILL
1 SPRUCE
26 SNOW IN SUMMER
3 YELLOW POTENTILLA
1 SASKATOON
1 BERGINIA
1 MEYER LILAC
5 PRECAST PAVERS
3 SMOOTH ASTER
4 GAILLARDIA
3 MUGO PINE
5 IRIS
1 RUSSIAN OLIVE
6 WHITE POTENTILLA
8 BLUE CHIP JUNIPER
TURF SEEDED WITH BRONCO KENTUCKY BLUEGRASS AND CREEPING RED FESCUE
23 STONECROP
4 YARROW
7 CORAL BELLS
12 PHLOX
6 SILVER MOUND
8 VAR. STONECROP
3 SCARLET MALLOW
5 HEN & CHICKS
6 3-FLOWERED AVENS
3 SHOWY STONECROP
3 CORAL BELLS
5 RUDBECKIA
2 YELLOW POTENTILLA
3 MORDEN CENTENNIAL ROSE
2 WALKER CARAGANA
2 BABY'S BREATH WITH 6 ORIENTAL POPPIES
5 PRINCE OF WALES JUNIPER
3 GAILLARDIA
3 MUGO PINE
WALK
11 WOOLY SPEEDWELL
1 ADELAIDE HOODLESS ROSE
24 SNOW IN SUMMER
3 BOULDERS
KLIMAN CRESCENT

TRUESDALE DRIVE

beds. Both mulches form mats and do not tend to blow or spread. Lawn edging was installed to define the shrub bed. A landscape fabric was installed below the mulch to reduce weed growth.

The site has an automated, full-coverage irrigation system. The two grassed areas on the side of the property use traditional pop-up fan spray heads. To ensure maximum water efficiency, the heads are equipped with pressure compensators to prevent misting and minimize wind drift and evaporation. The timer is set to deliver several short periods of water application to allow deeper penetration and reduce runoff.

Shrub and perennial beds are watered with a drip emitter system. The multi-outlet emitters are located in small sleeves throughout the bed below the mulch. The lawn uses a subsurface irrigation system consisting of a polyethylene tube with drip emitters pre-spaced at regular intervals inside the pipe at the time of manufacture. It is installed in a series of offset rows at a 15 cm (6 in.) depth. This allows a slow infusion directly into the root zone so no water is lost to evaporation.

The controller for the system was selected for versatility. It provides extended periods of operation for the emitters and a series of short cycles for the pop-up sprinklers.

A parking lot surrounded by a mixed tree-shrub border of drought-tolerant species provides beauty, screening, and shade.

water use. The program was initiated by the city water engineer and aimed at homeowners, professionals, and land developers. In 1993 the City of Regina set as its goal to reduce peak and overall per capita water use by 15 percent by the year 2011. They are already on their way to meeting that goal.

The program was supported by local home builders, private developers, the University of Saskatchewan, and a film production company that produced a television series on xeriscaping (see suggestions for further reading at the end of chapter 1). Well-informed media coverage was abundant, and the city has garnered much public support through brochures, fact sheets, free public workshops, and a demonstration project (see p. 209).

Regina has reduced mowing and irrigation in many of its coarse-grassed buffer strips and open areas and carried out a mulching program for trees and shrubs. Irrigation is applied at night and in the early morning. Berms and knolls in parks are no longer being built as they require excessive water to prevent browning. Irrigated grass center medians in streets have been largely eliminated and replaced with mulched trees watered with drip irrigation.

Regina promotes xeriscape as "the natural choice"—a low-water, low-maintenance landscape that is the environmentally responsible way to a beautiful, practical yard that saves time and cuts water bills.

Edmonton

Edmonton has an average of 35 cm (14 in.) of precipitation per year. During the growing season, 50 percent of the water used by the average family living in a single-family dwelling is for landscape irrigation.

Edmonton actively supports the efficient use of its water and is committed to a reduction of consumption by providing information and technical assistance to its customers. In 1994, it set a goal to reduce per capita water consumption by 10 percent by 1997. By the spring of 1996, they had already achieved a 14 percent reduction in consumption.

In the greater Edmonton area, the xeriscape concept is called "ecoscape." Its benefits are promoted as water conservation, low maintenance, and an attractive and useful landscape that saves time, money, and effort. The use of native plants is emphasized.

The City of Edmonton Water Branch (AQUALTA) meters all water users. Total residential and industrial consumption averages 390 L (100 U.S. gal.) per day per person. The per capita water use in Edmonton is about half that of Calgary

The public xeriscape: Parking lots to parks

Over the past few decades, we've become accustomed to barren parking lots and municipal facilities marked by signs that are in themselves urban eyesores. Conventional landscaping requires too much water and maintenance to be practical in these areas, but the innovative use of xeriscape design can make these facilities attractive without the associated maintenance.

Above and below: Facility sign planting at the Saskatoon Field House.

Downtown parking lot and facility sign plantings in Saskatoon
by Terry Klassen

Downtown parking lot and facility sign plantings in Saskatoon were installed early in the summer of 1992. Only two of the nine sites were irrigated and little difference was noted between the irrigated and nonirrigated beds.

The beds were excavated to a depth of 45 cm (18 in.). The existing soil was replaced with a herbicide-treated soil mixture for weed control and planted with mature containerized perennials and the occasional shrub (with the pots removed prior to installation). Wood fiber mulch was installed. During the first summer, both irrigated and nonirrigated beds were watered two to three times a week depending on natural moisture conditions.

Plants used for these projects include: daylily *(Hemerocallis),* common yarrow *(Achillea millefolium* 'Cerise Queen'), coral bells *(Heuchera),* spike speedwell *(Veronica spicata),* blanket flower *(Gaillardia aristata),* bearded iris *(Iris* x *germanica),* wormwood *(Artemisia schmidtiana* 'Silver Mound'), golden marguerite *(Anthemis tinctoria),* sneezewort *(Achillea ptarmica* 'The Pearl'), Colorado spruce *(Picea pungens),* shrubby cinquefoil *(Potentilla fruticosa* 'Coronation Triumph'), 'Cuthbert Grant' rose *(Rosa* 'Cuthbert Grant'), shasta daisy *(Chrysanthemum* x *superbum),* bergenia *(Bergenia crassifolia),* and 'Adelaide Hoodless' rose *(Rosa* 'Adelaide Hoodless').

Terry Klassen is owner of KLA Group, Inc., Saskatoon.

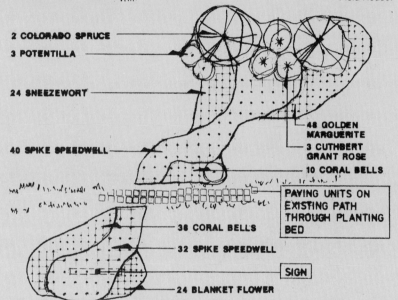

2 COLORADO SPRUCE
3 POTENTILLA
24 SNEEZEWORT
40 SPIKE SPEEDWELL
48 GOLDEN MARGUERITE
3 CUTHBERT GRANT ROSE
10 CORAL BELLS
PAVING UNITS ON EXISTING PATH THROUGH PLANTING BED
36 CORAL BELLS
32 SPIKE SPEEDWELL
SIGN
24 BLANKET FLOWER

Left and right: Two downtown parking lots in Saskatoon.

(which is only partially metered). AQUALTA regularly implements odd/even watering (restricting watering according to residential street numbering), and a total ban is imposed when reservoir levels fall.

The xeriscape demonstration garden at Summerland, British Columbia, has a wide range of labelled, drought-tolerant plantings.

Kamloops

Kamloops has an average of 25 cm (10 in.) of precipitation annually. The average citizen uses 450 L (120 U.S. gal.) of water per day in winter, and as much as 2,000 L (525 U.S. gal.) on hot summer days. Kamloops has had an extensive water conservation program since 1992, with the goal of reducing peak period demands by 25 percent without instituting universal metering. The city has a xeriscape demonstration garden and distributes xeriscape brochures emphasizing low maintenance, water and money savings, the attractive and functional nature of xeriscape landscapes, and their environmental appropriateness.

Ornamental Plant Charts

| Trees & Shrubs | LIGHT | | | TYPE | | HEIGHT | | | | | | | FOLIAGE | | | | | | |
| | | | | | | | | | | | | | Color (F = fall color) | | | | | | |
Botanical Name	Sun	Partial Shade	Full Shade	Conifer/Evergreen	Deciduous	Under 30 cm (1 ft)	30 cm–1 m (1–3 ft)	1–2 m (3–6 ft)	2–5 m (6–16 ft)	5–10 m (16–33 ft)	10–15 m (33–50 ft)	15–20 m (50–65 ft)	Variegated	Green	Gold/Yellow/Orange	Purple/Red	Blue	Grey	Compound Leaves
Acer ginnala	•	•			•					•				•	F	F			
Acer negundo	•				•						•			•	F				•
Amelanchier alnifolia	•	•			•				•					•	F	F			
Amorpha canescens	•				•			•						•				•	•
Amorpha fruticosa	•	•			•			•						•					•
Arctostaphylos uva-ursi	•	•		•		•								•		•			
Caragana arborescens 'Lorbergii'	•				•				•					•					•
Caragana arborescens 'Pendula'	•				•		•	•						•					•
Caragana arborescens 'Sutherland'	•				•				•					•					•
Caragana arborescens 'Walker'	•				•			•						•					•
Caragana frutex 'globosa'	•				•			•						•					•
Caragana pygmaea	•				•		•							•					•
Corylus cornuta	•	•			•			•						•	F				
Cotoneaster adpressus	•	•			•	•								•					
Cotoneaster integerrimus	•	•			•			•						•	F				
Cotoneaster lucidus	•	•			•				•					•	F	F			
Crataegus arnoldiana	•				•				•					•					
Crataegus chlorosarca	•				•				•					•					
Crataegus chrysocarpa	•				•				•					•					
Crataegus columbiana	•				•				•					•					
Crataegus crus-galli	•				•				•					•	F	F			
Crataegus x 'Snowbird'	•				•				•					•					
Cytisus pilosa 'Vancouver Gold'	•				•									•					

Ornamental Bark	Ornamental Flowers	Ornamental Fruit/Seeds/Cones	Fragrant	Edible Landscape	Shelter for Wildlife	Food for Wildlife	Native Plant	Pre-treatment (d = day, m = month, r.t. = room temperature, h.w. = hot water)	Sow Outdoors In	Budding/Grafting	Stem Cuttings	Layering	Suckers	Root Cuttings	Division	Page Number	Common Name
	•					•		4 m @ 5°C	Fall							97	ginnala maple, Amur maple
						•	•	45 d @ 5°C	mid-Sept							97	Manitoba maple, box elder
	W		•	•	•	•	•	5 m @ 5°C	Fall	•	•		•			98	saskatoon berry
	B					•					•	•	•			98	leadplant
	B				•	•		scarified 3 m @ 5°C	Fall		•					99	false indigo
	W/P	•				•	•				•					99	bearberry, kinnikinnick
	Y									•						99	fern-leafed caragana
	Y									•						100	weeping caragana
	Y									•						100	'Sutherland' caragana
	Y									•						100	'Walker' caragana
				•									•			100	globe caragana
	Y			•					Fall							100	pygmy caragana
			•	•	•	•		3 m @ 5°C								100	beaked hazelnut
	•					•		3–5 m @ r.t. + 3 m @ 5°C	early July							101	creeping cotoneaster
	•				•	•		3–5 m @ r.t. + 3 m @ 5°C	early July							101	European red-berried cotoneaster
•					•	•		3–5 m @ r.t. + 3 m @ 5°C	early July							101	hedge cotoneaster
	W	•			•	•			July							102	'Arnold' hawthorn
•	•				•	•			July							102	chlorosarca hawthorn
	W	•			•	•	•		July							102	roundleaf or fireberry hawthorn
	W	•			•	•	•		July							102	Columbian hawthorn
	W	•			•	•	•		July							102	cockspur hawthorn
	W			•						•						102	'Snowbird' hawthorn
	Y	•									•					103	'Vancouver Gold' broom

LANDSCAPE USE (B = blue, P = pink, Pu = purple, W = white, Y = yellow)

PROPAGATION — Seed / Vegetative

Trees & Shrubs	LIGHT			TYPE		HEIGHT							FOLIAGE						
														Color (F = fall color)					
Botanical Name	Sun	Partial Shade	Full Shade	Conifer/Evergreen	Deciduous	Under 30 cm (1 ft)	30 cm–1 m (1–3 ft)	1–2 m (3–6 ft)	2–5 m (6–16 ft)	5–10 m (16–33 ft)	10–15 m (33–50 ft)	15–20 m (50–65 ft)	Variegated	Green	Gold/Yellow/Orange	Purple/Red	Blue	Grey	Compound Leaves
Elaeagnus angustifolia	•				•					•								•	
Elaeagnus commutata	•				•				•									•	
Fraxinus pensylvanica var. *subintegerrima*	•	•			•						•			•	F				
Genista tinctoria	•				•		•							•					
Halimodendron halodendron	•				•				•					•					•
Hippophae rhamnoides	•				•				•									•	
Juniperus communis	•	•		•			•	•						•		F			
Juniperus horizontalis	•	•		•		•								•		F	•		
Juniperus sabina	•	•		•			•	•						•		F			
Juniperus scopulorum	•			•					•	•				•			•	•	
Larix sibrica	•			•	•							•		•	F				
Lonicera caerulea var. *edulis*	•	•			•			•						•					
Lonicera 'Cameo'	•	•			•				•					•					
Lonicera 'Flamingo'	•	•			•				•					•					
Lonicera maackii	•	•			•				•					•					
Lonicera 'Miniglobe'	•	•			•		•							•					
Lonicera 'Sunstar'	•	•			•				•					•					
Lonicera tatarica ('Arnold Red')	•	•			•				•					•					
Lonicera (tatarica x xylosteum)	•	•			•			•						•					
Malus baccata	•				•					•				•					
Malus (hybrids)	•				•					•				•	F	F			
Philadelphus lewisii 'Waterton'	•				•				•					•					
Physocarpus opulifolius	•	•			•				•					•					

LANDSCAPE USE
(B = blue, P = pink, Pu = purple, W = white, Y = yellow)

PROPAGATION

Ornamental Bark	Ornamental Flowers	Ornamental Fruit/Seeds/Cones	Fragrant	Edible Landscpae	Shelter for Wildlife	Food for Wildlife	Native Plant	Pre-treatment (d = day, m = month, r.t. = room temperature, h.w. = hot water)	Sow Outdoors In	Budding/Grafting	Stem Cuttings	Layering	Suckers	Root Cuttings	Division	Page Number	Common Name
		•				•		3 m @ 5°C			•					103	Russian olive
		•			•	•	•	2-3 m @ 5°C		•	•		•			103	wolf willow, silverberry
					•	•		3 m @ 5°C			•					104	green ash
	Y								when ripe		•					104	dyer's greenweed, broom
	P								when ripe	•			•			105	salt bush
	•			•		•		3 m @ 5°C or 24 h in h.w.				•		•		105	sea buckthorn
	•				•	•	•	3 m @ r.t. 3 m @ 5°C			•		•			106	common juniper
	•					•	•	3 m @ r.t. 3 m @ 5°C		•	•	•				106	creeping juniper
	•				•	•				•	•		•			106	savin juniper
	•				•	•				•	•					106	Rocky Mountain juniper
	•							3 m @ 5°C	when ripe							107	Siberian larch
	Y/W	•		•		•		3 m @ 5°C			•				•	108	sweetberry honeysuckle
	W		•			•					•				•	108	'Cameo' honeysuckle
	P		•			•					•				•	108	'Flamingo' honeysuckle
	W		•					3 m @ 5°C			•				•	108	Amur honeysuckle
											•				•	108	'Miniglobe' honeysuckle
	W		•			•					•				•	108	'Sunstar' honeysuckle
	P		•			•		3 m @ 5°C			•				•	108	'Arnold Red' honeysuckle
											•				•	108	'Clavey's Dwarf' honeysuckle
	W	•	•			•		2 m @ 5°C			•					108	Siberian crabapple
	P/W	•	•	•		•				•						109	crabapple hybrids
	W		•						when ripe		•				•	109	'Waterton' mockorange
	•								when ripe		•				•	110	common ninebark

Botanical Name	LIGHT			TYPE		HEIGHT							FOLIAGE Color (F = fall color)						
	Sun	Partial Shade	Full Shade	Conifer/Evergreen	Deciduous	Under 30 cm (1 ft)	30 cm–1 m (1–3 ft)	1–2 m (3–6 ft)	2–5 m (6–16 ft)	5–10 m (16–33 ft)	10–15 m (33–50 ft)	15–20 m (50–65 ft)	Variegated	Green	Gold/Yellow/Orange	Purple/Red	Blue	Grey	Compound Leaves
Picea glauca 'Densata'	•			•								•		•					
Picea pungens	•			•								•		•			•	•	
Picea pungens 'Glauca Globosa'	•			•			•										•	•	
Pinus banksiana	•			•							•			•					
Pinus cembra	•			•							•			•					
Pinus contorta var. latifolia	•			•								•		•					
Pinus flexilis	•			•						•				•					
Pinus mugo	•			•				•	•	•				•					
Pinus ponderosa	•			•								•		•					
Pinus sylvestris	•			•								•		•					
Potentilla 'Abbotswood'	•				•		•							•				•	•
Potentilla 'Coronation Triumph'	•				•		•							•				•	•
Potentilla 'Elizabeth'	•				•			•						•				•	•
Potentilla fruticosa	•				•			•						•					•
Potentilla 'Goldfinger'	•				•		•							•				•	•
Potentilla 'Katherine Dykes'	•				•		•							•				•	•
Potentilla 'Snowbird'	•				•		•							•				•	•
Potentilla 'Yellowbird'	•				•		•							•				•	•
Prinsepia sinensis	•	•			•			•						•					
Prunus x cistena	•				•		•									•			
Prunus fruticosa	•				•			•						•					
Prunus padus var. commutata	•				•					•				•		•			
Prunus pensylvanica	•				•					•				•	F				

Ornamental Bark	Ornamental Flowers	Ornamental Fruit/Seeds/Cones	Fragrant	Edible Landscpae	Shelter for Wildlife	Food for Wildlife	Native Plant	Pre-treatment (d = day, m = month, r.t. = room temperature, h.w. = hot water)	Sow Outdoors In	Budding/Grafting	Stem Cuttings	Layering	Suckers	Root Cuttings	Division	Page Number	Common Name
		•			•	•		2 m @ 5°C								110	Black Hills spruce
		•			•	•		1 m @ 5°C		•	•					111	Colorado spruce
										•						111	'Glauca Globosa' spruce
		•			•	•	•		when ripe							112	jack pine
		•		•	•	•		3 m @ 5°C								113	Swiss stone pine
		•			•	•	•		when ripe							113	lodgepole pine
		•			•	•			when ripe							113	limber pine
		•			•	•			when ripe		•					114	mugo pine
•		•			•	•			when ripe							114	ponderosa pine
•		•			•	•			when ripe							115	Scots pine
	W				•						•				•	116	'Abbotswood' potentilla
	Y				•						•				•	116	'Coronation Triumph' potentilla
	Y				•						•				•	116	'Elizabeth' potentilla
	Y				•						•					115	potentilla
	Y				•						•				•	116	'Goldfinger' potentilla
	Y				•						•				•	116	'Katherine Dykes' potentilla
	W				•						•				•	116	'Snowbird' potentilla
	Y				•						•				•	116	'Yellowbird' potentilla
	Y	•	•			•		2 m @ 5°C + 2.5 m r.t.			•					116	cherry prinsepia
											•					117	cistena cherry
	W	•		•		•		4 m @ 5°C			•		•			117	Mongolian cherry
	W	•	•	•	•	•		5 m @ 5°C			•					117	mayday tree
	W	•		•		•	•	5 m @ 5°C		•			•			118	pincherry

Trees & Shrubs Botanical Name	LIGHT			TYPE		HEIGHT							FOLIAGE Color (F = fall color)						Compound Leaves
	Sun	Partial Shade	Full Shade	Conifer/Evergreen	Deciduous	Under 30 cm (1 ft)	30 cm–1 m (1–3 ft)	1–2 m (3–6 ft)	2–5 m (6–16 ft)	5–10 m (16–33 ft)	10–15 m (33–50 ft)	15–20 m (50–65 ft)	Variegated	Green	Gold/Yellow/Orange	Purple/Red	Blue	Grey	
Prunus tenella	•	•			•		•							•					
Prunus tomentosa	•				•			•						•					
Prunus triloba 'Dropmore'	•				•				•					•		•			
Prunus virginiana var. *melanocarpa*	•	•			•					•				•		F			
Pyrus ussuriensis	•				•					•				•					
Quercus macrocarpa	•				•							•		•	F				
Rhus glabra	•				•				•					•		F			•
Rhus trilobata	•				•		•							•		F			
Ribes alpinum	•	•	•		•			•						•	F				
Ribes aureum	•	•			•			•						•	F				
Ribes oxycanthoides	•	•			•		•							•	F	F			
Rosa acicularis	•				•			•						•					•
Rosa arkansana	•				•		•							•		F			•
Rosa 'Hansa'	•				•			•						•					•
Rosa 'Hazeldean'	•				•			•						•					•
Rosa 'Marie Bugnet'	•				•		•							•					•
Rosa 'Morden Centennial'	•				•			•						•					•
Rosa 'Prairie Youth'	•				•			•						•					•
Rosa rubrifolia	•				•			•								•			•
Rosa spinosissima var. *altaica*	•				•			•						•					•
Rosa 'Theresa Bugnet'	•				•			•						•					•
Rosa woodsii	•	•			•			•						•					•
Sambucus racemosa	•	•			•				•					•	•				•

Ornamental Bark	Ornamental Flowers	Ornamental Fruit/Seeds/Cones	Fragrant	Edible Landscape	Shelter for Wildlife	Food for Wildlife	Native Plant	Pre-treatment (d = day, m = month, r.t. = room temperature, h.w. = hot water)	Sow Outdoors In	Budding/Grafting	Stem Cuttings	Layering	Suckers	Root Cuttings	Division	Page Number	Common Name
	P							5 m @ 5°C			•		•			118	Russian almond
	P	•		•	•	•		5 m @ 5°C								119	Nanking cherry
	P			•				5 m @ 5°C								119	'Dropmore' double flowering plum
	W	•	•	•	•	•	•	5 m @ 5°C			•		•			120	chokecherry
	W		•	•				3 m @ 5°C								120	Ussurian pear
	•				•	•			Fall							121	bur oak
	•					•							•			121	smooth sumac
	•					•		5 m @ 21°C + 3 m @ 5°C					•			121	lemonade sumac
			•	•	•			3 m @ 5°C			•					122	alpine currant
	Y		•	•	•	•	•	3 m @ 5°C			•	•				122	golden currant
			•	•		•	•		Fall		•		•			123	wild gooseberry
	P	•	•	•		•	•	5 m @ 5°C			•		•			123	prickly rose
	P	•	•	•		•	•	5 m @ 5°C			•		•			123	prairie rose
	Pu	•	•	•		•					•		•			123	'Hansa' rose
	Y										•					123	'Hazeldean' rose
	W		•								•					123	'Marie Bugnet' rose
	P	•		•		•					•					123	'Morden Centennial' rose
	P										•					124	'Prairie Youth' rose
	P	•		•		•		5 m @ 5°C			•		•			124	red-leafed rose
	W	•	•	•		•		5 m @ 5°C			•		•			123	Altai rose
	P		•								•					124	'Theresa Bugnet' rose
	P	•		•		•	•	2 m @ 21°C + 3 m @ 5°C			•		•			123	woods rose
	W	•			•	•					•					124	European red elder

Trees & Shrubs — Botanical Name	LIGHT			TYPE		HEIGHT							FOLIAGE Color (F = fall color)						Compound Leaves
	Sun	Partial Shade	Full Shade	Conifer/Evergreen	Deciduous	Under 30 cm (1 ft)	30 cm–1 m (1–3 ft)	1–2 m (3–6 ft)	2–5 m (6–16 ft)	5–10 m (16–33 ft)	10–15 m (33–50 ft)	15–20 m (50–65 ft)	Variegated	Green	Gold/Yellow/Orange	Purple/Red	Blue	Grey	
Sheperdia argentea	•				•				•									•	
Sorbaria sorbifolia	•	•	•		•			•						•					•
Spiraea trilobata	•				•			•						•					
Symphoricarpos occidentalis	•	•			•		•	•										•	
Syringa x hyacinthiflora	•				•				•					•					
Syringa meyeri	•				•			•						•					
Syringa patula 'Miss Kim'	•				•			•	•					•					
Syringa x prestoniae	•				•				•					•					
Syringa reticulata	•				•					•				•					
Syringa villosa	•				•				•					•					
Syringa vulgaris	•				•				•					•					
Viburnum lantana	•	•			•				•					•					
Viburnum lentago	•	•			•					•				•		F			

Ornamental Bark	Ornamental Flowers	Ornamental Fruit/Seeds/Cones	Fragrant	Edible Landscape	Shelter for Wildlife	Food for Wildlife	Native Plant	Pre-treatment (d = day, m = month, r.t. = room temperature, h.w. = hot water)	Sow Outdoors In	Budding/Grafting	Stem Cuttings	Layering	Suckers	Root Cuttings	Division	Page Number	Common Name
	•		•	•		•	•	3 m @ 5°C			•					125	silver buffaloberry
	W										•		•		•	125	Ural false spirea
	W								when ripe		•				•	126	three-lobed spirea
	P/W	•			•	•	•	5 m @ 5°C					•			126	western snowberry
	Pu/W		•			•					•		•			127	hyacinth-flowered lilac
	P/Pu		•			•					•		•			128	Meyer lilac
	P		•			•					•		•			128	'Miss Kim' lilac
	P		•			•					•		•			128	Preston lilac
	W		•			•					•		•			128	Japanese tree lilac
	P		•			•		2 m @ 5°C + 75 d @ 21°C			•		•			128	late lilac
	Pu/B		•			•					•					127	common lilac
	W	•						5 m @ 22°C + 3 m @ 5°C	when ripe		•					129	wayfaring tree
	W	•				•					•					129	nannyberry

Perennials

Botanical Name	Full Sun	Partial Shade	Full Shade	Mat-like (<30 cm/1 ft)	30–60 cm (1–2 ft)	60 cm–1 m (2–3 ft)	1–1.2 m (3–4 ft)	Over 1.2 m (4 ft)	White	Yellow	Orange	Red	Pink	Purple	Blue	Early	Mid	Late	Fresh	Dried
	LIGHT			**HEIGHT RANGE**					**FLOWER — Color**							**Season of Interest/Bloom**			**Cut**	
Achillea millefolium	•				•				•			•	•	•			•	•	•	•
Achillea ptarmica	•				•				•								•	•	•	•
Achillea tomentosa	•			•						•						•				
Aegopodium podagraria 'Variegatum'	•	•			•				•							•	•	•		
Alcea rosea	•						•	•	•	•		•	•	•			•	•		
Anemone sylvestris	•	•	•		•				•							•		•		
Antennaria rosea	•			•					•				•			•	•			•
Anthemis tinctoria	•				•					•							•			
Arabis spp.	•	•		•					•				•			•				
Artemisia ludoviciana	•					•		•								•	•	•		•
Artemisia schmidtiana	•				•				•							•	•	•		
Artemisia stellerana	•			•	•					•						•	•	•		
Aurinia saxatilis	•			•						•						•				
Baptisia australis	•						•								•		•	•	•	•
Bergenia cordifolia	•	•	•	•	•								•	•		•				
Bromus inermis 'Skinner's Golden'	•	•				•										•	•	•		
Campanula carpatica	•	•		•					•						•		•			
Campanula cochlearifolia	•	•	•	•					•						•		•			
Centaurea macrocephala	•	•					•			•								•	•	•
Centaurea montana	•	•			•				•				•		•		•			
Cerastium tomentosum	•			•					•							•	•			
Coryphantha vivipara	•			•									•				•			
Dianthus deltoides	•			•					•				•	•			•			
Dianthus plumarius	•			•	•				•				•	•		•	•		•	

224 • *Creating the Prairie Xeriscape*

Long-flowering	Fragrant	Grey Foliage	Variegated Foliage	Naturalizing	Invasive	Poisonous	Birds	Butterflies	Bees	Native Plant	Seed	Self-seed	Division/Rhizomes	Stem Cuttings	Root Cuttings	Tissue Culture	Page Number	Common Name
•	•			•	•			•		•	•		•	•			131	common yarrow
				•							•		•	•			131	sneezewort
		•											•				131	dwarf woolly yarrow
			•		•								•				132	goutweed
							•	•	•			•					132	hollyhock
				•							•	•	•				133	wind flower, snowdrop anemone
		•								•			•				133	pussytoes, antennaria
	•			•							•	•	•	•			133	golden marguerite, chamomile
		•	•					•			•		•	•	•		134	rockcress
	•	•		•	•								•	•			134	'Silver King' artemisia
	•	•											•	•			135	'Silver Mound' artemisia
		•		•	•							•	•	•			135	'Silver Brocade' artemisia
		•									•		•	•			135	perennial alyssum
								•			•						136	false indigo
		E									•		•	•			136	bergenia
			•	•	•								•				137	'Skinner's Golden' bromegrass
•											•		•				137	Carpathian bellflower
•				•							•		•				137	creeping bellflower
											•	•	•				138	globe centaurea
				•				•	•		•		•				138	perennial cornflower
•		•		•							•		•	•			138	snow-in-summer
										•	•			•			139	pincushion cactus
•											•		•	•			139	maiden pinks
•	•	•									•			•			139	grass pinks

Perennials

Botanical Name	LIGHT			HEIGHT RANGE					FLOWER Color							Season of Interest/Bloom			Cut	
	Full Sun	Partial Shade	Full Shade	Mat-like (<30 cm/1 ft)	30–60 cm (1–2 ft)	60 cm–1 m (2–3 ft)	1–1.2 m (3–4 ft)	Over 1.2 m (4 ft)	White	Yellow	Orange	Red	Pink	Purple	Blue	Early	Mid	Late	Fresh	Dried
Dictamnus albus	•					•			•				•				•			
Echinops ritro	•						•								•			•		•
Elymus arenarius	•					•										•	•	•		•
Erigeron speciosus 'Pink Jewel'	•					•							•				•		•	
Eryngium spp.	•					•									•			•	•	•
Erysimum asperum	•	•			•					•	•					•	•			
Euphorbia cyparissias	•				•					•						•				
Festuca ovina var. *glauca*	•	•		•	•					•						•	•	•		
Gaillardia aristata	•				•	•				•	•	•		•			•		•	
Geranium macrorrhizum	•	•	•		•				•				•				•			
Gypsophila paniculata	•						•		•				•				•			
Gypsophila repens	•			•					•				•				•		•	
Hemerocallis spp.	•	•	•		•	•	•			•	•	•	•	•		•	•	•		
Heuchera spp.	•				•								•			•	•		•	
Iris spp.	•			•	•	•			•	•	•	•	•	•	•	•				
Leontopodium alpinum	•	•		•					•	•						•				•
Limonium spp.	•					•									•		•	•	•	•
Linum perenne.	•				•				•						•		•			
Malva spp.	•	•				•	•		•				•	•			•		•	
Nepeta x *ucranica* 'Dropmore'	•	•			•									•		•	•	•	•	
Oenothera missouriensis	•				•					•							•	•		•
Opuntia polyacantha	•			•						•							•			
Paeonia spp.	•					•			•	•		•	•	•		•			•	

226 • *Creating the Prairie Xeriscape*

Long-flowering	Fragrant	Grey Foliage	Variegated Foliage	Naturalizing	Invasive	Poisonous	Birds	Butterflies	Bees	Native Plant	Seed	Self-seed	Division/Rhizomes	Stem Cuttings	Root Cuttings	Tissue Culture	Page Number	Common Name
											•				•		140	gasplant
				•				•	•		•	•			•		140	globe thistle
			•	•	•								•				140	blue lyme grass
•								•			•		•	•			141	'Pink Jewel' Oregon fleabane
											•		•	•	•		141	sea holly
•				•							•	•					141	Siberian wallflower
				•	•	•					•		•	•			142	cypress spurge
											•		•				142	blue fescue
•				•				•	•	•	•	•	•		•		142	gaillardia, blanket flower
•	•			•							•		•	•	•		143	bigfoot geranium
•				•	•						•						144	babysbreath
•											•					•	143	creeping babysbreath
	•			•			•	•	•		•		•				144	daylily
•										•			•				145	coral bells
			•								•		•				146	bearded iris
											•		•				146	edelweiss
•											•				•		147	sea lavender
•				•							•			•			147	perennial flax
•								•			•	•		•			148	malva hollyhock, musk mallow
•	•								•				•	•			148	'Dropmore' catmint
•				•			•				•		•	•			149	Missouri evening primrose
				•						•	•			•			149	prickly pear cactus
	•										•		•				149	peony

Appendix 2: Ornamental Plant Charts • 227

Perennials — Botanical Name	LIGHT — Full Sun	Partial Shade	Full Shade	HEIGHT RANGE — Mat-like (<30 cm/1 ft)	30–60 cm (1–2 ft)	60 cm–1 m (2–3 ft)	1–1.2 m (3–4 ft)	Over 1.2 m (4 ft)	FLOWER — Color — White	Yellow	Orange	Red	Pink	Purple	Blue	Season of Interest/Bloom — Early	Mid	Late	Cut — Fresh	Dried
Papaver nudicaule	•				•				•	•	•		•			•	•	•		
Papaver orientale	•					•			•		•	•	•	•		•			•	•
Phalaris arundinacea var. *picta*	•	•	•			•										•	•			
Phlox spp.	•	•		•					•				•	•		•				
Polygonum bistorta 'Superbum'	•	•			•				•				•				•		•	
Potentilla spp.	•			•	•					•						•	•			
Salvia x *superba*	•				•									•	•		•		•	
Saponaria ocymoides	•			•									•			•	•			
Sedum spp.	•	•		•	•					•	•		•			•	•	•		
Sempervivum spp.	•			•					•				•			•	•	•		
Silene vulgaris var. *maritima*	•			•					•							•	•	•		
Solidago hybrids	•					•				•							•	•	•	
Sphaeralcea coccinea	•			•								•				•				
Stachys byzantina	•				•									•		•	•			
Stachys grandiflora	•	•			•									•			•		•	
Symphytum officinale	•	•	•			•							•		•	•	•	•		
Tanacetum vulgare	•	•				•				•							•	•	•	•
Thermopsis caroliniana	•						•			•							•		•	
Thymus spp.	•			•					•				•	•		•	•			
Verbascum nigrum	•					•				•							•	•	•	
Veronica spp.	•			•	•								•		•		•			
Viola canadensis		•	•	•	•				•							•				
Viola tricolor	•	•	•	•					•	•					•	•	•	•		
Yucca glauca	•					•			•							•	•	•		

228 • *Creating the Prairie Xeriscape*

Long-flowering	Fragrant	Grey Foliage	Variegated Foliage	Naturalizing	Invasive	Poisonous	Birds	Butterflies	Bees	Native Plant	Seed	Self-seed	Division/Rhizomes	Stem Cuttings	Root Cuttings	Tissue Culture	Page Number	Common Name
•				•							•	•					150	Iceland poppy
											•		•		•		150	Oriental poppy
			•	•	•								•				151	ribbon grass
													•	•			151	Arctic or moss phlox
•				•							•		•	•			152	knotweed
				•	•					•	•		•				152	orangespot cinquefoil, silverweed
•											•	•	•	•			152	salvia 'Superba'
											•	•	•	•			153	rock soapwort
			•					•			•		•	•			153	stonecrop
													•				154	hens and chicks, house leek
•				•							•	•		•			154	sea campion
•				•	•		•	•	•	•			•	•			154	goldenrod
										•	•		•				155	prairie mallow
		•									•		•				155	lambs ears
											•		•				155	big betony
•			•	•	•						•		•		•		156	comfrey
•				•	•						•		•				156	common tansy
				•							•						156	false lupine, thermopsis
•	•	•						•	•		•		•	•			157	thyme
•				•							•	•			•		157	verbascum, dark mullein
		•							•		•		•	•			157	veronica, speedwell
	•			•	•					•			•				158	Canada violet
•				•	•						•	•					158	johnny-jump-up
		•								•	•		•		•		159	yucca

Appendix 2: Ornamental Plant Charts • 229

Vines — Botanical Name	TYPE		LIGHT			HEIGHT		LANDSCAPE VALUE — Flowers						Other	
	Perennial	Annual	Sun	Partial Shade	Shade	1.5–4.5 m (5–15 ft)	4.5–9 m (15–30 ft)	White	Yellow/Orange	Red	Pink	Purple	Blue	Ornamental Fruit/Seed	Autumn Color
Celastrus scandens	•		•				•	•						•	•
Clematis ligusticifolia	•		•	•		•		•						•	
Clematis tangutica	•		•	•			•		•						
Clematis macropetala	•		•	•		•							•		
Clematis 'Markham'	•		•	•		•					•				
Clematis 'Bluebird'	•		•	•		•							•		
Clematis 'Maidwell Hall'	•		•	•		•							•		
Clematis 'Snowbird'	•		•	•		•		•							
Clematis 'White Swan'	•		•	•		•		•							
Clematis 'Prairie Traveller's Joy'	•		•	•		•		•							
Clematis 'Blue Boy'	•		•	•		•							•		
Clematis 'Rosy O'Grady'	•		•	•		•					•				
Clematis alpina	•		•	•		•							•		
Clematis 'Pamela Jackman'	•		•	•		•							•		
Clematis 'Ruby'	•		•	•		•				•					
Clematis 'Willy'	•		•	•		•					•				
Clematis 'Francis Rivis'	•		•	•		•							•		
Echinocystis lobata		•	•	•		•		•						•	
Humulus lupulus	•		•				•	•						•	
Ipomea tricolor		•	•			•		•		•	•	•	•		
Lonicera x brownii 'Dropmore Scarlet Trumpet'	•		•	•			•		•						
Parthenocissus quinquefolia	•		•	•	•	•								•	•
Tropaeolum majus		•	•			•			•	•					
Vitis riparia	•		•	•	•		•							•	

Native Plant	Seed — Pre-treatment (m = month)	Seed — Sow	Seed — Biodegradable Pots	Vegetative — Stem Cuttings	Vegetative — Layering	Vegetative — Suckers	Vegetative — Root Cuttings	Vegetative — Division	Page Number	Common Name
		When ripe		•	•				160	American bittersweet
•	3 m @ 5°C								160	western virgin's bower
	3 m @ 5°C								160	golden clematis
	3 m @ 5°C								160	big petal clematis
				•					161	'Markham' clematis
•				•					160	'Bluebird' clematis
				•					161	'Maidwell Hall' clematis
				•					161	'Snowbird' clematis
				•					161	'White Swan' clematis
				•					161	'Prairie Traveller's Joy' clematis
				•					160	'Blue Boy' clematis
				•					161	'Rosy O'Grady' clematis
	3 m @ 5°C								161	alpine clematis
				•					161	'Pamela Jackman' clematis
				•					161	'Ruby' clematis
				•					161	'Willy' clematis
				•					161	'Francis Rivis' clematis
•	nick and soak overnight	directly outdoors							161	wild cucumber
•		when ripe in fall						•	162	hops
	nick or soak sow @ 21-30°C								162	morning glory
				•					163	'Dropmore Scarlet Trumpet' honeysuckle
	3m @ 5°C				•	•	•		163	Virginia creeper
	19°C	directly	•						163	nasturtium
•				•		•			164	riverbank grape, Manitoba grape

Annuals Botanical Name	Full Sun	Partial Shade	Full Shade	Mat-like (<30 cm/1 ft)	30–60 cm (1–2 ft)	60 cm–1 m (2–3 ft)	1–1.2 m (3–4 ft)	Over 1.2 m (4 ft)	White	Yellow	Orange	Red	Pink	Purple	Blue	Fresh	Dried	Grown Primarily For	Grey	Variegated	Fragrant	Aggressive	Poisonous
Ageratum houstonianum	•	•		•	•				•				•		•								
Amaranthus caudatus	•					•	•					•				•	•						
Ammobium alatum	•					•			•	•							•		•				
Anagallis monelli var. *linifolia*	•			•	•								•	•	•								
Arctotis stoechadifolia	•				•				•	•		•	•	•	•								
Argemone grandiflora	•					•			•														•
Argemone mexicana	•					•				•	•											•	•
Calendula officinalis	•	•			•					•	•					•							
Catharanthus roseus	•	•		•					•		•		•	•									
Celosia cristata	•	•		•	•				•	•	•	•	•			•	•						
Centaurea cineraria	•			•	•														•				
Centaurea cyanus	•	•			•	•			•				•	•	•	•							
Chrysanthemum parthenium	•	•		•	•				•	•													
Clarkia unguiculata	•	•				•			•				•	•		•							
Cleome hasslerana	•	•						•	•				•	•							•		
Coreopsis tinctoria	•			•	•	•				•	•	•	•	•		•							
Cosmos bipinnatus	•				•	•	•		•	•	•	•	•	•		•							
Craspedia spp.	•	•				•				•						•	•		•				
Cynoglossum amabile	•	•			•	•			•						•	•					•		
Datura spp.	•						•	•	•	•		•			•							•	•
Dianthus chinensis	•	•		•	•				•			•	•	•		•					•		
Dimorphotheca sinuata	•				•				•	•	•												

Birds	Butterflies	Bees	Native Plant	Directly Outdoors	Soil Temperature	Light	Dark	Weeks Before Setting Out	Self-seeds	Comments	Cuttings	Page Number	Common Name
	•				21°C	•		6–8				168	ageratum, flossflower
					24°C			6		biodegradable pot		168	love-lies-bleeding
				•	21°C			6				169	winged everlasting
					21°C			6				169	flaxleaf pimpernel
					21°C			3				169	blue-eyed African daisy
					21°C			6		biodegradable pot		170	prickly poppy
					21°C			6		biodegradable pot		170	Mexican poppy
	•			•	18°–24°C		•	3–4	•			170	calendula
					21°–30°C		•	10–12			•	171	vinca, Madagascar periwinkle
					21°–25°C	•		4–6		biodegradable pot		171	cockscomb
					16°–21°C	•		10			•	172	dusty miller
				•			•		•			172	bachelor's button, cornflower
					21°C	•		8				172	feverfew, matricaria
				•	21°C			6				173	clarkia
•		•			20°–30°C	•		6–8	•			173	cleome, spider flower
				•	21°C		•	6	•	biodegradable pot		174	coreopsis, tickseed
	•	•		•	24°–27°C	•		4–6	•			174	cosmos
					21°C			5–6				175	drumstick flower
				•					•			175	Chinese forget-me-not, hound's tongue
					21°C			10				175	trumpet flower, angel's trumpet
•					21°C			8				176	China pink
					13°–16°C			4–6				176	African daisy, cape marigold

Appendix 2: Ornamental Plant Charts • 233

Annuals	LIGHT			HEIGHT RANGE					LANDSCAPE VALUE														
									Flower Color							Cut		Foliage			Special Features		
Botanical Name	Full Sun	Partial Shade	Full Shade	Mat-like (<30 cm/1 ft)	30–60 cm (1–2 ft)	60 cm–1 m (2–3 ft)	1–1.2 m (3–4 ft)	Over 1.2 m (4 ft)	White	Yellow	Orange	Red	Pink	Purple	Blue	Fresh	Dried	Grown Primarily For	Grey	Variegated	Fragrant	Aggressive	Poisonous
Dorotheanthus bellidiformis	•			•					•	•	•	•	•	•									
Dyssodia tenuiloba	•			•						•						•							
Emilia javanica	•				•						•	•				•							
Eschscholzia californica	•	•			•				•	•	•		•	•									
Euphorbia marginata	•	•			•				•							•				•			•
Gaillardia pulchella var. picta	•				•					•	•	•		•		•							
Gazania ringens	•				•				•	•	•		•										
Gomphrena globosa	•			•	•				•	•	•		•	•		•	•						
Gypsophila elegans	•				•				•				•			•	•				•		
Helianthus annuus	•	•			•	•	•	•	•	•	•	•		•		•	•						
Helichrysum bracteatum	•				•				•	•	•	•	•	•		•	•						
Helipterum spp.	•				•				•	•		•	•			•	•						
Kochia scoparia var. trichophylla	•				•	•												•		•		•	
Limonium sinuatum	•				•				•	•		•	•	•	•	•	•						
Mesembryanthemum crystallinum	•			•					•	•			•						•	•			
Nolana paradoxa	•	•		•											•								
Papaver rhoeas	•				•	•			•		•	•	•			•	•						
Pelargonium x spp.	•				•				•		•	•	•							•			
Perilla frutescens 'Crispa'	•	•			•													•					
Petunia x hybrida	•	•		•	•				•	•		•	•	•	•						•		
Phacelia campanularia	•			•											•		•						•
Portulaca grandiflora	•			•					•	•	•	•	•	•									

Birds	Butterflies	Bees	Native Plant	Directly Outdoors	Soil Temperature	Light	Dark	Weeks Before Setting Out	Self-seeds	Comments	Cuttings	Page Number	Common Name
					15°–21°C		•	10				177	livingstone daisy
					21°C			12		very fine seed; place on surface and cover with tin foil		177	Dahlberg daisy
				•	21°C			5				177	tassel flower
				•					•	does not transplant easily		178	California poppy
					21°C			6–8	•	pre-chill seeds @ 5°C for 2 m		178	snow-on-the-mountain
		•		•	21°–30°C	•		4–6				178	gaillardia, blanket flower
					21°C			8–10		basal cuttings	•	179	gazania
					21°–30°C		•	6–8		soak seeds in water		179	globe amaranth
					21°C	•		4–5	•			179	annual babysbreath
•		•		•					•			180	sunflower
					16°–24°C	•		6–8				180	strawflower
				•	21°C			6		biodegradable pots		181	acrolinium
					18°–24°C	•		6–8		soak seeds; biodegradable pots		181	burning bush, summer cypress
	•				16°–21°C			8–12		biodegradable pots; use cleaned seed		181	statice
					30°–35°C			10–12				182	iceplant
					21°C			8–10		biodegradable pots		182	Chilean bellflower
				•					•			183	corn poppy, Shirley poppy
•					21°–30°C			14–16			•	183	geranium
					21°C			4–6			•	184	'Crispa' perilla
•					21°–30°C	•		10–12		sow very fine seed on surface		184	petunia
		•		•	21°C			4–6	•	biodegradable pot		184	California bluebell
				•	21°C	•		6–8		pre-chill 14 d @ 5°C		185	portulaca, rose moss

Annuals Botanical Name	LIGHT			HEIGHT RANGE					LANDSCAPE VALUE														
									Flower Color							Cut		Foliage			Special Features		
	Full Sun	Partial Shade	Full Shade	Mat-like (<30 cm/1 ft)	30–60 cm (1–2 ft)	60 cm–1 m (2–3 ft)	1–1.2 m (3–4 ft)	Over 1.2 m (4 ft)	White	Yellow	Orange	Red	Pink	Purple	Blue	Fresh	Dried	Grown Primarily For	Grey	Variegated	Fragrant	Aggressive	Poisonous
Psylliostachys suworowii	•				•	•			•				•	•		•							
Salvia farinacea	•	•			•				•						•	•	•						
Salvia viridis	•				•				•				•	•		•							
Sanvitalia procumbens	•			•	•					•	•												
Senecio cineraria	•			•	•													•	•				
Tagetes spp.	•			•	•				•	•	•												
Tithonia rotundifolia	•					•	•	•		•	•					•							
Ursinia anethoides	•				•					•	•												
Venidium fastuosum	•				•	•			•		•			•					•				
Xeranthemum annuum	•					•			•				•	•		•	•						
Zinnia elegans	•			•	•	•			•	•	•	•	•	•		•							

Birds	Butterflies	Bees	Native Plant	Directly Outdoors	Soil Temperature	Light	Dark	Weeks Before Setting Out	Self-seeds	Comments	Cuttings	Page Number	Common Name
	•				21°C			8		biodegradable pot		185	Russian statice
					21°C			8–10			•	185	mealycup sage
				•	21°C			4–6	•			186	clary sage
				•	21–30°C	•		4		biodegradable pot		186	creeping zinnia
					21°C	•		10–12			•	186	dusty miller
•	•	•		•	21°–30°C	•		3–4	•			187	marigold
					21°C			6		biodegradable pot		187	Mexican sunflower
					21°C			6–8				188	dill-leaf ursinia, jewel-of-the-veldt
					21°C	•		6–8				188	cape daisy, monarch-of-the-veldt
					21°C			8		biodegradable pot		188	immortelle
•	•			•	18–21°C	•		6		biodegradable pot		189	zinnia

Botanical Name	Full Sun	Partial Shade	Full Shade	<30 cm (1 ft)	30–60 cm (1–2 ft)	60 cm–1 m (2–3 ft)	Over 1 m (3 ft)	White	Yellow	Orange	Red	Pink	Purple	Blue	Spring	Summer	Native Plant	Seed	Self-seed	Division of Bulb	Bulb	Bulblets/Bulbils	Page Number	Common Name
	LIGHT			LANDSCAPE Height Range				FLOWER Color							Bloom			PROPAGATION						
Allium aflatunense	•				•	•							•			•		•			•		165	Aflatun onion
Allium caeruleum	•				•									•		•		•			•		165	blue globe (azure) onion
Allium flavum	•				•				•							•		•			•		165	flavum onion
Allium karataviense	•			•								•			•			•			•		165	karataviense onion
Allium moly	•			•					•						•			•			•		165	golden garlic
Allium oreophilum	•			•								•				•		•			•		165	ostrowsky onion
Allium x 'Purple Sensation'	•					•							•			•					•		165	'Purple Sensation'
Allium schoenoprasum	•				•								•			•		•	•		•		165	chives
Allium senescens	•				•							•				•		•			•		165	curly onion
Allium sphaerocephalon	•				•						•					•		•			•		165	drumstick onion
Fritillaria pallidiflora	•	•	•		•				•							•		•	•		•	•	166	Siberian fritillary
Fritillaria michailowski	•	•	•										•	•				•	•		•	•	166	Michailovsky fritillary
Lilium spp.	•	•				•	•	•	•	•	•	•				•		•	•	•	•	•	166	lilies
Scilla sibirica	•			•				•						•	•						•		167	Siberian squill
Tulipa x Darwin	•				•			•	•	•	•	•	•		•					•	•		167	Darwin tulips
Tulipa kolpakowskiana	•			•					•	•					•				•	•	•		167	kolpakow-skiana tulip
Tulipa tarda	•			•				•	•						•				•	•	•		167	tarda tulip
Tulipa turkestanica	•			•					•	•					•				•	•	•		167	Turkestan tulip
Tulipa urumiensis	•			•					•						•				•	•	•		167	Urumia tulip

Appendix 3

Glossary

AAS — All-America Selections (see below).

acclimation — the process whereby woody and herbaceous perennial plants become hardened for winter survival.

acidic soil — soil that is below 7.0 on the pH scale.

aerate — to allow air to enter (the soil).

aggregation — the formation of many individual soil particles into a single cluster or crumb.

agronomic — dealing with agricultural crops.

alkaline soil — soil that is above 7.0 on the pH scale.

All-America Selections — a North American organization that tests and selects new flower and vegetable cultivars and recommends outstanding performers for home garden use.

allelopathic — the release by a plant of a chemical that inhibits the growth of nearby plants and thus reduces competition.

amend — to change or add to; usually the addition of organic matter to soils.

amendment — a material such as peat moss, compost, or aged manure which is added to soil to improve properties such as its workability, water-holding capacity, or tilth.

anaerobic — occurring without oxygen. Anaerobic decomposition occurs when compost piles have not been turned to allow sufficient oxygen; it is usually smelly.

anther — part of a stamen of a flower on which pollen is produced.

aquifer — layer of underground water often used as a source of potable water or for irrigation.

aster yellows — a plant disease caused by a mycoplasma common in over 40 plant families. Symptoms are excessive branching, leaf yellowing, and floral deformity. It is spread by sucking insects.

awl-type leaf — small, sharp-pointed leaves, such as those found on common juniper; they resemble the awl of a carpenter.

awn — a stiff bristle projecting from the seed heads of grasses, as in bearded wheat.

axils — the angle created where a leaf arises from a stem.

basal — from below or at the base of a plant, as in basal leaves.

basic soil — soil that is above 7.0 in the pH scale (alkaline soil).

biennial — a plant that lives for two years, producing vegetative growth in the first season and flowering in the second.

black knot — a fungal disease of chokecherry, Mayday, and some other members of the plum family. It is characterized by black, sooty, swollen growths on the stems.

bloom — a waxy or powdery coating on the surface of fruit (such as plums) or conifer needles.

bract — a modified leaf. Members of the genus *Euphorbia* (poinsettia and cypress spurge) have colorful bracts which are commonly mistaken for flower petals.

broadleaf weed — a dicot or non-grassy weed such as a dandelion or thistle.

calyx — outermost whorl of flower parts which protects the closed flower bud. They are generally green but can be parchment- or petal-like in the lily family.

canopy tree — a tree that does not branch near its base but has upper branches that extend laterally to provide shade.

capillary action — the movement of water within the larger pore (macropore) spaces of the soil, or up through the plant xylem.

catchment area — an area within a landscape such as a pond where water is encouraged to collect and from which it may later be used for irrigation purposes.

catkin — tight, often pendulous spikes of petalless flowers of one sex, as in the flowers of willow or birch.

chlorosis — yellowing of plants when chlorophyll fails to develop.

clay — the smallest soil particle, usually less than 0.002 mm in diameter.

companion plant — a plant used in the landscape in combination with a another plant for aesthetic or functional reasons. Perennial geraniums, bergenia, and catmint are often used as companion plants to roses in England.

compound leaf — a leaf that is divided and consists of two or more separate leaflets.

cool-season grass — a grass that grows vigorously during the spring and fall but slows or ceases growth during the heat of summer.

crown — part of a plant, usually at ground level, from which roots and stems emerge.

cultivar — a cultivated variety. A plant with distinguishing characteristics originating and persisting under human cultivation. Cultivar names are capitalized and enclosed within single quotation marks (eg., 'Thunderchild' crabapple, 'Sweet 100' tomato).

deadhead — to remove faded flowers, thereby preventing seed set and encouraging a prolonged period of flowering.

desiccation — drying-out, usually associated with excessive heat, wind, or drought.

diagonal drift — a diagonal planting within a bed or border of an early-flowering perennial such as an Oriental poppy surrounded by later-blooming perennials which hide its dying or yellowing foliage.

dioecious — with male and female flowers found on separate plants, as in Manitoba maple or sea buckthorn. To ensure fruit set, plants of each sex should be planted in close proximity.

disc flower — the small, fertile flowers in the center of a composite or daisy-like flower such as a sunflower.

dormant/dormancy — a general term denoting a lack of growth, often due to factors in the plant's environment; the "rest" or non-active growth periods plants enter prior to winter.

double flower — a flower with two or more times the normal number of petals.

drip line — the area of soil below the outermost extent of a tree's branches, often corresponding with the extent of its feeder roots within the soil.

emitter — the component in an irrigation system from which water is emitted.

endophyte — the genetically "built-in" biological controls of some plants against insects and diseases.

escape from cultivation — cultivated plants that have naturalized in an area to which they are not native.

evapotranspiration rate — loss of water, from a given area during a specific time period, due to the combined effects of evaporation from the soil and transpiration from plant leaves.

feeder roots — finely branched roots near the soil surface that are active in water- and nutrient-absorption.

fertilizer — any organic or inorganic material added to soil to supply elements essential to the growth of plants.

flax shives — the chopped by-product of flax straw that has been processed for paper. Flax shives make a long-lasting mulch.

field capacity — water remaining in a soil a few days after rain or irrigation and after free drainage has ceased.

floriferous — producing many flowers.

foundation planting — landscape plantings placed adjacent to the foundations of a building, usually to conceal it.

friability — the ease with which soils are crumbled or worked.

genus — the major subdivision of a plant family. The first term in a botanical plant name.

glacial till — glacial deposits consisting of a mixture of clay, sand, gravel, and boulders.

glaucous — dull greyish-green or blue, often due to a fine coating of wax or bloom.

granulation — soil structure in which individual particles are grouped into larger structures called crumbs or aggregates. A well-granulated soil is considered ideal for most plants.

hardpan — a hardened soil layer which impedes root penetration and water percolation.

hardscape — nonplant parts of the landscape, such as decks, ponds, gates, walls, fences, and patios.

hard surface — nonplant flooring in the landscape, such as paths, walks, driveways, patios, and decks.

hardwoods — deciduous trees, as contrasted with coniferous or evergreen trees.

hybrid — the offspring produced from the crossing of two plants of different genetic make-up.

hydrogel — a synthetic soil amendment that has the ability to absorb many times its weight in water and is sometimes added to the media in containers, decreasing the need for frequent watering (also called a polymer).

infiltration — the downward movement of water into and through the soil.

inorganic — composed of materials that were never alive.

leach — the washing through or removal of materials such as fertilizer from the soil.

iron chlorosis — an iron deficiency caused by a high pH, which limits the availability of iron for the production of green pigment. It is characterized by dark green veins and a light green or yellow leaf blade.

leaflet — a single unit or division of a compound leaf.

leaf margin — the edge of a leaf. Leaf margins may be wavy, incised, or variegated.

legume — a member of the pea family.

lignin — a waxy deposit in the cell walls of trees and shrubs which makes them rigid and woody.

loam — soil having approximately equal proportions of sand, silt, and clay.

mixed border — a border or bed planted with a combination of annuals, biennials, perennials, vines, bulbs, shrubs, and trees.

microclimate — the localized climatic conditions of a small area, where wind, temperature, and evapotranspiration may differ from its surroundings. Examples would be a sheltered part of a yard, the area below a spruce, or a city center. Microclimates may enhance or hinder plant growth.

monocarpic — dying after flowering once.

mushroom compost — compost made from manures and straws that are first steamed and then used to grow several crops of mushrooms.

naturalize — plants introduced to an area and then allowed (either intentionally or by accident) to spread through seed, suckers, or rhizomes in a natural or uncontrolled manner.

nematode — microscopic worms that are abundant in some soils and attack and destroy plant roots. They are not common in most prairie soils.

nitrogen fixation — the ability of certain plants, such as legumes, to convert nitrogen from the atmosphere into forms readily used by plants.

nomenclature — a system of naming. The scientific names of plants consist of genus and species or specific epithet. Manitoba maple is *Acer negundo*.

noxious weed — a plant regulated or identified by law as being undesirable, troublesome, and difficult to control. *Lythrum salicaria* is a noxious weed in Alberta and Manitoba; *Gypsophila paniculata* and *Kochia scoparia* are noxious weeds in Manitoba.

oedema — rupturing of a lower leaf surface; it is caused by internal water pressure due to over-watering or prolonged wet conditions and is characterized by scabby or corky spots. *Pelargonium* are particularly susceptible to oedema (edema).

organic — from living organisms.

organic matter — materials such as manures, leaves, compost, or bone or blood meal, which are derived from something that was once living.

overseed — to seed over an existing lawn without removing or destroying it.

palmately compound leaf — a leaf with leaflets radiating outward from a single point, like fingers from the palm of one's hand, such as those of the Ohio buckeye.

panicle — a branched, elongated flower cluster.

perched water table — an underground body of water held in place by an impermeable layer, usually of clay.

percolation — the downward movement of water through soil.

perfect flower — a flower with both male (stamens) and female (pistil) parts.

perlite — an inorganic soil amendment made of expanded volcanic silica rock. It is added to potting mixes to increase soil aeration and drainage.

permanent wilting point — level of soil moisture where water is no longer available to plants and they wilt and die.

PFRA — Prairie Farm Rehabilitation Administration, a federal agency that encourages and assists soil conservation and shelterbelt development.

pharmacopoeia — a book containing a list of drugs, including plants, with directions for their use. The first one was written in Germany in 1542.

photosynthesis — the process by which the energy of sunlight is used by green plants to make sugar from carbon dioxide and water.

phytotoxic — poisonous to plants.

pinnately compound — compound leaves with the leaflets arranged along both sides of a common axis, in a similar pattern to that of a feather.

polymer — see hydrogel.

porosity — the degree to which soil allows the infiltration of air and water.

precipitation rate — the rate at which a sprinkler delivers water to the landscape, expressed in inches or centimeters per hour.

psi — pounds per square inch; a measurement of water pressure.

raceme — a type of flower cluster on which individual flowers are attached to a central stalk by small, unbranched stalks.

ray flower — the petal-like flowers often on the outside of a composite or daisy-like flower such as a sunflower.

rhizome — an underground stem capable of producing roots and shoots at each node. Plants often spread and are propagated by rhizomes.

runoff — water applied to the landscape that is not absorbed by the soil or used by plants and instead drains to another location, usually ending up in storm sewers or ditches.

rust — a fungal disease of plants, often characterized by orange pustules, which often needs two alternate host plants in order to survive. Saskatoon-juniper rust is an example.

saline soil — soil with a salt content high enough to inhibit plant growth.

salinity — the presence of salts in soils.

samara — a winged seed pod typical of maple and ash trees.

sand — soil particles of 0.05–2.0 mm, which can be seen with the naked eye.

saturation point — the point at which the pore space of a soil is filled with water.

scale-type leaf — a small leaf typical of some cedars and junipers.

scarification — injuring the seed coat mechanically or with acid so that germination can take place.

selective herbicide — a herbicide that kills one type of plant but will not harm another type. Those registered for domestic use usually kill broadleaf plants (dicots) but will not harm most grasses (monocots).

sepal — one of the separate parts of the calyx of a flower; it is often green and protects the flower bud.

sessile — directly attached, without a stalk.

shelterbelt — a planting of trees consisting of several rows; shelterbelts are planted to protect fields from wind erosion, catch snow, or shelter farmyards. More recently, shelterbelts have been designed for wildlife enhancement and agro-forestry.

silt — a soil particle between 0.05 and 0.002 mm in diameter, a size between that of clay and sand.

soil texture — the relative proportion of sand, silt, and clay particles in a soil.

solarization — the process of covering soil with clear plastic and allowing heat from the sun's rays to build up in order to kill the vegetation below it.

species — a group of similar but distinct plants capable of breeding to produce offspring similar to themselves. The species is indicated by the second part of a botanical name.

specimen plant — a plant used within the landscape by itself as a focal or interest point rather than as a part of a grouping.

sport reversion — the reversion of a sport or mutant plant (such as a variegated goutweed) back to its original (green) form.

sterile — not capable of producing viable seeds. Sterile plants give gardeners the advantages of a long flowering period and no unwanted seedlings, but they must be propagated vegetatively.

stolon — a horizontal stem on or above the surface of the soil that is capable of rooting and producing shoots or plants at each node. Stolons are often called runners, as in strawberry runners.

stomates — the microscopic openings in leaves through which water evaporates and carbon dioxide is absorbed (stomata).

subsoil — the soil layer below the topsoil; it typically has less organic matter, but minerals leached from the top soil accumulate there.

sucker — a shoot arising from the roots. Shrubs such as saskatoons and lilacs often have a suckering growth habit.

swale — a dry stream bed or shallow ditch that directs water to catchment areas or planting beds.

sward — an expanse of short grass.

tannins — organic compounds found in plants. Those found in the bark of some trees are used to tan animal hides.

target area — area toward which irrigation water is directed.

tendril — a modified leaf or leaf part, usually slender and coiled, used by some vines (such as a pea) to cling to a support.

thatch — a layer of decaying vegetation, mostly grass clippings, left on the soil surface among the living leaf blades. A thatch layer over 1 cm (0.5 in.) can be detrimental to a lawn.

tillering — the production and growth of new vertical shoots of grass. A tiller is a stem that develops from the crown of the parent plant and is immediately adjacent to other stems within the crown.

tilth — the physical condition of the soil as related to its ease of tillage.

tomentose — covered with small hairs, usually on the leaves or stems, often giving plants a grey or silver appearance.

top dress — to cover with a shallow layer. Lawns are sometimes top dressed with screened manure. Grass clippings used as mulch are often top dressed with coarse peat moss.

topsoil — the upper layer of the soil surface; topsoil generally contains more organic matter than the subsoil below.

trajectory angle — the angle above ground level at which irrigation water is projected, usually 23° to 26°.

transpiration — the loss of water through evaporation from the stomates of leaves.

turgor — the rigidity or stiffness of plants due to internal water pressure within individual cells.

umbel — a flower head in which the individual flower stalks arise from one point to form an umbrella-like flower cluster, such as in dill.

2,4–D — a selective herbicide used to kill broadleaf weeds in lawns.

underplanting — the placement of shorter plants under taller ones. Creeping juniper can be used as an underplanting below pines.

variegated — leaves having marks, stripes, blotches, or margins in a color different than that which predominates (usually green.) Variegation is often white, cream, yellow, or pink.

vermiculite — particles of mica that have been heated and expanded. Vermiculite is added to potting mixtures to increase their water-holding ability. It contains some potassium and magnesium.

warm-season grass — a grass that thrives in the heat of midsummer but is less active in spring and fall.

water sprouts — vigorous young shoots that arise randomly from large branches or the trunk of a tree.

wetting front — the movement of water after rain or irrigation from the soil surface downward through the pore spaces.

xylem — cells that carry water and dissolved minerals from the soil upward to the tops of trees.

Index

Symbols

2,4–D   67, 81, 83

A

acrolinium   181, 235
aeration   24, 31, 35
African daisy   176, 233
ageratum   168, 233
allium   165. *See also* onion
alumroot   145, 194
alyssum, perennial   12, 135, 225
amaranth, globe   12, 179, 235
American bittersweet   160, 231
anemone   225
   Canada   194
   cut-leaved   194
   snowdrop   133
angel's trumpet   175, 233
annuals   168–89
antennaria   133, 225
apples   34
arabis   134. *See also* rockcress
artemisia   10, 94, 134, 225
   'Silver Brocade'   19, 135, 225
   'Silver King'   23
   'Silver Mound'   12, 135, 225
ash, green   10, 12, 18, 29, 47, 94, 104,
     191, 194, 196, 217
aspen   194, 196
aster
   hairy golden   194
   Lindley's   194
   smooth   194, 195
avens, three-flowered   190, 194, 195

B

babysbreath   192, 227
   annual   179, 235
   creeping   143, 227
bachelor's button   172, 233
bacteria   34, 35, 64

banks   81, 82, 193
bark chips   38, 63
bark, decorative   67, 68
barley   18
basket-of-gold   135. *See also* alyssum
bearberry   99, 215
beardstongue
   blue   190
   lilac flowered   194
   smooth blue   194
bedstraw, northern   194
bellflower
   Carpathian   13, 137, 225
   creeping   137, 225
bergamot   194, 195
bergenia   12, 16, 27, 136, 211, 225
betony, big   155, 229
birch   48, 196
birds   18, 24, 29
black-eyed susan   194
blanket flower   142, 178, 194, 211, 227,
     235
blazingstar   194, 195
blood meal   37
blossom end rot   200
blue-eyed African daisy   169, 233
bone meal   37
box elder   97, 215
broom   104, 217
   'Vancouver Gold'   103, 215
broom weed   194
buckbrush   127
buffaloberry   12, 18, 34, 196
   Canada   194
   russet   125, 195
   silver   125, 194, 223
bulbs   165–67
burning bush   181, 192
bylaws   14, 49, 80, 208

C

cactus
   brittle prickly pear   194
   pincushion   139, 194, 225
   plains prickly pear   149, 194, 227
calendula   12, 170, 233
California bluebell   184, 237
calliopsis   174
cape daisy   188, 237
cape marigold   176, 233
caragana   5, 12, 29, 34, 99, 215
catmint, 'Dropmore'   148, 227. *See also*
     Nepeta
centaurea, globe   138, 225
chamomile   5, 133, 225
chelated iron   34
cherry   196
   cistena   10, 117, 219
   Mongolian   117, 219
   Nanking   119, 199, 221
   prinsepia   116, 219
Chilean bellflower   182, 235
Chinese forget-me-not   175, 233
chives   238
chokecherry   18, 29, 94, 120, 191, 194,
     195, 221
cinquefoil   115, 152. *See also* potentilla
clarkia   173, 233
clay   32, 39, 48
clematis   13, 26, 29, 160, 231
cleome   173, 233
cockscomb   171, 233
comfrey   23, 156, 229
compost   36–37, 38, 67
coneflower, prairie   194, 195
cool-season crops   201
coral bells   10, 12, 13, 145, 211, 227
coreopsis   174, 233
corn   18

cornflower 12, 172, 233
   perennial 23, 138, 225
cosmos 12, 174, 233
cotoneaster 12, 18, 29, 101, 215
cottonwood 26
cover crops 38
crabapple 12, 16, 18, 26, 27, 94, 108, 199, 217
cranberry, American highbush 13
creeping zinnia 12, 186, 237
crocus, prairie 194
currant
   alpine 12, 18, 122, 221
   golden 12, 18, 29, 95, 122, 221

D
Dahlberg daisy 177, 235
daylily 12, 13, 16, 23, 27, 78, 144, 211, 227
decks 17, 19, 25, 26, 75
deficit irrigation 200
delphinium 48
demonstration gardens 208, 209, 210, 212
dianthus 12, 176
dill-leaf ursinia 188, 237
dogwood 13, 48, 194, 196
drip irrigation. *See* irrigation
drip line 52
driveways 11, 15, 49
drumstick flower 233
dusty miller 12, 172, 186, 233, 237
Dutch elm disease 67
dyer's greenweed 104, 217

E
edelweiss 146, 227
elder 18, 124, 221
elephant ears 94
elm 26, 34, 47
erosion 81
evaporation 42

F
false indigo 99, 136, 215, 225
false lupine 156, 229
false spirea, Ural 126, 223
fertilizer 3, 4, 35, 74, 81, 83
   formulations 83
fescues. *See* grasses: bunch
feverfew 172, 233
field capacity 43
fir 196
flax
   perennial 147, 227
   shives 69, 71
   wild blue 194, 195
flaxleaf pimpernel 169, 233
fleabane
   'Pink Jewel' Oregon 141, 227

smooth 194, 195
   tufted 194
fleece flower 152
flossflower 168, 233
focal points 13
foundation plantings 15
fritillary 166, 238
fruit 203
fungi 34, 35

G
gaillardia 5, 12, 23, 142, 195, 227, 235
   annual 178
garland flower 173
garlic, golden 238
gasplant 140, 227
gaura, scarlet 194
gazania 179, 235
geranium 183, 235
   bigfoot 27, 143, 227
   sticky 195
giant rockfoil 136
glyphosate 72, 78, 79
golden bean 194
golden fleece 177
golden marguerite 5, 10, 23, 133, 211, 225
goldenrod 23, 154, 194, 229
gooseberry 18, 123, 195, 221
goutweed 23, 27, 28, 132
grading 15, 17, 47, 48, 79
grape
   Manitoba 18, 26, 27, 164
   riverbank 24, 164
grass clippings 36, 66, 196
grasses 32, 77, 84
   bunch 75, 77, 84, 85
      Canada bluegrass 87
      chewings fescue 84, 86
      crested wheatgrass 87
      fescues 86
      hard fescue 87
      Russian wild ryegrass 88
      sheep fescue 84, 86, 89, 142, 193
      streambank wheatgrass 88
      wheatgrass 84, 87
   cool-season 76, 81, 84, 85
   native 88
      awned wheatgrass 194
      big bluestem 89
      blue grama 89, 194
      Canada wild rye 89, 193
      fringed brome 89, 193
      Indian grass 193
      Indian rice grass 89
      June grass 194
      little bluestem 89, 193
      needle and thread 89
      northern wheatgrass 88, 89, 194

plains rough fescue 194
   reed grass 89
   ribbon grass 23
   speargrass 194
   switch grass 89
   tufted hair grass 89
   western wheatgrass 89, 194
ornamental 26, 77
   blue fescue 12, 16, 23, 142, 227
   blue lyme grass 23, 140, 227
   ribbon grass 16, 26, 27, 151, 229
   'Skinner's Golden' bromegrass 23, 137, 225
rhizomatous 84, 85, 194
turf
   creeping red fescue 84, 85, 86
   Kentucky bluegrass 80, 84, 85
warm-season 84
green manures 38
ground covers 26
ground plum 194

H
hard surfaces 26, 75
hardpans 33, 44
hardscape 11, 13
harebell 190, 194, 195
hawthorn 18, 29, 34, 102, 194, 215
hazelnut, beaked 100, 194, 215
heart-leaved alexander 194
hedges 24
hens and chicks 94, 154, 229
herbicides 78
holding pond 49
holding tanks 49
hollyhock 132, 225
honeysuckle 12, 18, 26, 29, 34, 107–8, 163, 217
hoof and horn meal 37
hops 162, 231
hosta 48
hound's tongue 175, 233
house leek 154, 229
humus 36
hydrogels 40
hyssop, giant 194

I
iceplant 182, 235
immortelle 180, 188, 237
Indian breadroot 194
indigo, wild blue 136
infiltration rate 43, 53
inoculants 36
iris 12, 13
   bearded 146, 211, 227
iron 34
iron chlorosis 34
irrigation 41–59
   drip 55–58, 70, 200

allowed length of run   57
   emitters   56, 57, 58
moisture sensors   51
rain shut-off devices   51
schedules   42, 49–51, 57
soaker hoses   58, 59, 200
sprinklers   42
   bubble heads   55
   fan spray heads   54–55
   portable   52, 53
   rotary stream heads   55
   trajectory of   54, 55
systems   22, 50, 52–59, 53–55
timers   50
zones   47, 48, 82

J
jewel-of-the-veldt   188, 237
johnny-jump-up   158, 229
juniper   10, 12, 13, 16, 18, 27, 34, 78,
   106, 191, 194, 195, 217

K
kinnikinnick   99, 215
knotweed   152, 229

L
lambs ears   155, 229
landscape fabrics   71
larch, Siberian   107, 217
lawn   16, 22, 24, 26, 73–89
layered mixed borders   9, 11, 12, 18, 23,
   77
leaching   42, 82, 83
leadplant   98, 215
leaf mold   38, 69
lilac   5, 12, 18, 48, 94, 127, 128, 223
lilies   12, 13, 16, 94, 166, 238
linden, little leaf   48
livingstone daisy   177, 235
loam   32, 48
locoweed, showy   194
love-lies-bleeding   168, 233
low everlasting   194

M
Madagascar periwinkle   171, 233
mallow
   musk   148, 227
   prairie   155, 229
   scarlet   194, 195
malva hollyhock   148, 227
manures   34, 37
maple
   Amur   12, 13, 34, 97, 215
   ginnala   97, 215
   Manitoba   10, 18, 26, 34, 47, 94, 97,
   215
marigold   12, 187, 237
mass plantings   23, 77
matricaria   12, 172

mayday tree   94, 117
mice   63, 69, 71
microclimates   9, 10, 16, 21, 22, 28, 48,
   50, 63
microorganisms   31, 33, 36
mixed layered borders. *See* layered mixed
   borders
mockorange, 'Waterton'   109, 217
moisture-holding capacity   32, 43
monarch-of-the-veldt   188, 237
morning glory   162, 231
mowing   81, 82
mulch   3, 24, 27, 51, 52, 60–72, 78, 196
   applying and maintaining   64–66
   benefits of   60, 61–63
   design functions   63
   inorganic   70–72
   organic   66–70
   problems with   63–64
   renewal   66
   summer   65
   types of   66–72
   winter   65
mullein, dark   157, 229

N
nannyberry   130, 223
nasturtium   163
native plants   191
naturalization   191, 192, 194, 195, 212
Nepeta   13, 19. *See also* catmint
newspapers   70
ninebark, common   110, 217
nitrogen   83
   deficiency   38, 64, 68, 69, 71
nutrient-holding capacity   32
nutrients   3, 34

O
oak   196
   bur   12, 13, 18, 27, 121, 191, 194, 221
onion, ornamental   165, 194, 238
organic matter   16, 31, 32, 33, 34, 35, 43,
   44, 78, 80
overseeding   78
overspray   42, 55
oxygen depletion   64, 65
Ozark sundrops   149

P
patios   17, 19, 25, 26, 49, 75
pea shrub   99
pear
   Manchurian   120
   Ussurian   120, 221
peat moss   27, 34, 37, 38, 67
peony   12, 13, 149, 227
perennial blue flax   23
perennials   131–59
perilla   184, 235
perlite   39

permanent wilting point   43
pesticides   4, 74, 83
petunia   12, 184, 235
PFRA   29
pH   33–34, 34, 37, 38, 72
phlox
   Arctic   151, 229
   creeping   151
   moss   151, 229
phosphorus   34
photosynthesis   46, 81, 82
phytotoxic, properties of trees   38
pincherry   18, 29, 94, 118, 191, 194, 195,
   199, 219
pine   18, 112
   bull   114
   jack   112, 195, 196, 219
   limber   113, 219
   lodgepole   113, 195, 219
   mugo   114, 219
   ponderosa   114, 219
   Scots   12, 16, 18, 94, 95, 115, 219
   Swiss stone   13, 113, 219
   western yellow   114
pinks   12
   China   176, 233
   cottage   139
   grass   139, 225
   maiden   139, 225
play area   11
plum, double flowering   119, 221
polymers   16
pond   11
ponding   43
poplar   26, 29, 47
poppy   16
   California   12, 178, 235
   corn   183, 235
   Flanders   183
   Iceland   23, 150, 229
   Mexican   233
   Oriental   12, 150, 229
   prickly   233
   prickly and Mexican   170
   Shirley   183, 235
pore structure   31
porous pipe   58, 59
portulaca   12, 185, 235
post peelings   27, 63, 67
pot marigold   170
potentilla   12, 16, 152, 219
   orangespot cinquefoil   229
   prairie cinquefoil   194
   shrubby cinquefoil   211
   silverweed   229
   white cinquefoil   194
precipitation rate   53, 54, 55
primrose, Missouri evening   149, 227
pruning   4

puddling 49, 54, 55
purple loosestrife 192
pussytoes 94, 133, 225

R
rain barrels 49
raised beds 20, 33
raspberry 34
rock gardens 24, 25
rockcress 12, 134, 225
rose moss 185, 235
roses 12, 13, 18, 29, 34, 48, 123–24,
194–95, 211, 221
runoff 24, 25, 42, 43, 48, 49, 54, 55, 61,
62, 81, 82, 83, 196
Russian almond 118, 221
Russian olive 12, 18, 29, 34, 95, 103, 217

S
sage 134
clary 5, 186, 237
mealycup 185, 237
purple 199
salinity 33, 34, 44, 46
salt 33, 44, 57
salt bush 34, 105, 217
salt-tolerant plants 34
salvia 152, 185, 229
sand 32, 39, 48
sandcherry, purple-leaved 117
saskatoon berry 12, 18, 29, 98, 194, 195,
196, 215
sawdust 38, 68
scale 13, 15
scattergun plantings 9, 11, 20
sea buckthorn 12, 18, 29, 34, 105, 217
sea campion 154, 229
sea holly 141, 227
sea lavender 147, 181, 227
sedum 27, 94
Shasta daisy 211
shelterbelts 29, 71, 200
shives 69, 71
silt 32, 48
silverberry 103, 194, 217
silverweed 229
site analysis 20, 21, 28
skunkbush 121
slopes 9, 24, 42, 48, 54, 57, 69, 79, 81,
82, 193
sneezewort 131, 211, 225
snow-in-summer 12, 23, 138, 225
snow-on-the-mountain 178, 235
snowberry 18, 127, 194, 223
snowdrop anemone 225

soaker hoses See irrigation
soapweed, small 159
soapwort, rock 153, 229
sodding 81
soil 22, 30–40
acidity 33, 34, 38, 64
aggregation 62
alkalinity 33, 34
amending 30
compaction 33, 44, 61, 62
erosion 62
layering 44
particles, aggregation of 31, 32, 35
texture 32–33, 43
soil amendments 20, 24, 33, 35–40
solarization 78, 79
speedwell 157, 211
sphagnum moss 67
spider flower 173, 233
spirea, three-lobed 126, 223
spruce 15, 18, 29, 47, 196
Black Hills 110, 219
Colorado 18, 111, 211, 219
'Glauca Globosa' 219
spurge, cypress 142, 227
squill 167
Siberian 238
star-of-the-veldt 176
statice 147, 181, 235
Russian 185, 237
stomates 45, 46, 74, 94
stonecrop 153, 229
stratification 44
straw 69
strawberry 34, 194
strawflower 180, 235
sulfur 34
sumac 121, 196, 221
summer cypress 181, 192, 235
sunflower 18, 180, 235
Mexican 187, 237
swales 24, 48, 49

T
tamarack 196
tansy 23, 156, 229
tassel flower 168, 177, 235
terraces 24
thatch layer 83
thermopsis 156, 229
thistle, ornamental 18, 140, 227
thyme 27, 157, 229
tickseed 174, 233
topography 9, 21
topsoil 38, 79

traffic patterns 11, 21, 22
transpiration 45, 46, 47
trees and shrubs 25, 97–130
trumpet flower 175, 233
tulips 94, 167, 238

U
umbrellaplant, yellow 194

V
verbascum 16, 157, 229
vermiculite 39
veronica 27, 48, 157, 229
vetch, ascending purple milk 194
vinca 12, 171
vines 160–64
violet
Canada 158, 229
early blue 194
Virginia creeper 10, 18, 24, 26, 27, 163

W
wallflower, Siberian 141, 227
water 45–46, 80
catchment 47, 48, 49, 64
catchment areas 28
waste 42
water-storing capacity 31, 36
wayfaring tree 129, 223
weeds 3, 61–62, 78, 79, 192
wetting front 42, 43
wheat 18
wild cucumber 161, 231
willow 26
wind flower 133, 225
winged everlasting 169, 233
winter landscape 15, 18, 22
wolf willow 18, 29, 34, 94, 103, 217
wolfberry 127
wood ash 38
wood chips 27, 38, 68, 71
wood products, toxicity of 64
wood shavings 68
wormwood 211

X
xeriscape, community implementation 206–12
xylem vessels 45

Y
yarrow 10, 23, 131, 211, 225
yucca 5, 12, 48, 159, 229

Z
zinnia 12, 189, 237

About the Author

With a passion for people, perennials, and puns, Sara Williams is the horticultural specialist with the Extension Division, University of Saskatchewan. She has gardened with limited water on 5 acres of sand for almost 20 years, and brings a wealth of practical experience and horticultural knowledge to the subject of xeriscaping.

Her other books include *Perennials for the Prairies, Commercial Saskatoon Berry Production on the Prairies,* and *Commercial Raspberry Production on the Prairies.* She is also editor of *The Saskatchewan Gardener* magazine, a well-known horticultural instructor, and has led numerous garden tours to the British Isles.